34072855

D0203475

The Case for Education: Contemporary Approaches for Using Case Methods

The Case for Education: Contemporary Approaches for Using Case Methods

Edited by

Joel A. Colbert
Peter Desberg
Kimberly Trimble

Allyn and Bacon
Boston · London · Toronto · Sydney · Tokyo · Singapore

This volume is dedicated to Judy Shulman for her pioneering efforts

and years of dedication to the advancement of

case study methodology in teacher education.

Vice President, Publisher: Nancy Forsyth
Editorial Assistant: Kate Wagstaffe
Production Editor: Catherine Hetmansky
Cover Administrator: Suzanne Harbison
Manufacturing Buyer: Aloka Rathnam
Marketing Manager: Anne Morrison

Copyright © 1996 by Allyn & Bacon
A Simon & Shuster Company
Needham Heights, Massachusetts 02194

ISBN: 0–205–17394–2

Printed in the United States of America
10 9 8 8 7 6 5 4 3 2 1 99 98 97 96 9

Table of Contents

Contents

Foreword I

A redheaded boy, playing in the block corner of his kindergarten classroom was once asked what advice he would give to a group of adults who was preparing to become teachers. After a moment, he stopped building his tower, grinned a toothless grin and declared, "Tell them to make their letters good!" Though clearly reflecting admonishments he'd heard before, his words offer sound advice for any teacher. We all need to make our letters good. We need to attend to the detailed processes of teaching as well as to the substance of teaching.

Sometimes it's hard to learn about the processes of teaching. This is due, in part, to the fact that teaching is riddled with uncertainties: "Should I answer Matt's question now or wait until after class?" "What's the most productive learning environment for Darnell?" "I wonder how Alicia interpreted my comment on her paper?" It also is difficult to learn about teaching because the culture of schools, both at the elementary and secondary and higher education level, fosters the view that teaching is a private affair. Teachers, even good ones, rarely discuss their teaching in public.

While teacher educators have proclaimed the virtues of case–based instruction for over a decade, few individuals, with the notable exception of C. Roland Christensen of Harvard University, have explicitly discussed the processes of teaching by the case method. Effective case method instruction requires extensive skill development and intensive practice. Just as the kindergartner must work deliberately to learn to print the alphabet before he can write his name, so, too, must faculty learn certain fundamental skills in order to lead effective case–based discussions.

At the college and university level, it is unusual for faculty to reflect, either in print or voice, about their teaching. It is in this context that *The Case for Education: Contemporary Approaches for Using Case Methods* makes such an important contribution to the developing body of knowledge about the processes of teaching. This is a book full of information, personal reflection, and creative improvisation about a powerful pedagogical approach — case–based instruction.

In this collection of essays, readers will find candid, honest descriptions of teaching by an extraordinary group of practitioners. The contributors open the doors to their classrooms and invite the reader to explore the intimate skills of case–based instruction. The work also provides a wonderful example of the wide range of techniques in instruction. Examples that utilize video, CD–ROM or hypermedia cases suggest the emergence of technology in case–based instruction. Other essays illustrate diverse contexts, from math in elementary classrooms to foundations courses at the graduate level, and disparate physical locations, from Alaska to Los Angeles. As a collection they paint a rich portrait of struggles and triumphs in the private world of teaching.

There are clearly identified skills in teaching with cases — skills honed through hours and hours of practice and reflection. Just as the kindergartner grips his stubby pencil and struggles to make an intelligible mark on the paper, so does the teacher work deliberately to create a lasting impression in the mind of the student. *The Case for Education: Contemporary Approaches for Using Case Methods* captures these deliberate efforts and offers an important opportunity for educators to reflect upon and develop a deeper understanding of the process of teaching with cases.

Katherine K. Merseth
Harvard University

Foreword II

Teacher education presents a set of challenges with which scholars and educators have grappled for many years. The results are sometimes successful, but more often than not, they border on failure. Case use in teacher education is a process that offers ways to approach the theoretical and practical dilemmas in teacher education. More importantly, the work represented in this book provides the often missing documentation of a promise in practice.

The challenge of preservice teacher education is to move students toward thinking like teachers and to help them begin to develop practical knowledge that will allow them to survive the reality of the classroom in their first several years of teaching. Preservice teacher education has been characterized as a weak intervention, sandwiched as it is between two extremely powerful forces: previous life as a student, and classroom experiences as a student teacher and teacher. Preservice classes tend to focus on formal knowledge, whereas it is classroom experience that allows teachers to develop practical knowledge. Cases have the potential to ground preservice students' formal knowledge in real–life classroom practice and teachers' practical knowledge, and provide students with ways of developing reflective capacities that will benefit their teaching for years to come.

Inservice teacher education has its own set of challenges. Teachers develop strong beliefs and practical knowledge about their teaching, but this knowledge is often tacit. At the same time, it exerts a powerful force on teachers' practices and willingness to change practices. The typical staff development programs in which someone from outside the classroom suggests practices that teachers should implement in their classrooms are often treated with scorn and are ignored. The challenge is to develop a staff development process that acknowledges and helps teachers articulate their expertise and practical knowledge, and introduces to the teachers new possibilities in ways of thinking and practices. Cases provide a mechanism for doing just this. Because they are close to practice, they are considered as legitimate by teachers who participate in their analyses. Further, when teachers write cases, they are articulating knowledge they did not know they had, and are therefore able to analyze their understandings for consistency and for the relationship between their understandings and their practices.

More important to the case movement than theoretical speculation about the benefits of case use in teacher education is documentation of the process. So often in education, we push for a new approach — competency based teacher education, professional development schools, reflective teacher education — but forget to provide information on implementation, potential barriers and successes. It is this information that allows and encourages others to implement the process, and to avoid some of the pitfalls that accompany the implementation. This book provides just this form of knowledge. As such, it will be extremely important for all those who are interested in introducing case use in their teacher education programs — either at the preservice or inservice levels.

Virginia Richardson
University of Arizona

Foreword III

Between narrative and experience two important relations arise. In one, the author constructs meaning from experience through storytelling. The verb here is evocative: We might replace "constructs" with "wrests" or "imposes on". The former suggests powerful experiences that the author wrestles with, seeking a coming to terms. Alternatively, the wrestling may ensue not from experience's emotional impact but from its ambiguity. The turn to stories may be an effort to collect understanding through a form of disciplined recollection. Narrative in the first instance may serve the author's desire for catharsis, in the second for understanding. In either, the emphasis rests on the experience in its powerful or puzzling aspects. The latter verb indicates an author engaged in a creative act, asserting his or her interpretation of experience. Author(ity) is paramount in this rendering, rather than the primacy of experience itself. We are authoring creatures, culture creators who build up the worlds we inhabit through the stories we tell, whose resonances intimate the universal in the particular, the sacred in the mundane, the depths beneath the surface.

The second relation between narrative and experience transpires in the reader's or listener's encounter with the story. The reader/listener brings his or her experience to the narrative, constructing an interpretation. This creative act, too, has its strong and weak forms. In its weak form, the narrative is accorded an autonomy that resides in canons associated with genres and in (much disputed) authorial intention. In this version, reader responses are more or less valid, depending on their observation of external standards and traditions of interpretation. The interpretive act is tethered to evidence proffered by the text. In its strong form, the narrative barely exists outside the reader's response; the reader writes the text. In this version, reader response swings free of received traditions and is a primary creative act grounded in the reader's perspectives, the validity of which is more or less independent of the narrative.

Contemporary literary theory, then, is provocative around questions of readers and writers, narrative and experience, standards and subjectivity. Such issues, I want to suggest, pertain as well to questions of case use in professional education. Some case users conceive professional knowledge *in the case*; others conceive the requisite knowledge as brought to bear *on the case* from other sources (e.g., "theory"). Some users carefully fabricate cases prior to instruction, then anchor discussion in those fabricated particulars. Others encourage students to create and share their own cases, shifting the case work from reader response to authorial production. Case users set cases into a range of instructional contexts, employing them as launching pads, as terrain for repeated visits, as practice sites, as culminating activities, as evaluation devices, and many others. Such invention and eclecticism is a healthy sign of a field that is actively creating its own practices.

Educators interested in case use might simply consult their imaginations for ideas, and this seems a promising starting point under present circumstances. But the experience of others with cases can serve to fortify the imagination, and that is the great value of the present volume. Authors of these chapters are not advocating imitation of their experiments. Rather, they offer their experience with case use as a stimulus for further invention. This is not a methods text; such would be counterproductive and misleading. Instead, this collection of reports operates more like a good network, in which individuals engage in mutual sharing of ideas and practices.

The construction of narratives — cases — from the viewpoint of author and of reader represents a complex and powerful means for learning from experience that many educators today are exploiting, stimulated not least by the existence of new technologies for case work. The reports assembled for this volume provide a rich sampling of this work and a welcoming invitation to build on and extend these forays.

Gary Sykes
Michigan State University

Preface

Why is there a growing interest in using case methods in teacher education? We think this question can be answered with one word: ***context***. Authenticity enhances the effectiveness of cases by adding context to theory. In all cases (sic), the overriding concern is to make cases real and to use authentic stories that illustrate key educational theories and bring up issues that are critical to the professional growth of teachers.

Cases represent an interesting paradox in that they are deeply personal, evolving out of an individual's experience, yet objective, in that they are designed to train teachers to function effectively in dealing with some of the most difficult problems they may face. This book is intended to deal with this duality. We sought leading case practitioners throughout the country and asked them for a personal account of how they do what they do. In keeping with the flavor of case methodology, one of our aims was to demonstrate the wide variety of case methodology applications. Another aim was to present a wide variety of strategies that other case practitioners could adapt or adopt.

As mentioned above, cases are attractive to educators because of their rich context and personal nature. We tried to reflect that attitude by asking each of our contributors to depart from traditional academic writing styles and make their chapters personal. We asked authors to address the following topics:

- Their personal histories with case methodology
- Procedures in using cases
- Original ways in which they use cases
- Their evaluations of case use
- Reflections and conclusions

About two years ago, in the Los Angeles area, several of us formed a Special Interest Group of the California Council for Education of Teachers. At one of our meetings, we discussed the possibility of case users telling their stories of how they use cases in their own local settings. After much discussion, we realized that there were some people around the country who are very active case users. Their tales of success and failure would be very compelling for potential and experienced case users alike. We contacted many of the leaders in this field and the result is this volume.

This book is the culmination of a journey that began in 1985. It was in 1985 that Joel Colbert first came to know Judy Shulman. He was working in the Los Angeles Unified School District and she was at Far West Labs, pioneering the use of case studies for teacher training. She proposed that they edit a book of cases written by a group of mentor teachers in Los Angeles. Thus began an interest in developing case studies in teacher education. Throughout Joel's involvement in the field, he noticed that many colleagues were also interested and case methods Special Interest Groups began to grow in pockets around the country. After working on two casebooks (*The Mentor Teacher Casebook* and *The Intern Teacher Casebook*) with Judy and presenting their work at conferences, there seemed to be a consistent call for some work on how people were actually using cases in their classes, with student teachers, in the staff development realm, and in other scenarios.

Peter and Kim met Judy by reading the two Casebooks, and later directly through conference participation. We all agreed that her contribution to the field of case methodology warranted special recognition. We would like to dedicate this collection to the person who first got us interested in using case methods in teacher education, Judy Shulman.

Joel A. Colbert, Peter Desberg, and Kimberly Trimble

Fostering Critical Analysis and Reflection Through Mathematics Case Discussions

Carne Barnett

Alma Ramirez

This chapter describes the reflections of a classroom teacher and a teacher educator to illustrate how case discussions can be structured to foster the growth of a critical and collaborative culture among teachers. Furthermore, it shows how this process serves as a model for classroom teaching that fosters such as an environment among students. We present an analysis of three key elements that are believed to be at the crux of these process: shared authority, intrinsic motivation, and the teacher's pedagogical–content knowledge.

We are beginning to believe that one of the most important purposes for case discussions may be to support "critical and collaborative teacher cultures which develop curriculum and pedagogical reform from within the profession" (Hargreaves & Dawe, 1990, p. 230). If case discussions are conducted in a way that teachers in the discussion group accept more responsibility for figuring things out and assign less responsibility to the facilitator as the "answer bearer," they become empowered. Once it happens to them, they seem eager to empower their own students in a similar way.

In this chapter, we discuss a professional development program that uses cases of mathematics teaching practice as a stimulus for reflective discourse among practicing teachers. We have evidence to support the claim that this program has many features that foster the growth of a critical and collaborative culture among teachers. An added benefit is that the case discussion process itself serves as a model for classroom teaching that fosters such an environment among students.

We are Carne Barnett, a researcher and teacher educator, and Alma Ramirez, a teacher with six years of experience teaching in sixth and seventh grade bilingual classrooms. Currently, Barnett is director of a professional development project called *Mathematics Case Methods* at Far West Laboratory for Educational Research and Development, and Ramirez teaches mathematics at a predominantly Latino community school in Oakland, California. Ramirez has participated for four years in the *Mathematics Case Methods Project* as a case discussion participant, a case discussion facilitator, a case writer and more recently as a teacher–leader in the project.

The *Math Case Methods Project* is a professional development program in which teachers meet monthly to discuss issues of mathematics teaching that are embedded in a case. Our cases are narratives, written by classroom teachers. They include information about the context and situation that occurred, examples of student work and dialogue, and reflections about what happened from the teacher's point of view. The case discussions are usually about 2 hours long and take place in a school setting. Typically, the group has from 6 to 15 teachers and is facilitated by someone who has prior experience as a case discussion participant and has had preparation to become a facilitator. Tyrrell School, Ramirez' former school in Hayward, California, opted to do curriculum development one afternoon per month in subject matter groups as part of their educational restructuring grant. Ramirez and her colleagues chose to focus on mathematics, and decided to use case discussions as their vehicle to examine on the teaching and learning of this subject matter.

In this chapter, we will relate two stories that are drawn from Ramirez's experiences at Tyrrell and Jingletown Charter Schools. They illustrate first, how case methods can foster critical analysis and reflection among teachers, and second, how these same dispositions also may be developed in students. The stories are followed by a discussion of what we believe are some of the key elements that contribute to critical analysis and reflection among teachers and their peers, and among teachers and their students. These elements — shared authority, intrinsic motivation, and the teacher's pedagogical–content knowledge — undergird the decisions we make about which cases we choose to discuss and the methodology we use to conduct the discussions.

The first story, narrated by Ramirez herself, is about her involvement as a participant in case discussions. The second story, also in Ramirez's voice, is about a lesson from her classroom. In it she describes how she sometimes feels like she is leading a case discussion with her students.

Ramirez: A Turning Point in the Case Discussions

When I first joined case discussions, I was a second year bilingual teacher. I look back on that year as the year I took it all in and tried to figure it out. Even though I met monthly to discuss mathematics cases for two hours with several 4th through 8th grade teachers from the district, I rarely spoke. The process was new to us all, and it took several months for us to begin to understand why we might be there and how this process was different from other professional development processes. I know now that Carne, who was our facilitator, was concerned that I was not interested or was not getting anything out of the process. The truth is that I was a bit intimidated by my lack of experience and also didn't feel I had anything new or different to add to the discussions. I did however, feel that the process was valuable to my development as a mathematics teacher.

Three teachers from our school participated in the case discussions that year. When Carne asked if any school would like to try having case discussions at their school site, our school volunteered. We had applied for a restructuring grant and felt that case discussions might help us think more deeply about how we wanted to restructure our math program.

Seven teachers from our school volunteered to participate in 30 hours of case discussions during that school year. Once again, we asked Carne to lead the case discussions because none of us felt ready to take on that responsibility. Our restructuring grant provided time on Wednesday afternoons to meet, and sometimes we had long meetings that extended into a potluck dinner.

Even at our fourth through sixth grade elementary school, the group was diverse. We had teachers with 25 years of experience to less than 2 years. Some of us were specialists in language acquisition, while others had math as their forte. Some of us were most comfortable with a fairly traditional approach, and some of us were already attempting newer methods such as those in current reform documents and our state framework.

Our first discussions were similar to those from the previous year. They were satisfying, but in retrospect, I feel we were still trying to please Carne. We were trying to figure out what she, as the "expert," wanted to hear and were looking to her for hints about the direction we should take. In our eyes, she was the expert, even though we didn't know much about her background at the time. These assumptions about our role as case discussion participants and Carne's role as a discussion leader were based on our previous professional development experiences.

Then something happened that made us see how truly different this process was. It occurred during a discussion of a case called *Zeroes Sometimes Make a Difference*. That case, like several others, focused on the teaching of decimals. We were looking at the manipulatives used in the case, and trying to figure out what the "best" one was. We tried money, measurement, base–ten blocks, and decimal grids… but nothing seemed to work. We left that session feeling frustrated, confused, and somewhat discouraged – but also feeling compelled to continue the discussion among ourselves.

The next month, Carne returned to us with a new case, but we had our own issues to deal with. We weren't finished with the decimal case from the month before. We had each brought along manipulatives we felt could help children understand decimals and continued the previous month's discussion. Each of us had evaluated the decimal teaching materials that we were using, and all of us were searching for something new: a new curriculum unit, a new manipulative, a new approach. We began to think that perhaps a combination of materials or approaches was a possibility. We carefully questioned our teaching and considered the difficult decisions we had to make. Everything has its trade–offs, but what was really important to us? What did we feel comfortable trying out?

I feel that here, as a group, our focus had shifted from trying to please Carne to trying to grapple with our own questions. Although we wanted to share our ideas with Carne, the tables had turned. The discourse changed from trying to convince the *facilitator*, to trying to convince our *peers* in the group. The facilitator still played an important part by pushing us to clarify our thinking, ask questions, defend our ideas, and consider other perspectives. But, instead of asking, "What does Carne want?" we began asking, "What is it that we need to figure out?" This became a new norm for our subsequent discussions, where the discussions were driven by what we felt was important for us as teachers, within the context of a mathematics case. We began to see ourselves and each other as authorities, and to share authority with the facilitator.

❊

Ramirez: I Feel Like I'm Leading a Case Discussion

Sometimes in our classroom, I feel like my students and I are having a case discussion. I wouldn't be able to describe it in this way or be able to execute this if I hadn't participated in case discussions myself. My ultimate goal has become for children to share authority with me. Instead of children looking to me as the base "of all knowledge" in our classroom, I want them to look to each other for answers to puzzling questions. I know this sounds naive, much more easily said than done, but I feel that this year we are close to reaching this turning point. Let me pose an example that I think illustrates the progress we are making toward that goal.

In my sixth and seventh grade bilingual mathematics classes, we were working on collaborative problem solving. In one lesson, students were given clues and asked to find the possible solutions to a problem in small group discussions. The problem for them turned out to be the clues themselves. My students had problems understanding a clue like "The difference between the digits is an odd number." "What was a 'digit'? What was meant by 'odd'?" they wanted to know. That night for homework, I had them write down what they thought certain phrases or words meant so that we could discuss them the next day.

What ensued was like a case discussion. For example, the students would say what they thought the word digit meant, I would write it on the chalkboard, and they would try to agree on the meaning. Examples and counterexample would fly across the room, until they were happy with the final product. We went on like this for sometime until we got to the meaning of odd number.

Rebecca, who is a socially and academically successful student, proudly raised her hand. She had gotten an answer from Ramon, a UC Berkeley engineering student who tutors them in math. "An odd number is a number that cannot be divided into two equal parts," she actually looked pretty triumphant as she said that. However, the other students had concerns about the wording.

I asked Rebecca if she'd like to change it, but she wouldn't budge. After all, a grown–up had given her that answer, so it had to be right. "Right?" she asked. I said I wasn't sure. Their conversation continued something like this:

"If I have 4 candy bars, and I keep two and you keep two, then it's even because it was divided into two equal parts. You can't do that with an odd number."

Four Candy Bars

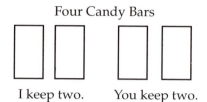

I keep two.   You keep two.

"Yes, you can" said Juan quickly.
"How?" demanded Rebecca.

Alejendro jumped in, *"If you have five candy bars, and you keep two and give me two, then we can split the last one in two and each of us keeps a half. That's two equal parts, and five is an odd number.*

Five Candy Bars

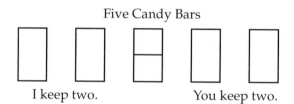

I keep two.   You keep two.

The last one we divide into two parts. Odd numbers can be divided into two equal parts.

"But that doesn't count," said Rebecca. *"You can't have any leftovers. Odd numbers can't be divided by two evenly."*

Lupe said from the back of the room, *"Anything can be divided by two, even fractions, even odd numbers."*

Rebecca was having a hard time convincing the class that she was right. Why were they disagreeing with her definition, which she had gotten from someone who was an authority in her eyes? At this point, I was pretty much out of this discussion.

The next day, I thought we'd wrap up the odd number controversy and get on with some "problem–solving." My students clearly had another idea in mind. They had gone home and continued their debates internally. Even though I was ready to go on, they weren't. So they discussed some more, and went back to Alejendro's five candy bar example. He showed how he could divide it evenly into two parts, so they refined their definition. What they came up with was that an odd number is a number that cannot be divided into two equal whole number parts. Then they were ready to go on.

It's not that I feel that odd numbers are a terribly important thing to cover in middle school, but I let the discussion go on just the same. Some important things were happening during their discourse. As in the our case discussion, they were looking to each other and within themselves for answers to their dilemmas. They were concerned about and motivated by their disagreements. Finally, mathematically, they were discussing part/whole relationships and division, as well as reevaluating myths about odd and even numbers that they had been carrying around since the first grade.

It has taken me a long time to decide that relinquishing some authority through discourse is something I want in my classroom. I have frequently heard that the teacher should be the "facilitator" and that there are questioning techniques that elicit discourse from students. This is a difficult thing to, however, and it still may not mean that the discussion is driven by the children.

I currently have a student teacher in my classroom. She did the same lesson with my Block 2 Math class. I could see that she was taught that discussion was a "good" thing. She tried to hold a discussion, and held her own fairly well. However, the ultimate authority rested with her, the final "meaning" was in her words, paraphrasing the students. It is difficult to explain to her that what I mean by *facilitating* is something different. All I can do is model. But the model for me was the process of being involved in case discussions.

Finally, part of the process of feeling comfortable sharing authority is truly believing that through time and discourse, and some guidance, children will negotiate meanings that will help them build conceptual understandings. Equally important is having a sense of what and how children are thinking, and being able to elicit that in a safe environment, one in which they are allowed to work things through at their own pace, and make changes in their thinking in their own time. In order to do this, a teacher must have a certain comfort level in her own conceptual understanding of the content, as well as his or her understanding of the student's thinking Without this comfort level, "letting go" becomes more challenging, as it is difficult to identify the importance of a particular discourse or reign–in a discussion.

✪

Elements and Conditions That Foster Critical Analysis and Reflection

Shared Authority

Judith Little (1993) proposes that one test of a teachers' professional development program is its capacity to "equip teachers individually and collectively to act as shapers, promoters, and well–informed critics of reforms" (p. 130). In other words, teachers must be partners in educational reform. The same could be said for students in the classroom. They must be partners in shaping their own educational experience. With the responsibility for making decisions, comes empowerment.

In both situations described in Ramirez's stories, we believe that one of the most important aspects was the development of shared authority. In the case discussion episode, the teachers did not see themselves as sharing authority with the facilitator in the beginning. The turning point for them was when they stopped viewing their role as "trying to find ways to please the facilitator" to "trying to figure out for themselves what was worthy of change." In the classroom episode, one can see the transition to shared authority was occurring for some students, but for Rebecca, the goal was still to respect adult knowledge more than her own or her peers.

In reflecting on how shared authority is developed through case discussions, we believe that the neutrality of the facilitator and the cases is a key aspect. If the facilitator or the cases promote a particular point of view or theory about teaching and learning, alternative views or theories will be less likely to surface for critical analysis in a discussion. Teachers who agree with the theory will feel validated, and teachers who disagree may either reject the ideas quietly or may openly resist the ideas. In either case, less popular or opposing ideas and beliefs do not get exposed and analyzed critically. We end up reinforcing the teachers who are already prone to reform and alienating those who are not.

We believe that developing shared authority may be a key aspect of a professional development process that values a culture of critical and collaborative thought and work. However, this calls into question the very basis on which many professional development programs rest. Is it possible to have *implementation* as a goal and not be in conflict with the goal of *shared authority*? It is common, for example, to find that professional development programs state their goal is to help teachers learn to *implement* the standards, a state framework, an innovative curriculum, a constructivist approach to teaching, or an approach to assessment. Yet, without additional qualification, implementation could imply the "uncritical adoption of preferred forms of action (new teaching styles) introduced and imposed by experts from elsewhere, in which teachers become technicians rather than professionals exercising discretionary judgment" (Hargreaves and Dawes, 1990, p. 230). Most of us would likely agree, in principle at least, that we must avoid this interpretation of *implementation*. However, it may be more difficult than one might think to design a professional development experience that has *implementation* as its goal, and that also encourages open discussion of, and possibly even disagreement with, the fundamental ideas that are to be *implemented*.

The case discussion process as it has been developed in the *Math Case Methods Project* has several aspects that safeguard against the uncritical adoption of ideas and strategies. First, the cases do not carry a presumption that the teaching they portray is either good or bad. It is up to teachers to decide this for themselves by carefully analyzing and reflecting upon the cases and their own experiences.

Second, the facilitator's job is not to lead teachers to implement a particular approach to teaching or a particular set of materials. Instead, the facilitator's role is to elicit alternative points of view and to provoke analysis of these alternatives. It is not the role of the facilitator to pass judgment on ideas or to promote his or her personal view. Again, teachers must decide for themselves what approaches they value and how much risk they are willing to take to change their practices, based on their own knowledge and confidence.

Third, although teachers are exposed to new ideas and new ways of thinking about teaching through the cases, *they* are the ones who are primarily responsible for seeking out the specific resources they need to change their practice. For example, they can call on each other for ideas and feedback, ask an "expert," request research articles, or look for new materials. There are other aspects that we could describe, but these are the most consequential ones from our point of view.

Intrinsic Motivation to Change

Cohen (1990) points out that educational change is unlikely to occur "unless the people who teach and learn want to change, take an active part in changing and have the resources to change" (p. 327). From a teacher's point of view, Ramirez puts it this way, "Changes take place when we're ready. We need discourse and time. We need to have experience looking at children's thinking over and over."

In the case discussions, we were totally surprised that two hours of discussion, once a month could be such a powerful motivator for change. We have five years of research to document changes in teachers' thinking, beliefs, pedagogical–content knowledge, and practice. We find ourselves wondering, "What motivates these changes?"

In the case discussions we see tremendous motivation arising from the teachers' consternation that "nothing works." In the case discussion that Ramirez described, teachers were frustrated that no manipulative was without its pitfalls for teaching decimal concepts. Teachers continued to search for something that would pacify the concerns that had arisen from their case discussions. They tried out different things in their classrooms through that year and the next. They created new curriculum units and adapted units developed by others. The change was motivated by the desire to understand and to assuage a nagging dissatisfaction with their current practices.

Likewise, from Ramirez's classroom situation, students were driven by the desire to express their ideas in such a way that they could stand up to the scrutiny of their classmates. They knew it was possible and were challenged by the possibility. Challenges, disagreement, conflict, and dissatisfaction are all seeds of intrinsic motivation to change.

While change that is extrinsically motivated may lead to desired results, we are struck by the powerful effect of intrinsically motivated change. Intrinsically motivated change is slower, more deliberate, and lasting change, one which comes from truly believing that this is worthwhile based on experience and analysis. We can only speculate about the relative value of change that is motivated intrinsically rather than extrinsically, but we believe that intrinsically motivated change may be more resilient to opposing influences. Teachers may be more willing to defend what they believe and practice if they are the ones who made changes based on their own inquiry and problem solving. We agree with Fullen (1993) who discusses a new paradigm for thinking about change, "It is a world where we will need generative concepts and capacities. What will be needed is the individual as inquirer and learner . . ." (p. viii).

Pedagogical Content Knowledge

Lee Shulman (1986) introduced the concept of pedagogical content knowledge and has helped us realize the difference between knowing content and knowing general pedagogical methods. The intertwining of the two represents a special kind of knowledge that is important for teachers. Ramirez alludes to this in her contrasts between the discourse that she elicits and that of her student teacher's. The student teacher has a general pedagogical strategy for engaging in discourse, but she has a limited knowledge of how that strategy applies to specific situations in mathematics learning. Ramirez, on the other hand, uses her deep pedagogical–content knowledge to pose counterexamples, to help her understand students' thinking, and to elicit alternative representations of the ideas.

Even if teachers question their methods of teaching and have a desire to change, many do not feel they have the resources to make a change. Some researchers are now suggesting that one of the most important resources that a teacher must have to risk change is a strong pedagogical–content knowledge base. Unless teachers can anticipate the tough spots and the complexities, understand children's thinking and know ways to deepen it, know the benefits and drawbacks of a variety of representations, and have a complex understanding of the interconnections among mathematical ideas, they will not adopt the teaching approaches that are strongly advocated in today's reform documents such as the NCTM Standards (1989, 1991). The cases in the *Math Case Methods Project* supports the growth of pedagogical content knowledge by focusing on student thinking and the related mathematical concepts and problems (Barnett, Goldenstein, Jackson, in press).

Our experience has shown that subject–specific cases can have an important role in expanding pedagogical–content knowledge, but we believe that our success is not incidental. We have selected and sequenced cases according to a theoretical stance advocated by Rand Spiro and his colleagues called cognitive flexibility theory (Spiro, Coulson, Feltovich & Anderson, 1988). In keeping with this theory, our cases focus on a relatively confined content domain, rational numbers. Because the domain is relatively narrow, the cases can be designed to elicit discussion about the same pedagogical–content issues and mathematical concepts again and again, each time in different contexts. By revisiting the same issues and concepts, we hope that teachers begin to connect the ideas and recognize them in new situations that they have not encountered before.

Change and Case Discussions

It is not unusual to hear comments from educational reformers and scholars that teachers are resistant to change. If professional development, however, were built on the premises we propose — shared authority, intrinsic change and strong pedagogical–content knowledge — we believe that resistance would not be an issue. In fact, as Richardson (1990) noted, "Teachers change all the time. Therefore the problem is not one of change or non–change. It centers on the degree to which teachers engage in the dialogue concerning warranted practice and take control of their classroom activities and theoretical justifications; and the degree to which these justifications relate to the socially constructed standards of warranted practice" (p. 16).

Our cases are constructed to portray actual situations that are messy and complex. They call for ongoing analysis and compromises rather than solutions. They are different from cases that are constructed to illustrate a preconceived point (Doyle, 1990, p. 10). It is our hope that by learning how to analyze critically and reflect on one's experiences one can respond to new situations with increased knowledge and better judgment. In the classroom, as opposed to some other professions, decisions are made minute by minute rather than day by day or month by month. One has to think on one's feet and accept that no solution is perfect. Cases offer one way that teachers can learn these ways of thinking and make well–informed decisions.

References

Barnett, C., Goldenstein, D. & Jackson, B. (1994). *Mathematics teaching cases: Fractions, decimals, ratios, and percents; Hard to teach and hard to learn?*, Portsmouth, NH: Heinemann.

Cohen, D. (1990). A revolution in one classroom: The case of Mrs. Oublier. *Educational Evaluation and Policy Analysis, 12*(3), 327–345.

Doyle, W. (1990). Case methods in the education of teachers. *Teacher Education Quarterly, 17* (1), 7–15.

Fullen, M. (1993). *Change forces, probing the depths of educational reform.* London: The Falmer Press.

Hargreaves, A. and Dawe, R. (1990). Paths of professional development: Contrived collegiality, collaborative culture, and the case of peer coaching. *Teaching and Teacher Education, 6*(3), 227–241.

Little, J. (1993). Teachers' professional development in a climate of educational reform. *Educational Evaluation and Policy Analysis, 15*(2), 129–151.

Merseth, K. (in preparation). Cases and case methods in teacher education. *Handbook on Teacher Education.* New York: MacMillan.

National Council of Teachers of Mathematics. (1989). *Curriculum and evaluation standards for school mathematics.* Reston, VA: NCTM.

National Council of Teachers of Mathematics. (1991). *Professional standards for teaching mathematics.* Reston, VA: NCTM.

Richardson, V. (1990). Significant and worthwhile change in teaching practice. *Educational Researcher, 19*(7), 10–18.

Shulman, L. (1986). Those who understand: Knowledge growth in teaching. *Educational Researcher, 15(4)*, 4–14.

Spiro, R. J., Coulson, R., Feltovich, P., & Anderson, D. (1988). Cognitive flexibility theory: Advanced knowledge acquisition in ill–structured domains. In *Tenth Annual Conference of the Cognitive Science Society*, 375–383, Hillsdale, NJ: Lawrence Erlbaum.

Carne Barnett joined Far West Laboratory in 1989 as Director of the Mathematics Case Methods project. Dr. Barnett's pioneering work with cases in a content area began as part of the Teacher Assessment Project at Stanford University. She currently helps guide Far West Laboratory research and development efforts as Associate Director of the Institute for Case Development. Dr. Barnett draws her expertise from a range of previous experiences in teacher education and teaching. She was a faculty member in the Graduate School of Education at the University of California, Berkeley, for eight years where she initiated and directed a K-12 Mathematics Specialist Credential Program, coordinated two preservice teacher education programs, and instructed several graduate level courses. Dr. Barnett has published in research journals, is the author of three mathematics textbook series, is co-editor of a casebook on mathematics teaching, and has written several resource books for mathematics teachers. She was a mathematics resource teacher and classroom teacher in urban settings for 10 years.

Alma Ramirez has been a classroom teacher for more than eight years. As well as teaching 7th and 8th grade, she has also been a mathematics methods instructor a the New College of California, a Family Math Mentor for the Lawrence Hall of Science, and a teacher–leader and case discussion facilitator for the *Math Case Methods Project*. Ramirez has co–led numerous presentations at various professional meetings and conferences. She is the author/consultant/reviewer for a mathematics textbook, and has co–authored research papers on math case duscussions. Ramirez currently teaches mathematics, science, and Spanish at Jingletown Charter School in Oakland, CA, and is working on her masters degree in mathematics education at San Francisco State University.

Creating A Shared Culture Through Cases and Technology:

The Faceless Landscape of Reform

Traci Bliss
Joan Mazur

Our project, Common Thread Cases: Teachers in the Midst of Reform, is a series of stories capturing how teachers transform practice in policy-driven reform. Our conceptual framework, based on art theory, suggests that positive images expand our perspective and inspire our creativity. In teaching and teacher education we have few such images, especially actual cases, of innovative of accomplished practice. The cases in our series provide rich depictions of good teaching and the dilemmas that so often accompany change. These images can help novice and experienced teachers to envision new possibilities for their own practice and the schools in which they teach.

By having the cases also available in a compact disc (CD-ROM) format, teachers have multiple ways of studying real images of good practice. Video clips, high quality graphics, photography, and audio narration intensify the reader's full participation in the story.

Introduction

My interest in the case method developed several years before I decided to become a teacher. As a graduate student at the LBJ School of Public Affairs, University of Texas, Austin in the mid 1970's, I experienced the case method as the foundation for critical thinking about policy issues and it provided an induction into a shared culture. Case discussions constituted at least 10–12 hours a week of the LBJ core curriculum. Years after graduation when LBJ classmates came together, our discussions often turned to specific cases decades after we had forgotten other aspects of the curriculum. The cases presented in–depth images of policy makers and discussions were usually intensely emotive with no easy answers. Perhaps because the case characters provided us with vicarious and dramatic experiences of our profession, the images have endured, helping us to talk with one another.

Some years later when I entered the Stanford Teacher Education Program, I was surprised to discover that cases were not used in preparing teachers. *Without cases* I wondered, *where would we collectively learn about how real teachers solve problems? Where would we see great moments in teaching to which we might aspire or about which we could disagree?* Without cases, ours was an idiosyncratic induction. We each had a world view too frequently defined by the relationship with a single mentor teacher. Weekly we would emerge from our methods classes with no truly shared experience of our profession. The history of classroom practice, a culture my colleagues and I were seeking to join, was for the most part, faceless.

The Faceless Culture of Reform

I moved to Kentucky in 1991, recruited to be part of the state's systematic reform effort. Acting under a court order, the state legislature passed the Kentucky Education Reform Act (KERA) of 1990, which mandated radical change in school governance, finance, and curriculum, accompanied by a tax increase considered essential to the reform's success[1]. The two most heavily funded reform initiatives were the development of a technology infrastructure linking every school in the state, and a performance assessment system for all students, K–12.

In the early years of reform, the difficulties of teacher preparation became readily apparent. The problem of thousands of new teachers a year entering a rapidly changing teaching profession is hardly unique to Kentucky, but the urgent need to address the problem is more pronounced here because of the statewide policy holding schools and teachers accountable for students' academic progress. For teacher educators it poses a unique challenge. We can engage new teachers in lengthy discussions about changes in classroom practice, but without authentic, concrete, and accessible images we mire them in abstractions.

Experienced teachers face a similar if more complex problem. The unrelenting pressure to change means leaving a familiar landscape for the new and unknown. Experienced teachers have no shared images of how their peers change pedagogy, no rich accounts of the struggles and accomplishments of teachers in the midst of policy–driven reform[2]. Their painful experiences of uncertainty were brought home to me rather dramatically this past year. When scheduled to play in a regional tennis tournament I learned the match would be on clay, a surface with which I was unfamiliar. I found a "clay pro" who confirmed that playing on clay was a very different game. But the pro took my basic strokes and showed me how to adjust them for clay. He demonstrated for me, for example, that I should angle my overheads to adjust to the slower pace of clay. I promptly forgot all this while losing badly in the regionals, but at least I had the images for what I might practice under less stressful circumstances.

This was an indelible lesson for what teachers really needed in the turbulence of transition. Policy–driven reform had provided directives for the "switch to clay," but had given no corresponding images of what the process for making that switch might look like. Teacher success stories are routinely published by the Kentucky Department of Education, but these focus on *what* teachers have accomplished, not the *hows* of transforming practice or the complex issues involved in the process.

The Need for New Cases

Within the teaching profession, two types of teaching cases are commonly used: controversy cases and good teaching/aspiration cases. A controversy case attempts to capture a controversial or problematic issue immediately relevant to teachers. It may or may not show how key characters attempt to solve the issue. Good teaching/aspiration cases present rich and extensive descriptions of innovative or accomplished teaching. In these compelling episodes of good teaching, the teacher's philosophy and various dimensions of the teaching context are also often presented. This type of case, however, is far more than a portrait; it tells a story of how a teacher handles an instructional dilemma.

While controversy cases abound, there is a dearth of good teaching/aspiration cases. This is due in part to the challenges of writing such cases. Rendering detailed pictures of good practice imbued with a true and engaging storyline is demanding work. It requires the rigor of qualitative research and the artistry of storytelling.

The power of these demonstrative cases, however, is apparent to anyone who has experienced them in the classroom. My own experiences using a good teaching/aspiration case in a course entitled Past, Present and Future of Education Reform, are illustrative. The course began with the history of 20th century reform efforts, followed by the history of the Kentucky reform: its philosophy, components and comparisons with other reform efforts. This was followed by a lengthy case discussion of *When is Enough, Enough?* (Bliss, 1995), the story of an award winning high school teacher, Elaine Temkin. Mrs. Temkin teaches U.S. History thematically, beginning her course with a unit on the Vietnam War and using primary source materials and cooperative learning extensively. She is emphatic on the issue of themes, "I don't think any teacher has a right to teach history without an overriding theme; mine is conflict and consensus." The story focuses on the way she motivates a low achieving student Mark, who wants to transfer to a less demanding course.

In the course, beginning teachers analyzed Temkin's approach of ignoring a student's prior records because she feels it diminishes her capacity to have high expectations for all students. As the story of the case unfolds, we see several examples of how this teacher integrates an extensive knowledge of history with a variety of teaching strategies. The case discussion included the following types of questions: In what ways is her teaching consistent or inconsistent with the goals of reform in Kentucky and elsewhere? What combination of teaching strategies enable her to successfully motivate students, especially students like Mark? Are certain student performance standards most obviously associated with her teaching? (For example, every graduating senior in Kentucky must demonstrate a knowledge of historical perspective and this teacher presents a unique example of teaching historical perspective.)

We revisited the case later in the course. In the unit on Urban Education we compared and contrasted Elaine Temkin with Jaime Escalante, using the movie *Stand and Deliver*, excerpts from *Escalante: The Best Teacher in America* (Matthews, 1985) and an article from *Education Week* (Hill, 1994). To balance the information on Escalante, students viewed film clips of Temkin discussing her teaching.[3] Thoughtfully and with considerable wit, she elaborates on points brought out in the case such as the use of thematic teaching as a way of giving students meaningful concepts for understanding history. In comparing Temkin and Escalante, students saw both in the context of large urban high schools yet involved in little interaction with their colleagues. Both have very high standards and expectations for their students and themselves, and both create a strong sense of group identity, but they have very different approaches to pedagogy. Students were asked to ponder both approaches, asking themselves the following questions: Why do both approaches seem to work? Is one necessarily better? Is it possible to make such a judgment? If so, on what basis? How would each respond to Kentucky's assessment mandates for high school students?

Students seem to benefit from these case discussions in a number of ways. Four months after the course students were asked to anonymously report what they recalled most about the Temkin case. Fifty percent of the students discussed Elaine's specific teaching methods such as thematic teaching, critical thinking and cooperative learning. The other half wrote about how the teacher challenged, encouraged, or motivated an at–risk student. Adjectives such as determination, persistence, and confidence appeared frequently in their responses. The case had conveyed a strong positive image, of both effective and character qualities that were never explicitly stated in the case.

The case seemed to resonate not only with history teachers, many of whom were interested in the details of her teaching a specific historical event, but also with teachers from other disciplines. A math teacher at a local high school commented, "I see several students like Mark...so I find the teachers who are good at motivating at–risk kids and watch them very closely." Similarly, a foreign language teacher commented:

> *I recall the way she presented group work, how she stressed conflict and consensus as a theme for her class, how she used many secondary sources as texts for her class. I remember her persistence with the problem student and her willingness to work with him until he got caught up with the rest of the class. I remember the student developing the skill of supporting his opinions and challenging the other students to support their opinions. I remember the student finally succeeding in the regular U.S. History class and the next year opting out of AP U.S. History because he thought it would be too challenging. I remember thinking these are the battles you win and lose in teaching.*

I also use this case very successfully in courses for more experienced teachers. Experienced teachers often recount Temkin's success with cooperative learning, intrigued by her strategies for individual accountability. Several teachers have said she inspired them to try more thematic teaching. This one good teaching/aspiration case, however, is insufficient for teachers eager for images of this new, emerging culture. For them, the teaching terrain, filled with years of recognizable practice, has all at once become unfamiliar. The "switch to a clay court" has meant that primary teachers are teaching multi–age, multi–ability classes for the first time; secondary teachers in math, history, and science are teaching writing for the first time; and English teachers are responsible for student portfolios. A reservoir of new and relevant positive images would seem to be required to encourage teachers to assume more risks in their teaching.

In a course entitled, The American High School, I decided that as a group, we would begin to create a shared culture. As a term project, each student wrote a case of an experienced secondary teacher, considered good by his/her peers, and how that teacher was handling a dilemma or multiple dilemmas related to reform. Every case depicted a teacher's philosophy, background, pedagogy and his or her approach to solving the dilemma. The case included an analysis drawing on course readings.

During the last month of the course, part of each class was devoted to students presenting their cases and leading a discussion among their peers. With each new case presented, the class was building its pictures of reform. These were not intended to be polished cases, but local stories of talented teachers and the complex issues they faced. Some issues, like the presence or absence of administrative support for teacher change, were common enough among the early cases that they became easily recognizable in the later ones. "Oh, that's really similar to the principal in Robert's case." Through this type of image, a shared culture was beginning to emerge; the "clay court" no longer seemed like foreign terrain. This was obvious in each class session as body language, levels of participation, and interest hinted at important changes. Teachers were eager to stay after class, late into the evening, to discuss the cases. They were particularly intent on knowing how other teachers approached specific problems, like incorporating extensive writing in high school math or preparing students for performance–based assessments. I was reminded of my own experience of professional bonding in public policy school.

What makes this bonding possible? My hunch is this: when a good teaching/aspiration case imparts a recognizable and positive image, it is giving concrete meaning to abstractions about pedagogy. For example, high expectations, a buzz word in Kentucky reform, become real and achievable through the story of Elaine Temkin and her student Mark. The story becomes the vehicle for translating the abstraction into qualities like caring and persistence; a once remote idea is made tangible.

Encouraged by teacher feedback on the good teaching cases, I became more intrigued by the idea of a shared culture. Assuming we could produce a sufficient number of good teaching cases, how could these ever be made accessible to the majority of teachers, especially teachers in remote geographic areas? By chance, I turned to a colleague who brought to bear the powerful world of technology to help transform my ideas into reality.

Creating a Shared Culture: Cases and Technology

While lingering over lunch at a local eatery in January 1994, reluctant to return to the residue of Kentucky's worst ice storm, I listened intently as Traci talked about cases, her experiences, and her vision of cases for shaping a shared culture. *How*, she asked, *could technology help this case idea?* Occasionally there are times, and it seemed to me this was one of them, when the presence of a like–minded colleague is completely apparent. In fact, using technology to effect change in a professional culture had been the goal of a development project I had recently been associated with. Prior to coming to Kentucky in 1993, I worked as part of a multimedia design team at Cornell developing a collaborative computing environment for engineers. It seemed that Kentucky's teaching culture in transition could make productive use of these same kinds of tools and resources. Moreover, my personal experience resonated with the needs of these teachers. In the 1970's I had spent several years as a junior high English teacher in rural, upstate New York, where access to subject area colleagues was impossible. Then, as a new teacher, filled with enthusiasm and doubt, I wondered about my teaching. What strategies did other English teachers use to engage parents or to motivate bored students? Were others experimenting, as I was, with the use of photography and drama to teach composition and point of view? What I would have given to be able to sit down after school and send off a quick e–mail to talk with other teachers.

Given our complementary paths, we continued to explore the concept of a shared culture. How could Kentucky's burgeoning electronic communication network be used as the infrastructure for virtual, online communities? A CD–ROM format for cases, combined with e–mail and Internet could give teachers unique access to each other in new and exciting ways. Our collaboration, *Common Thread Cases: Teachers in the Midst of Reform*, was born.

The project's title derives from *The Thread That Runs So True*, Jesse Stuart's widely acclaimed narrative about teaching in Appalachian Kentucky (Stuart, 1949). Stuart took his title from the chant of a mountain folk game. In the game, the thread winds its way throughout a circle of children; each child eagerly anticipates the next move in order to be drawn into the circle. Stuart saw the fun and adventure of the game as analogous to teaching, in that there is a never–ending challenge to engaging each child. The idea of the *Thread That Runs So True*, is similar to what David Cohen (1988) describes as "adventurous learning." For teachers in the midst of reform, adventure is a key word. In its truest sense, adventure stresses the excitement or thrill associated with change, applicable to either the event or its emotional effects.

The first step in our collaboration following the "ice-storm lunch" was to involve like-minded colleagues at the University of Louisville in our effort and collectively to clarify project goals.[4] We agreed:

1. We would produce a series of true story cases, capturing the types of dilemmas and accomplishments teachers experience in policy–driven reform.

2. Each case would be related to one or more of the state– adopted teacher performance standards, not as a formula, but as an illustration consisting

of rich and detailed depictions of classroom practice. Consistent with our project title, teacher performance standards would be referred to as the "common threads" of changing practice.

3. Cases would be available in hard copy and compact disc formats with a major focus on the latter.

4. Our overriding purpose in developing the cases would be to provide views of the possible, what we refer to as images of aspiration.

By the late spring, we had received project funding from the University of Kentucky/University of Louisville Joint Center for the Study of Education Policy, the Gheens Foundation of Louisville and the Bell South Foundation of Atlanta. Kentucky Educational Television had joined us as a full partner contributing all the video production services necessary for development of the interactive CD–ROM.

Common Thread Cases:
Program Description

The thematic metaphor for the Common Thread Cases interactive computing program is weaving. This image runs through the conceptual task of weaving the teaching standards relevant to the case into thinking about classroom experience, as well as through the visual and structural organization of the program.

When the program begins, a vibrant graphic of interwoven threads is displayed on the screen. From this initial screen, shown in Figure 1, the user can

Figure 1: Common Threads Cases Initial Screen

select from three "buttons" that lead to distinct parts of the program. Selecting the KERA Context Button, for example, launches a presentation of historical and descriptive information about the Kentucky Education Reform Act.

Clicking on the True Story Case Button begins the teaching case. The full text of the animated case, enhanced by audio or video segments is presented. The narrative of each case is animated through the use of video clips, high quality graphics, photography, audio narration, and original music. The user can read the complete narrative, hear commentary by the case subject, or listen to remarks by other teachers concerning the case. Various online features can be used during one's exploration of the case. In Figure 2, several of these features, including multimedia representations of the case content, and several interactive tools and resources, are shown.

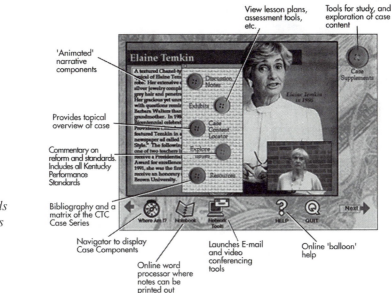

Figure 2: Case threads and features

Another feature, the Case Content Map (see Figure 3), displays the wealth of pedagogical information available to the interested teacher. This arrangement of case topics enables the user to navigate strategically throughout the case for specific content. The Content Map also marks sections already visited by shading in the display box. These features are especially helpful during subsequent uses of the case when a teacher may be examining one problem or approach in a focused study.

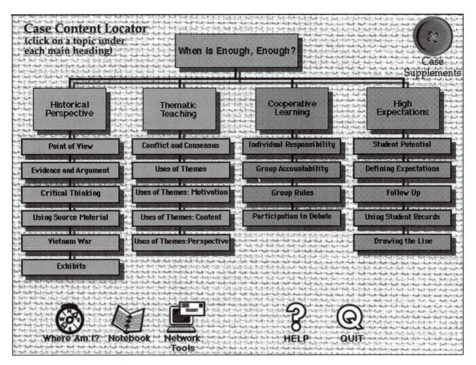

Figure 3: Case Content Map

The Common Thread Case interface is designed to function in two significant ways. It is an online storyteller that sets a context and presents a narrative embellished with multimedia representations to provide recognizable images of good teaching. Also, the interface is a communication tool that supports teacher discourse about common issues in transforming practice.

Prospective Uses of Compact Disc Cases

We anticipate that the Common Thread CD–ROM cases can be used to meet an array of professional needs. First, the CD–ROM versions of cases should enhance teacher preparation. The visual imagery provides a far richer understanding of the issues, with extensive teacher comments on pedagogy and transformative efforts. After the case discussion, students working alone or in groups can continue to explore the multimedia case and its resources such as the online notebook.

CD–ROM case materials can also be used for distance learning. The facilitator can conduct the case discussion via interactive video, simulating the immediacy of a classroom. Networked computers can enable case viewers at physically separate locations to share screens and work simultaneously on the same case. Again, proximity and spontaneity can be achieved through the CD, even though the participants may be at considerable distance from one another.

The compact discs can be used as part of ongoing professional development for experienced teachers. The program's e–mail and Internet video conferencing tools can link experienced teachers at diverse geographic locations. Through informal conversations teachers can discuss the issues raised in the case that are pertinent to their implementation of reform. Beginning teachers can also interact with experienced teachers throughout the state or nation on topics of mutual interest. Mentoring relationships no longer need to be confined to a single classroom or school. These collaborative activities underscore how even a self–contained CD–ROM can preserve the key feature of the case method: intense participation in the discussion of professional dilemmas and pedagogical issues.

Empty Infrastructure or Professional Culture?

We believe, for many reasons, that technology can help support the creation of a shared culture. First, vivid positive images create a sense of familiarity with the new and unknown. The highly visual CD–ROM presents cases as animated multimedia narratives. According to students' feedback, Elaine Temkin talking about her teaching in conjunction with the case narrative makes the situation more real and intensifies the images of good teaching.

Second, Internet tools make it possible for teachers to engage informally in case conversations even when they work at great distances from one another. When weary of formal inservice, teachers are now able to control their own professional development using a CD–ROM on the desktop at school or home. The convenience is extended by the e–mail tool on the CD–ROM, enabling teachers to have thoughtful discourse that is safe and private when struggling to implement new approaches. With the accessibility provided by these tools, teachers have the opportunity to engage in spontaneous and personal online discussions.

A major obstacle to such a professional community, however, is the very problem we began with: an absence of true stories of talented teachers in various disciplines and at different grade levels. To meet the needs of teachers and conduct formal research on good teaching cases, a reservoir of compelling stories is prerequisite. These narratives, focused on pedagogy, are the essence of our work. Without these expressive positive images, technological enhancements may be premature, perhaps even specious. As advocates of this idea, to date we have produced eight multimedia cases and are eager for others to develop more of such cases.

The technological infrastructure for CD–ROM cases and for spontaneous online personal communications already exists. This suggests the ability to galvanize our profession through the creation of electronic associations among teachers discussing stories of other teachers. The issues facing Kentucky's educators are not confined to a specific geographic area, but are common to teachers anywhere attempting to transform practice.[6]

The conditions are ripe for changing the faceless landscape of changing schools. Use of the case method, systemic reform, and technological innovation are synergistic nationwide movements. For us, they present an unprecedented opportunity to support and inspire classroom teachers as they are challenged by the hard work of reform.

Notes

[1] The Council for Better Education (CBE) filed its suit in 1986 alleging that Kentucky's entire system of common schools was inequitable and therefore unconstitutional. Bert Combs, former Governor of Kentucky, represented CBE before the Kentucky Supreme Court in 1989–90. The court found for the plaintiffs in *Council for Better Education versus. Rose* (1989).

[2] Policy–driven reform is used to differentiate the type of reform underway in Kentucky from reforms that teachers elect to participate in, such as the Coalition of Essential Schools. In Kentucky, a comprehensive performance assessment system includes accountability, e.g., rewards and sanctions for all schools.

[3] These film clips, produced by Kentucky Educational Television for specific use in our case development project, are then converted to a digital video format for the CD–ROM.

[4] Ric Hovda, professor of Early and Middle Childhood Education at the University of Louisville, is a co–director of the Common Threads Cases project. He is also the Associate Director of the Center for Collaborative Research at the University of Louisville.

⁵ For example, the case may be animated with audio narration that punctuates the oral storytelling with the immediacy of tone of voice, patterns of speech, or perhaps regional accents. Background music conveys mood and pace, among other qualitative aspects of context (Mazur, 1993).

⁶ The Common Thread Cases is available in both hardcopy and CD–ROM through the University of Kentucky/University of Louisville Joint Center for the Study of Educational Policy. Through the use of this non–profit distribution system, we can offer cases at a very reasonable price.

References

Bliss, T. (1995). *When is enough, enough?* Lexington, KY: The University of Kentucky/University of Louisville Joint Center for the Study of Educational Policy.

Cohen, D. K. (1988) Teaching practice: Plus ça change…In Jackson, P. (Ed.), *Contributing to educational change: Perspectives on research and practice* (National Society for the Study of Education Series on Contemporary Issues). Berkeley, CA : McCutchan.

Hill, D. (March 30, 1994). Stand and deliver: Act II. *Education Week*, 20-23.

Matthews, J. (1988). *Escalante: The best teacher in America.* New York: Holt.

Mazur, J (1993). *The interpretation and use of visuals in an interactive multimedia fiction program.* Unpublished doctoral dissertation. Cornell University.

Stuart, J. (1949). *The thread that runs so true.* New York: Charles Scribner's Sons.

Acknowledgments

For their insights and valuable criticisms we thank Judith Kleinfeld, Doug Smith, and Cynthia Ingols. For their reviews of our final draft, we appreciate the precision of our graduate students Caroline Fahrney, Toni Bishop, and Jenny Lynn Varner.

Traci Bliss is a faculty member in the Department of Curriculum and Instruction at the University of Kentucky and the Director of the project, Common Thread Cases: Teachers in the Midst of Reform. Her research with Joan Mazur describing the effects of the Common Thread Cases on beginning teacher priorities appears in *The Report of the First International Conference on Standards and Assessment*, University of North Carolina, Chapel Hill, 1995.

Joan M. Mazur is an assistant professor of instructional design and technology at the University of Kentucky and co-director of the Common Thread Case Project. She specializes in the design and research of interactive, networked multimedia programs. Previous work at the Interactive Multimedia Group at Cornell University included collaborative design interfaces for engineers, an interactive fiction program for Spanish language learning, and a hypermedia database for entomologists. Her current work has focused on the applications of these emerging technologies to teacher preparation and development in the context of systemic reform. Her research has been published in *The Journal of Educational Computing Research*, *The Journal of Research on Computing in Education*, and *Educational Technology*.

Cases in Context

Joel A. Colbert

In this chapter, I shall describe how I currently use cases in a generic secondary teaching methods course. As the title suggests, I use cases in a contextual setting, i.e., I integrate cases throughout the course when appropriate to the topic at hand.

First, I shall describe the cases and the context in which they are utilized in the class. Second, I'll describe the process by which students reflect on their own experiences and offer solutions to problems that might occur based on the situation posed in the case.

There are two types of cases I use with students. First, there are mini–cases, or caselettes, based on my own experiences and those of my students. These are typically anecdotal in nature and illustrate critical events in the lives of beginning teachers. Second, there are full blown cases from the two casebooks I co–edited with Judy Shulman (1987,1988), the Primis series (Silverman, Welty, and Lyon, 1993), and a new form of electronic interactive case, developed by Desberg, Colbert, and Trimble (1995).

Introduction

I shall use a narrative form of writing in this chapter, similar to one I use when I compose vignettes (cases) for use in my courses. This chapter is not research in and of itself, but the application of research on using case studies in teacher education.

I have been using cases in this context since 1988. Prior to that I worked with Judy Shulman, of Far West Laboratory, in developing two of the first casebooks for use in teacher education (Shulman and Colbert, 1987; Shulman and Colbert, 1988). During the initial design of these two publications, we had many discussions about how teachers share their "war stories" with each other in the cafeteria, over a beverage after school, and with colleagues in the teacher's lounge. These stories were rarely used for training purposes. Thus, there wasn't a record or legacy left by teachers that could be used for training beginning teachers. As a result of our work, the two casebooks have been extensively used in a variety of settings, e.g., college classes, staff development programs, etc. Since that time, cases have become much more widely used in the teacher education setting, as evidenced by works such as this book.

In this chapter, I shall describe how I currently use cases in a generic secondary teaching methods course. As the title suggests, I use cases in a contextual setting, i.e., I integrate cases throughout the course when appropriate to the topic at hand. Before I describe the course setting (again, context is an important part of this entire treatise), I will describe the students who enroll in this course.

Description of Students

There are two categories of students who enroll in teaching methods courses. First, there are students completing their credential coursework who will be student teaching the following semester. While enrolled in my class, they are observing in classrooms and, in many instances, helping teachers by working with small groups of students or with a student who needs extra help. Their classroom experience is limited, but not totally lacking.

The second group of students are classified as interns. An intern is a full-time classroom teacher who is completing his or her credential on the job. Interns are hired by local school districts, e.g., Los Angeles, Long Beach, and Compton Unified School Districts, who have teacher shortages in specific fields and who issue an emergency teaching credential to hire teachers who have not yet completed credential requirements. The stipulation is that emergency credentialed teachers must complete at least six semester units per year. In most instances, these teachers enroll in a credential program, and at California State University, Dominguez Hills, we have a special intern program for them so that they can complete the preliminary credential requirements in three semesters.

Since these two groups of teachers are quite different, i.e., one group is full–time teachers and the other has not even student–taught yet, it adds a unique dimension to a methods class. I try to use the experiences of the interns when we have case discussions to make the cases more relevant to the students. I try to use the actual experiences that the interns face on a daily basis to provide insight in solving problems that the interns are currently facing and will face as a prelude of things to come for the future student teachers.

Course in Context

The teaching methods course is part of a two semester methods course sequence. The first semester is generic and covers such topics as motivation, learning modalities, lesson planning, scope and sequence, various instructional strategies, logistics (rollbook, audiovisual, roles and responsibilities, paperwork, etc.), and problem–solving. The second semester of teaching methods is content area specific, e.g., science. While I also use cases in the content specific course, I shall describe my use of cases in the first semester course here.

Case Use I: Mini–Cases or Caselettes

Over the years, I have compiled mini–cases, or caselettes, based on my own experiences and those of my students. I differentiate between cases and caselettes in that the former should be well developed "stories", and may serve to illustrate larger principles, as well as describe events, problems, or situations. The latter serve to illustrate events that occur more spontaneously and, very often, are not well developed, and do not include a clear beginning, middle, and end. For example, I begin the semester with the following situation:

> It is your first day of school. You receive your class enrollment lists and, on your way to Period 1, realize that you are about to have 65 students enter your classroom, which comfortably holds 35. You call the head counselor, who sympathizes with you and says that the problem will be solved within the next two weeks. How would you handle this situation and what steps would you take to deal with the 65 students who are now entering the room?

This caselette is based on an actual experience I had, and one that many beginning teachers face, although not necessarily to that extreme. At the beginning of class, I pose the caselette, ask students to think about it and write down some of their thoughts while I take care of attendance, necessary paperwork and logistics. We then use the first ten to fifteen minutes of class for discussion of the caselette. I use a large class discussion setting in this context, since I do not want to spend a lot of time on the discussion, using it mainly as a warm–up and to focus the class. On occasion, the discussion continues over the allotted time, usually because students want to share their own similar experiences. I feel that this type of reflection is important, not only for those who want to share their experiences, but for all class members because I do not want my students to feel isolated in their classroom and to realize that *all* teachers have problems.

I like to use the class as a forum for sharing and reflection. In many instances, I record their own caselettes for use in future semesters, thus adding a heavier dose of reality and expanding my collection. When possible, I try to use caselettes that are relevant to the class topic that day.

A typical example of a student–generated caselette would be:

> You are a member of the curriculum committee at your school. The committee's role is to assist in the decision–making process regarding instructional programs. Before the committee is a motion to initiate a silent reading program during homeroom. The committee is split regarding a decision. One of the teachers writes a letter expressing his views about the program and distributes copies of the letter by placing them in all of the teachers' mailboxes. You believe that the letter is biased and decide to respond by writing your own letter and distributing it in the same manner.
>
> The day after you distribute the letter, you get a note from the principal asking you to report to the office after school. At the meeting, you are accused of improperly using teachers' mailboxes and the principal is going to write a letter of reprimand that will be placed in your personnel file. What is your reaction? What is your strategy for dealing with the situation?

I would use a caselette like this on a day when I am addressing logistical topics such as the rollbook, substitute folder, and, using faculty mailboxes.

In my course evaluations, I have consistently received positive feedback concerning my use of caselettes such as those described above. Samples of student comments include:

> *"I could really relate to the situation, since I have been in the same situa
> tion."*
> *"I never thought I would face such a problem, but I have spoken to
> other teachers who have and now I feel more prepared."*
> *"Now I know what to do the next time I am faced with a similar problem."*

Case Use II: Teaching Methods I: Secondary

I currently have three sources for cases that I use in the methods class: The
two casebooks I co–edited with Judy Shulman (1987,1988), the Primis series
(Silverman, Welty, and Lyon, 1993), and a new form of electronic interactive
case, developed by Desberg, Colbert, and Trimble (1995). This latter case is
more fully described in another chapter of this book (see Desberg and Fisher).

First, I shall describe the cases I use, and the context in which they are used
in the class. Second, I'll describe the process I use to cause students to reflect on
their own experiences, and offer solutions to problems that might occur based
on the situation posed in the case.

In addition to the caselettes described above, which I use at the start of most
class sessions, I use at least four larger cases, to which I devote approximately
one hour of class time. I always use *Descent from Innocence* (Shulman and Colbert,
1988). In this case, a new teacher describes his induction into teaching. He was
hired on an emergency credential without any teacher training. He stated,

> *My descent from innocence was swift and brutal. I was given a temporary
> roll sheet, assigned a room — actually three different rooms — and with little
> other preparation was thrust into the world of teaching. Suddenly, I was faced
> with classes populated by unruly students, gang members, and other children
> with only rudimentary scholastic skills.*

He then describes how his attempts to teach a unit on the metric system
failed miserably, but that he learned some valuable lessons.

I use this case since I have many students in class who are interns, and to
more fully prepare those who are student teaching candidates. I want them to
understand that they are not the only teachers who have problems; that many,
if not most, beginning teachers face the same kind of problems involving classroom organization, management, and instructional planning that is appropriate for the students' ability levels.

A second case I always use is called "The Breaking Point" (Shulman and
Colbert, 1988). In this case, the beginning teacher describes her problems establishing rapport with her students. She stated,

> *I felt the easiest way for me to do this was to establish peer relationships between my students and myself; however, I have never been more wrong in any decision I have since made as a teacher.*

She then describes how difficult it was to change the relationship, one where she was in charge, and not her students. She concluded,

> *When it comes to peer relationships in school, teachers are definitely not students' peers. When I saw that my co–workers had much more control and much less discipline problems because of their manner, I realized that I needed to change my own manner.*

One of the first topics I address in class is establishing rapport with students, and this case has been very useful is providing a forum for discussion on the topic. The interns share their revelations with us and the student teachers gain valuable insight in what to do and what not to do.

Another case I always use is "Breaking the Barrier" (Shulman and Colbert, 1988). In this case, the beginning teacher describes how difficult it was to motivate his students to read Dante's *Inferno.* He stated,

> *The problem, I decided, lay in the difference between how I had learned to approach Dante and how these students would have to approach him. Intellectualization...would not work. As soon as I had discarded my own notions about what the students must know in order to appreciate the poem, they began to respond...*

This case is a powerful example of how difficult it can be to motivate students to study what you, the teacher, feels is exciting, but which they do not. It provides a powerful forum for students to discuss their own ideas about motivation.

A fourth case I use is "Leigh Scott" (Silverman, Welty, and Lyon, 1993). In this case, a teacher gives a mainstreamed student a grade based, to some extent, on effort and attitude. Another student, who is African American, confronts the teacher because his grade was lower than the mainstreamed student even though the two students' test scores were identical. The student accuses the teacher of being racist. There are myriad issues in this case and I use it to demonstrate the complexity a teacher faces with every decision he or she makes. For example, the issue of fairness is a very complex topic for the beginning teacher to consider, and this case clearly delineates many of the issues involved.

Instructional Strategies Using Cases

I use two basic types of teaching strategies when using cases in the methods class. One format is the large group discussion and the other is small group discussion using a cooperative learning approach.

Large Group Discussion

When using this strategy, I have students read the case at home prior to class. I use three questions to generate discussion, which I put on the board or overhead projector prior to beginning the case analysis:

1. Who are the players in the case? Describe them. I point out that they should consider all of the players, those with major and minor roles.
2. What are the issues in this case?
3. How would you address/solve the issue/problem(s) in the case?

I instruct students to respond to these questions in their interactive journals, which I require them to keep. Following about 10 minutes of writing in the journals, I ask for volunteers to respond to the first question, and, because of the richness of the cases, the discussion is usually very energetic. As we address all three questions, students will reflect on their own experiences and share how they have resolved similar situations. Finally, I ask students to write their reaction to the discussion in the journal as a homework assignment.

Small Group Discussion

I often use cooperative groups and cooperative learning strategies in the methods class. When using cases in this context, it is very easy to generate discussion of the issues in the case. First, I have students form into their groups of four or five. Second, using the same three questions listed previously, I ask students to discuss them one at a time [Each group has a group leader, recorder, reporter, materials handler (gofer), and custodial engineer (cleanup specialist)]. Following the group discussion, I ask reporters to share their responses with the whole group. We then open the discussion up and share individual views. Finally, I ask students to react to the discussion in their journals. I have found that the writing activity adds much more reflection and richness to the oral discussion.

In both strategies, I also record student responses on the board, writing their responses verbatim. I find that other students, particularly those who are more visual learners, will then have more data to reflect on. I try to incorporate all learning modalities during the discussion: auditory (verbal discussion), visual (data recorded on the board or overhead projector), and kinesthetic (journal writing). I also focus discussion on the students' own experiences, often asking them to share similar experiences and describe how they handled them.

I decide which strategy to use based on the content of the case. If a case is more generic in nature, i.e., presents a problem that would impact most or all students, I would probably use a large group discussion and encourage as much active student involvement as possible. If the problem was very specific, I employ cooperative groups to come up with a specific solution(s) to the problem.

The Integration of Cases and Theory

Students in the methods course read a substantial amount of theory and research as part of their regular class assignments. Before using cases, it was hard for students to see how the theory and research could be applied in the real world of classrooms, other than through the use of their limited classroom exposure or by relating my own experiences, which, of course, is not necessarily contextual for my students.

What case studies have brought to my courses is the ability to interact with classroom incidents that are well developed, contextual, and relevant to most, if not all, students. By reflecting on their own experiences and tying in the relevant theory and research, students can realize how to handle situations they will face by applying relevant educational theory and research.

Conclusions

I have been actively using cases in my university courses for the past six years. The response from students (both from informal conversations and as reported on course evaluations) has been overwhelmingly positive. They love to reflect on their own experiences, thus putting their "war stories" to good use. Furthermore, they enjoy reflecting in their journals, and, when faced with similar problems at their own schools, have been able to resolve situations before the problems have escalated out of control. Before integrating cases into my classes, students reported that they saw little connection between theory and practical application. Now they report that the connections are clear and that they are very encouraged when they know that problem solving in the real world of classrooms is grounded in sound educational and psychological theory.

Personally, I have significantly decreased my speaking in class and have turned the discussion over to the students. When I don't use cases, I definitely spend more time directing instruction. When I use cases, the students direct the instruction. The students feel more empowered, less isolated, and less bewildered by their problems.

References

Shulman, J.H. & Colbert, J.A. (1988). *The intern teacher casebook*. Eugene, OR: ERIC Clearinghouse on Educational Management, University of Oregon, and San Francisco: Far West Laboratory for Educational Research and Development.

Shulman, J.H. & Colbert, J.A. (1987). *The mentor teacher casebook*. Eugene, OR: ERIC Clearinghouse on Educational Management, University of Oregon, and San Francisco: Far West Laboratory for Educational Research and Development.

Shulman, L.S. (1986). Those who understand: Knowledge growth in teaching. *Educational Researcher*, *15*(4), 4–14.

Silverman, R., Welty, W., & Lyon (1993). *Case studies for teacher problem solving*. NY: McGraw–Hill.

Joel A. Colbert is Professor of Teacher Education at California State University, Dominguez Hills. He teaches classes in teaching methods in science, computer graphics, and supervises student teachers and interns in secondary schools in the Los Angeles area. He is also a third degree black belt in Tae Kwon Do and teaches Martial Arts (Beginning and Advanced) in the Physical Education Department at the university. He has been heavily involved in using case methods in teacher education for about 10 years. Previously, he collaborated with Judy Shulman in co–editing *The Mentor Teacher Casebook* and *The Intern Teacher Casebook*. Most recently, he co–authored, with Peter Desberg and Kim Trimble, *Interactive Cases in Education*, which are interactive, multimedia, computer–based cases.

Using Technology in Case Methodology

Peter Desberg

Farah Fisher

This chapter presents two examples of using technology in case methodology. Examples of video–based cases on CD–ROM and an electronic database are presented. The introduction of video into a text–dominated area brings with it many changes. The differences between the two formats, the relative advantages and disadvantages of the two methodologies and issues and challenges for the use of video in cases are discussed.

Prologue

The collision of technology and case methodology was inevitable. This chapter discusses how technology can be used with case methodology, and some of the issues that it has generated. The majority of cases to date have been presented as text. The burden fell on a case writer to decide what content and context went in, and what was excluded. Then the reader had to piece together, from this description, what happened in the case. The text writer faced the difficult task of being complete enough to provide the context necessary to present a case authentically, yet not burden the case with so much description that it became unwieldy and distracting. It is at this point that cases presented as videotapes, laserdisks and CD–ROM disks emerged with a big advantage, but video brought its own problems.

One of the first issues a case author/editor faces is deciding the extent to which the cases are edited, or scripted. There is also a decision concerning when and how the case video is recorded. Unless there is a camera going eight hours a day, five days a week, it will be impossible to record truly authentic cases. Furthermore, in most instances, it takes a good bit of reflection and conceptualization to generate a good case. If cases must be recorded as they actually happen, this analysis and conceptualization becomes impossible. On the other hand, even if there is a camera going all the time…will it be able to catch the action if it occurs in a corner of the room? There are many new issues raised in using technology with cases.

In this chapter we make no attempt to do a complete review of the literature, but we will begin with a few noteworthy examples of the way technology has been used, and in doing so, see how these, and other issues have been dealt with. Then, a more in depth view of two different types of projects will help to show the range of possible uses. The first looks at a way to present cases using an interactive multimedia format. QuickTime™ movies (digitized video) are used to present the case material, and an interactive format permits the user to identify key issues, browse through many layers of commentary and make entries in an electronic journal which may be printed out and brought to the case discussion. In the second format, the computer is used to catalog cases either in video format or as a database of case information, and serve as a database and information source using hot text (key words and terms that can be clicked on to obtain definitions and elaborations).

Throughout the chapter, case issues emerge and are discussed in context. The authors believe that this is the beginning of a new era in case methodology. To the scholars who have braved this new frontier, or are about to, remember the old saying, "Pioneers are people with arrows sticking out of their backs."

Examples of Current Uses of Technology in Cases

Although the use of technology has tended to move beyond the boundaries of text–based cases, it has affected them also. Today, as publishing has moved onto the computer, it has become more fluid. This has enabled instructors to make custom order case texts for teacher education (Silverman and Welty, 1994; General Education Case Series, 1996). Publishers now offer case users a catalog of cases from which instructors may select the ones they want, and receive them bound and ready for use in their classes.

Technology has influenced text–based cases, but the most dramatic influence has come from the domain of video. Until the use of video, the reader had to picture a case through the writer's eye. Although there are many skilled case writers who managed to capture the essence and spirit of an incident on paper, it is difficult to compare that to being able to see the body language or expression on the face of a student or teacher. A written case may contain two sets of biases: (1) the case writer's language, and (2) the decision about which elements to include and which to omit. If a writer wants a case to be viewed in a certain way, or have specific elements stand out, it is difficult to exclude these influences in writing at some level. Video–based technology could lessen these biases by letting students view a case first hand. This offers them the opportunity to extract the information that appears relevant to them. I personally dislike watching sports on television because I want to select the elements I follow. I do not like a camera operator and director telling me how to view a play. When I go to a game, I select the aspect of the game that is meaningful to me and focus on it. For similar reasons, I do not like to watch an opera on television either.

Multicultural Cases on Videotape

One of the most interesting uses of video–based cases was presented by McNergney (1994). He and his colleagues traveled to five countries: Singapore, India, South Africa, Denmark and England. These countries were selected because English was one of the major languages used in their schools. Their video cases contained three components:

- real educational environments from multicultural settings
- teaching notes for instructors that provided them with suggestions to facilitate reflection by students in their classes
- expert interpretations of the video presented as text

The video cases were designed to be used as a vehicle for problem solving. After viewing a videotape, the instructor asked students to identify issues, map theory onto those issues and propose a variety of solutions. Because the cases are multinational and multicultural, there was also heavy emphasis on comparisons between the way these schools operate, and how U.S. schools do. Students were encouraged to identify elements in these videos that might be incorporated into their instructional settings. The videos enabled students to observe the different practices and their direct effect on students.

In a way, this project did not have to deal with some of the production issues that cases done here would necessitate. They were able to shoot actual classroom examples, and did not have to be concerned with issues of scripting and authenticity. They were not concerned with capturing dramatic moments of tension or specific types of interactions. Their goal was to secure the essence of multicultural approaches to instruction. This permitted them to portray the way students and teachers from other cultures interacted. Much of the interaction and reflection of their cases came from comparisons between these new pedagogical environments and our own. They dealt with cross cultural comparisons, and the insights that American students could get by analyzing these foreign settings. This is truly ground–breaking, innovative work that is driving a whole new methodology.

New Math Standards on CD–ROM

A team of educators at Vanderbilt University (Barron et al., 1994; Barron et al., 1995) have incorporated video cases in a CD–ROM format. They have made a strong commitment to the area of math reform. The CD–ROM disk contains several elements:

- QuickTime™ movies of lessons and interviews with teachers
- Students work
- Teacher lesson plans
- Information from the NCTM Standards
- Related literature references and abstracts

Cases on the disk were organized around five areas: planning, the role of the teacher, growth of student learning, assessment and mathematics content. Because of the large storage capacity of CD–ROM disks, instructional materials were presented along with the digitized case videos. This work focused on teaching geometry to fifth graders while illustrating the changing role of the teacher from information dispenser to coach or facilitator. The cases gave students a chance to view sound instructional exemplars and gave them the opportunity to reflect and discuss issues that this new view of mathematics instruction carried with it.

In the movies of these "minicases," one of the authors was the teacher in the sample lesson. When cases are more oriented toward positive examples and demonstration, there is less of a problem with cases being scripted. Their authenticity is guaranteed by the fact that a practitioner is modeling the actual methodology directly. Even in such cases, the goal is not to teach methodology so that students will blindly adopt it. This would make the movie a video lecture. The movie served as a springboard for reaction and reflection by the students who viewed it. It is intended to help teachers to "better anticipate and interpret students' thinking."

Preservice Reading Cases on Videodisc

Risko and Kinzer (1994) selected the area of reading instruction because courses in this area were traditionally taught by lecture. Instructors often taught procedures without presenting issues about how to use or adapt those procedures to meet needs in a variety of settings and contexts. Risko and Kinzer pointed out that even case methods have their limitations. Their success depends largely on the "coherence and richness of the data presented." They also pointed out that videotaped cases are limited by their linearity. To address this problem, they presented video cases on laserdisk format which provided random access, permitting the user to find any part of any case very rapidly. Furthermore, cases may be cross–referenced for easy location.

In their videodisc–based cases, they emphasized macrocontexts that present several problems simultaneously, and then examine solutions from multiple perspectives. This is in sharp contrast to many cases that are limited to one specific incident (i.e., microcontext). Teams of project staff and classroom teachers met and viewed many hours of videotapes to determine which would be best to edit into the half hour videos on the laserdisks.

Risko and Kinzer also noted that seeing an actual incident provided more information than any text–base description ever could. They point out, as an example, that if there were physical constraints involved in a problem, viewing the case would make those constraints much clearer than any verbal description. They believe that videotape is useful for an initial viewing, but for the purpose of analysis, it is more problematic than a disk–based system. Long rewinding times, and the difficulty of precise access to specific sections often make videotaped cases frustrating for the user. Written cases may oversimplify complex information, inhibiting the opportunity for true problem solving in meaningful situations.

John Bransford and his colleagues (Bransford et al., 1988) found that video based contexts were better teaching tools and increased transfer because they provided a richer source of information than a written text can provide. Videos more closely matched the environment in which teachers would find themselves. Furthermore, they liked videodisk technology because it provided random access and freeze frame capabilities.

For a more complete review of the literature see Sykes and Bird (1992). They have provided an excellent overview of the ways in which they and others have already used video with cases. In addition, the chapter in this volume by Bliss and Mazur shows another interesting use of video cases in CD–ROM format.

Interactive Cases in Teacher Education

I became interested in case methodology after reading the two teacher education case books by Judy Shulman and Joel Colbert (1987, 1988). As both a clinical psychologist and a technology educator, I saw interesting possibilities for combining case–based instruction with state–of–the–art technology. Coincidentally, at a meeting held at the Far West Laboratory to discuss using case studies in teacher education, the same topic was being discussed by Gary Sykes and Lee Shulman. Joel Colbert, who attended that meeting, and I began a prototype for a digitized video case presentation at that time. Along with our colleague, Kim Trimble, we designed a case presentation format that was truly interactive.

In our software presentation of cases, we let students see the case as a QuickTime™ Movie. A QuickTime™ movie permits viewing video on the computer screen. QuickTime™ is Apple Computer's digital video compression format that permits any NTSC video source (e.g., videotape, laserdisk or even a direct TV broadcast) to be digitized and played back on a computer. This technology enabled us to record critical classroom interactions such as a student defying a teacher and students cheating on an exam. The cases were entered as digital video so students could interact with our software in a number of ways described below. Because much of the essence of case methodology is group discussion, and we had students sitting at a computer, there were several points we had to reconcile. These issues will be discussed as we present the goals of the project.

Goals of the Project

Although the goals centered around the Interactive Cases project, it became apparent that the issues we dealt with were the ones that confront many applications of technology to case methodology. We established several goals for our software.

The Software Should Have Multiple Uses

Cases are used in a multitude of ways as can be seen in this volume. Cases are often used as a form of *process–oriented* instruction where other learning can be applied to it. Many instructors use cases as the capstone activity in classes such as educational psychology and curriculum or methods courses (Silverman and Welty, 1992). Students are often asked to provide analyses of cases and recommend courses of action. Here cases are used as simulations which invite *what–if* scenarios. Both of these uses are to be based on, or supported by, a theoretical position and empirical data. Cases are designed to help bridge the gap between theory and practice. They provide a way of thinking rather than a set of prescriptions.

Cases are also used as *content*, where the material in a case and its analysis represents the content to be learned. Students carry away with them both the many possible solutions to a problem and the methodology used in those solutions. These two views, content and process, are not mutually exclusive, and in the best applications, both emerge.

The Software Should Be Usable in a Variety of Settings

We have designed these cases to be used as stand–alone cases, or as adjuncts to be used with teacher training textbooks. Here are the settings in which we believe the software can be used:

- **The software should be usable by individual students or small groups on individual computers.** Students can sit at the computer and interact with the cases. They may make judgments and have the computer provide feedback. In addition, they may chronicle their work in an on–screen journal which may be stored there, edited, printed out and later brought to class to promote discussion.
- **The software should also be usable in classes on a single computer used with an LCD panel and an overhead projector.** Here the entire class may view the case simultaneously. As a group, the class would select each direction to take through the case. The students may suggest the path to be taken through the software, or the instructor can have a preplanned lesson. The computer could then take a back seat to a discussion about case elements at any time.
- **The software should be usable in classes without a computer being in the room.** The software was designed so that students could view it individually, on their own time, either at home or at a library or computer

laboratory. The software permits them to keep notes in an electronic journal, to be described later in this chapter. Later, they can meet as a class, with the printouts of their journals, and discuss the case.

The Software Should Be Interactive

The most common criticism of the lecture method (even the highest forms of it...such as when *we* do it) is that the students in our classes remain passive. Anyone who has been driven somewhere a number of times, and then gotten lost the first time they tried to find it alone understands the need for an interactive learning platform. One of the hallmarks of case methodology is that students get much more out of active participation than passive listening.

The software itself is an example of hypermedia. A student can always select his/her own path and activities at any point in time. There are four main interactive elements, two of which give direct feedback, and two which contain activities that are student–generated.

Direct Feedback

In the two activities that present direct feedback, the student makes a response, and then gets confirmation about his/her choice. Even in these closed–end situations, the student has the opportunity to enter comments and reflections in a journal (see next section for an explanation of journal use). The direct feedback activities involve using the QuickTime™ movies and identifying key issues.

QuickTime™ Movies

There are two ways in which QuickTime™ movies are used in these cases. In one, the student has the option to view (or stop) the entire movie as often as desired. They may also drag a scroll bar around to see specific details as often as they like. In the other form discussed here, the student is shown a portion of the movie, and must identify when the teacher is doing something with which they do not agree. If the student's response falls within the proper time range, he/she is given confirmation. If it does not, the student is offered a choice of continuing or trying again. Cases are broken down into three or four sections, each of which provide this opportunity. Again, the student is encouraged to reflect about this in an interactive journal.

Key Issue Identification

After viewing each section of the video, and identifying where there are problems, the student is shown a list of classroom issues, some of which have nothing to do with the present case, and some of which are relevant to it. The student is asked to identify the relevant ones. Although this is also closed–ended, the student is encouraged to make a journal entry immediately after the choice. This is one of the places where students are encouraged to merge theory and practice. Each section of the case has two sets of these issues. One is from the teacher's point of view, and the other is from the student's point of view. The student not only gets feedback, but is given a writing prompt about the issue he/she selected in the journal to facilitate active reflection.

Student Generated Activities

In the Direct Feedback activities, the student responds and the computer provides feedback. Even though the activities require the student to make inferences and the computer acts as a teacher/leader surrogate, these activities are not typical of the way case methodology is used. Cases are open–ended and exploratory. To this end, we included the Journal and Comments sections.

Journals – At any time, the student may call up a journal, located on every screen of the software. The student may make entries in a scrolling text field located on each card. These entries may be as long as the student wants. All of these journal entries are copied into one, final scrolling text field. A scrolling text field is familiar to all Macintosh users. It contains arrows at the top and bottom of the text so that the user may scroll up or down to see more, or review previous text. The contents of the journals can be printed out, or transferred to a word processor, edited and then printed out. These journal entries can then be brought to a class or a small discussion group. They provide a safe, private place to reflect, rethink and edit before presenting ideas to a larger group. It is through these journal entries that we hope students can apply and explore alternative points of view, and examine the consequences of their ideas.

Comments – One of my favorite movies was Rashomon, written and directed by Akira Kurasawa. In this movie, several witnesses to a crime each recount their experience. Each one tells a totally different story based on his/her own point of view. It was Kurasawa's wish that people would give up the notion that there is one objective or correct way to view things. This view is at the very cornerstone of case methodology, and was certainly one of the aspects that first attracted me to it. In this section, the student's interactivity comes from the browsing options. They may read any set of comments in any order that they find useful. A student may track one individual's comments successively, or read each comment for a given section of the case, or any combination in between. These comments hopefully stimulate reflection, which may also be recorded in the student's journal entries.

The use of case commentaries is not unanimously accepted within the community of case users. Lee Shulman (1992) views commentaries in the same way that we do, and summarized their value as follows:

> *The claim that there is something intrinsically simplifying about a case commentary fundamentally misconstrues the potential role of multiple interpretations in the examination of a text. Perhaps the skeptics confuse commentaries with answer keys or with the discussion notes that follow some cases, which appear to provide a concise "resolution" to the complexities of the puzzle. I view commentary as an opportunity to take a particular case — whether apparently straightforward or undeniably perplexing — and to provide alternative lenses for viewing it (p. 12).*

For each section of the case, there is a view from the teacher's side and the student's side. Once a student selects the comments, looking at the teacher's perspective, there is an option to examine five very different points of view:

- **Teacher Educator** – This represents a university faculty member involved in teacher training. These faculty usually present the more theoretical point of view, as well as the integration of it into practice. Quite often, these faculty also supervise student teachers in the field, and interface with mentor teachers.
- **Mentor Teacher** – These are the exemplary teachers into whose classrooms students teachers are placed. They are in the same environment as the teachers in the cases. They are experienced in the classroom, and bring that experience to bear in their analyses.
- **Beginning Teacher** – The perspective of new teachers is very important for several reasons. It lets other new teachers know that they are not alone. This perspective mirror the fears of most new teachers. They believe and reflect the myths found at each school, serving a cathartic function. They provide a great deal of empathy for the student going though the case.
- **Administrator** (School Principal) – It is very helpful for new teachers to know how their behavior is looked at by a school administrator. The principal sets the tone for the classroom management of a school, as well as serving as the ultimate arbiter of it.
- **Psychologist** – The school psychologist is the other member of the team who contributes a theoretical, as well as practical view of the case. In addition, the psychologist adds a professional dimension not available to the other commentators.

The student is then given a chance to select the appropriate issues from the student's point of view. There are three student points of view represented as comments:

- **Michael** (A High Achieving Student) – High achieving students care about school. They have very little patience with ineffective teachers. They do not like unfair situations, or students getting away with anything. They do their work!
- **Richard** (A Very Disruptive Student) – This student is affectionately know as *every teacher's nightmare*. This student points out how much he likes to see teachers in trouble. He points out how he benefits from it. We find it very helpful to represent this point of view for teachers who are inconsistent, yell or get easily distracted by misbehavior. For most new teachers, this is a very enlightening set of comments.
- **Theresa** (An Average Student) – This student shows how the silent majority in the class is viewing the case. Because this group is rarely vocal, their point of view is also very helpful for the teacher.

It should always remain clear that the comments of these eight individuals are just that…their comments. They are never represented as the correct solutions to the case situations. Their function is to model the notion of alternative points of view on an issue.

Courses in Which We Have Tried the Software

To date, we have previewed the software in three classes: teaching methods, classroom management and an advanced graduate technology course. We have shown it to each class as a whole either on a large screen TV or with an active matrix color LCD panel. The results have been very favorable in the science methods and classroom management classes. I personally was most interested in the reaction of the graduate technology course. I presented it to these students strictly as another piece of technology handiwork, and I was startled by the results.

The students did not want to discuss the technology aspects. They immediately got into a heated discussion about the case itself. There was an immediate polarization of students, and they wanted to argue/discuss the merits of the positions of the teacher and student involved in a confrontation. The results were very compelling. Most recently, we have been presenting the software to faculty groups at teaching and multimedia workshops, and have received a great deal of interest. They have immediately recognized the potential of the process and want to begin developing modules in their own academic disciplines.

It is obvious to anyone using case methodology that traditional norm–referenced, paper–and–pencil (or even worse…op scan answer sheet–based) tests are not appropriate. The key to evaluating students using this software is the Journal. We ask students to include the following things:

- the major issues;
- appropriate solutions;
- alternative solutions (or contingency plans if their initial strategies do not work); and,
- the theoretical underpinnings for those solutions.

As we evaluate the success of our use of cases, we are looking for two types of data:

- *student performance* – Problem solving and course content applications.
- *affective responses* – Student input through university–based evaluation measures, our own affective questionnaires, and direct conversation and inquiry .

Technological/Case Issues to be Resolved

If cases are to be presented on video (or digitized in QuickTime™) how should this be done? There are many issues dealing with production values of the video, scripting and authenticity. Rather than to offer a solution, we prefer to present several alternative solutions and choices about which the reader may reflect.

Keep a Camera Running at all Times

A camera could be set up in a class, and running full–time in the same way a security camera works in convenience store. The obvious advantage of this method is *guaranteed authenticity*. Deborah Ball (1994) showed an excellent example of this technique. She was able to "catch" the actual event occurring in real time in the classroom. The viewer was actually there, seeing everything.

There are several disadvantages to always having the camera on. You would have to be changing video tapes many times a day, and monitoring them to keep track of when they needed changing. You would have to spend massive amounts of time viewing and then editing the tapes. In order to take in the entire classroom at one time, the quality of the video would be poor. The subject would be defused, and the lighting and sound would be of equally poor quality. Also, the teacher could become very self conscious knowing that every move was being recorded for later analysis. This would affect the spontaneity, and therefore the authenticity of the video. Students could also feel like they were acting for the camera. They might also find it very obtrusive, wondering if it will later be shown to parents and administrators.

Another problem with using actual classroom video footage is the ethical issue of anonymity. In a written case, students' names and obvious identifying characteristics are usually masked, but this is not possible in an actual video case. If a child is put in an embarrassing or compromising position, most parents would not sign a release form.

Reenact Cases

It is possible to reenact a case as it actually occurred. Although this would take a bit of the spontaneity out of the case, it could build in the same elements that originally occurred, and increase the production value of the video, making it easier to view the critical events clearly. The major risk is that the recreation on the event might not be faithful to the original.

Create Composite Cases

You could build a composite case based on several true incidents that occurred to broaden the generalizability of the case. These are cases that are not based on a single, specific incident, but rather a group of events that most commonly occur in a particular context. University faculty who are committed to cases are in a unique position. As they recount their own experiences and confer with students, they hear many recurrent stories, incidents and themes. Each is unique, yet over time, there are many commonalities. There is general agreement that one of the cornerstones of effective cases is authenticity…cases must be based on true incidents. One of the areas that needs to be researched is the question of the validity, effectiveness and generalizability of single specific incidents versus composites of several related specific incidents, all of which actually occurred.

It is clear that as each issue gets solved, the solution creates several new problems. The introduction of video into case methodology presents many new challenges to case writers and users. Next, we present a more stable use of technology that offers much to users of cases.

Electronic Databases in Case Studies for Special Education

A totally different application of technology to case methods is to use it for data management and synthesis of information. Case studies have long been an accepted part of special education training courses. Individuals with special needs are, or should be, a topic studied by all teachers. Whether teaching a special education class, participating in a mainstreaming situation, or simply explaining differences to regular classroom students, teachers must have at least a working knowledge of exceptionality.

Special education case studies follow a fairly traditional format. Each includes personal and demographic information, test scores (often with the interpretation of test results), and narratives of class performance, often involving specific behaviors.

Case studies of special education students can be used in several ways in teacher training. At the lowest level, case studies can be used by beginning teachers to examine the behaviors and test scores of various disability categories. In this way, teachers can learn to recognize individual students in need of referral. For example, a case study of a learning disabled student assists regular education teachers in discriminating between a truly disabled student and one whose educational problems stem from other sources. Preservice special education teachers can begin to see patterns of special educational needs as they compare case studies.

At a slightly more advanced level, students with intermediate training or experience with special education students can use case studies to practice the prescription of teaching methods based on the test scores and narratives found in a case study. Special education teachers are a creative lot; they search out and use methods that will work with individual students. Case studies can assist in learning the techniques of diagnosis and prescription.

Inservice special education teachers may receive advanced training to become consultants for other teachers or specialists in a particular disability category. Such teachers, along with preservice school psychologists, are often required to create case studies. Using examples and partially completed case study templates have obvious educational value for these individuals.

One of the largest barriers to the use of case studies in special education teacher training is the interpretation of test results. A wide variety of assessment instruments may be used to identify disability categories and determine educational needs. Even within a single school district, many tests may be commonly used. If students transfer in from another district, the matter becomes even more complicated. School psychologists are thoroughly trained in the administration and interpretation of tests, but special education teachers are often called upon to explain test results to parents and teachers, and to recommend or implement teaching methods based on assessment results.

To address the various levels of case study use in special education and the problem of assessment interpretation, a program called *Case Studies in Special Education* was created by Farah Fisher and Carrie Ann Blackaller. This HyperCard stack, the first in a planned series of three, contains several special education case studies and information about commonly used assessment instruments. Case studies in the program were created by combining results from a number of actual cases to show examples of developmental and learning disabilities.

Case Studies in Special Education is best characterized as providing *illuminated* case studies. The general information for each case is presented on the screen in text form — the student's name, age, placement, as well as the test results, and narratives about specific behaviors. The illumination comes through the use of *hot text* — the user can click on words or numbers within a case for further explanation. Some examples include:

- Clicking on **WISC–R** brings up information about the Wechsler Intelligence Scale for Children, including an annotated list of subtests.
- Clicking on a **test score** shows the placement of that score (if appropriate) on a normal curve.
- Clicking on the name of a **disability category** displays a definition and typical criteria for classifying students in that category.

Case Studies in Special Education was designed to be used at the beginning and intermediate levels described above. Preservice teachers in regular and special education can use *Case Studies in Special Education* to learn to discriminate between disability categories. Such users concentrate on the explanations included in the case, and attempt to determine the disability label by examining all the given information. For these students, a brief look at the case is all that is necessary. They may use a few of the informational features to understand more fully the differences between exceptionalities.

Special education teachers with intermediate training or experience use *Case Studies in Special Education* as a foundation to begin the process of prescribing educational techniques which may be effective with a particular student. Intermediate users need to look at the case in much more depth, and will, therefore, need to use more of the information contained in the program.

Like the more traditional print cases, *Case Studies in Special Education* is only a starting point for instruction. It is not meant to teach, but rather to encourage discussion and exploration. The computer makes the cases easier to understand, and thus more useful. The challenges that such electronic cases provide have to do with epistemological issues. The computer can help analyze data, but someone has to decide on what kinds of data are necessary. Should the data be based more on standardized tests , with their many threats to validity, or should the data come from observation? If we use more observational data, what do we observe and for what duration, and under what conditions? These are the issues that will be the basis for fruitful discussions in classes or small groups.

References

Ball, D. (1994). *Multimedia case demo: mathematics and teaching through hypermedia (math)*. Paper presented at conference for Constructing Cases for Reflective Practice: Using Story, Narrative, Video, and Hypermedia, Tucson.

Bransford, J. D., Sherwood, R., & Hasselbring, T. (1988). The video revolution and its effects on development: Some initial thoughts. In Foremann, G. & Putfall, P. (Eds.), *Constructivism in the computer age* (pp. 173–201). Hillsdale: Erlbaum.

Desberg, P., Colbert, J.A. and Trimble, K. (1995). *Interactive cases in teacher education*. Boston: Allyn and Bacon.

General Education Case Series (1996). Boston: Allyn and Bacon.

Goldman, E., Barron, L., Bassler, O., Cobb, P., Bowers, J., McClain, K.,Robinson, C., St. Clair, J., Wilson, A., Harwood, J., & Altman, J. (1994). *Investigations in teaching geometry* [CD–ROM program]. Nashville, TN: Vanderbilt University.

Goldman, E.,Barron, L., Cobb, P., Bowers, J., McClain, K., Martin, M.,Robinson, C., St. Clair, J., Altman, J., & Harwood, J. (1995). *Investigations in teaching geometry: Developing a CD–ROM learning environment for teacher education students*. Symposium session conducted at the annual meeting of tne American Educational Research Association, San Francisco.

McNergney, R.B. (1994) Videocases: A way to foster a global perspective on multicultural education. *Phi Delta Kappan*, 76(4), p. 296–299.

Shulman, J.H. & Colbert, J.A. (Eds.) (1987). *The mentor teacher casebook*. San Fransisco: Far West Laboratory for Educational Research and Development.

Shulman, J.H. & Colbert, J.A. (Eds.) (1988). *The intern teacher casebook*. San Fransisco: Far West Laboratory for Educational Research and Development.

Shulman, L.S. (1992) Toward a pedagogy of cases. In Shulman, J.H. (ed.), *Case methods in teacher education.* New York: Teacher's College Press.

Silverman, R. & Welty, W.M. (1994) *Case studies for teacher problem solving.* New York: McGraw–Hill Primis.

Silverman, R., Welty, W.M., & Lyon, S. (1992) *Case studies for teacher problem solving.* New York: McGraw–Hill, Inc.

Sykes, G. & Bird, T. (1992) Teacher education and the case idea. *Review of Research in Education, 18.* Washington, DC: American Educational Research Association.

Peter Desberg is a clinical psychologist and coordinator of the Computer-Based Education Program at California State Univesity, Dominguez Hills. He is the author of twelve books and numerous book chapters, journal articles and conference presentations. He recently co-authored *Interactive Case Studies in Education,* an interactive CD-ROM disk of classroom management cases.

Farah Fisher is an Associate Professor of Graduate Education at California State University, Dominguez Hills, where she teaches courses in computer-based education and research methods. The mother of two disabled children and a former special education teacher, she has always had an interest in the use of technology with special needs students. Current projects in this area include workshops in assistive technology, the use of technologically enhanced special education case studies, telecommunications use by special needs students, and increasing the computer literacy of special education personnel.

Using the Case Method to Translate Theory into Practice

Gordon E. Greenwood

The case study approach developed and used in courses in the college of Education at the University of Florida since 1967 for the purpose of helping students learn how to translate theory into practice is described. With a focus on helping preservice and inservice teachers develop their decision-making skills, the approach helps students learn to analyze and resolve cases from the course while working in small groups. Both the college instructor's role and evaluation procedures are presented as well as a sample case, a small group paper, and the evaluation of the paper.

Sanford's (1962) position on university teaching decades ago that "the colleges will change only when more knowledge of what they do and of what they might do has been produced and made available to educator's" (p. 1012) seems as relevant today as it did then. In spite of conclusions like that of Dunkin and Barnes' (1986) in the third *Handbook of Research on Teaching* that "the innovatory methods of teaching discussed have in most cases been found slightly superior to conventional teaching methods," (p. 774) it is probably safe to say that the vast majority of college professors still primarily use the lecture method of teaching. While many have heard of the case study method of teaching, few have actually used it in their classes, and still fewer use it on a regular basis.

Introduction to Case Methodology

My discovery of what is now called case methodology dates back many years. As a doctoral student at Indiana University, I had the good fortune to work with David Gliessman, who had developed an innovative approach to college teaching called Group Independent Problem Solving (GRIPS).

Gliessman believed that students in small groups of 3–6 members using problem solving procedures would learn as much and at a higher cognitive level than students taught with traditional lecture–discussion methods. Gliessman's approach involved presenting a problem teaching situation to the students, having them generate and evaluate possible solutions. Students would learn to go beyond textbooks, lectures, and discussions to use the entire library as their knowledge base. Using a list of references as starter material, they create their own framework for defining the nature of the problem and possible solutions. The end product was typically a group or individual paper.

Gliessman also believed that if an entire course were taught in this way, students would learn and retain problem solving skills in addition to traditional course content. He felt this approach would help students begin to view teaching as problem solving, and that they would be able to apply these skills to actual teaching situations.

Gliessman developed a series of films, *Critical Moments in Teaching* (1970), to introduce problem situations to students, in which I participated. When the films were used in educational psychology classes, students needed to view the films over and over to determine exactly what the problem situation was. To address this problem, Gliessman gave the students the film scripts to work with. It was at that point that the value of written case material became apparent to me.

When I joined the University of Florida faculty in 1967, I began to use these films and film scripts in the learning and cognition and human growth and development courses that I taught. With few case materials available for classroom use, I began to collect written and interview materials from practicing teachers. In collaboration with Tom Good and Betty Siegel, these twenty cases were published as *Problem Situations in Teaching* (1971). These situations represented either the most difficult or the most frequently recurring type of situation the teacher had faced. We chose the cases so that they covered a wide variety of issues, including a spectrum of grade levels, problems dealing with individuals and groups, and cases from beginning and experienced teachers.

Since the three authors were all psychologists, the book's focus was primarily upon educational psychology. Believing that case methodology might be applicable to other areas in teacher education, I wrote a second case study book (*Case Studies for Teacher Decision Making*, 1989) with Forrest Parkay centering on curriculum and instruction. The thirty cases in the book were obtained in essentially the same way as the first book. The illustrative introductory material and the "starter" questions intended to stimulate initial group discussion, and a theory grid that matched cases with possible theories and principles had as much of a curriculum and instruction flavor as an educational psychology one. Such an inter–disciplinary team approach makes real sense when cases are used as applicational vehicles.

As has been indicated, cases have been used in the College of Education at the University of Florida primarily as applicational vehicles and for only part of the course. Further, the instructor typically works with the students in small groups of 4–6 students instead of working with the entire class as a group. Most of the case method demonstrations that I have observed or participated in have involved a large group and a skilled discussion leader who often, it strikes me, uses many "encounter group" techniques of the 60's and 70's. Since both our purpose and methodology are quite different, it may help to begin with our assumptions underlying the methods used.

It should be noted that our use of case studies focuses on teacher education. We agree with Shavelson (1973) that decision making is the "basic teaching skill" and our purpose is to help preservice and inservice teachers become more effective decision makers. We also agree with Broudy (1990) that case studies can be designed to represent the professional core knowledge base necessary for teaching to become a profession. However, some of our students are freshmen and sophomores and are novice decision makers at best.

A common model in using the case method is to focus on the following steps: (1) identify the educational issues involved; (2) think about the case from multiple points of view (e.g.: teacher, parent, student, principal); (3) use professional knowledge (e.g.: classroom management principles, learning theory) to discuss the case; (4) project courses of action that might solve the problem; (5) determine the consequence that might follow from each course of action generated; (6) after evaluating each, choose the courses of action to be followed and decide how to evaluate the effectiveness of the plan.

The first assumption we make is that it takes experience to examine a situation from multiple perspectives. It is often a problem for a beginner to use one framework (e.g.: theory, set of principles, model) well, much less three or four. We generally ask our students to begin by using only one framework for case analysis.

Our second assumption follows from the first one: that teacher education majors should focus on the perspective of the teacher. They should learn this perspective before shifting to that of the principal or parent or even the student. Even if one framework is being used, it is often difficult at the beginning to shift from what a teacher might look for in the classroom to how a parent might view the situation at home. Taking multiple perspectives is a long–term goal, not a beginning exercise.

A third assumption is that teacher education majors should use frameworks that they are studying in their courses. The goal is to learn to apply to case material what is being learned. For example, the student might use a learning theory from an educational psychology course or a classroom management model from a methods course to analyze a case. Analyzing the same case from a different theory or model may very well lead to a different decision about how to the case should be handled by the teacher. It is often useful to keep these two steps separate.

Fourth, as students learn to analyze a case in terms of a framework, they need to learn to defend their analysis by citing evidence appropriate to the framework. The kind of evidence appropriate to defend an operant analysis would be quite different from that required for a humanistic psychological analysis in an educational psychology course, for example.

The fifth assumption is that the courses of action that are generated to solve the problem should be consistent with the way the student analyzes the case and should be operationally stated (spelled out in terms of specifics) and reasonable to implement (feasibility) in the context of the situation. We often tell the students to pretend they are explaining to the teacher what to do. What they tell the teacher should be both clear and specific as well as reasonable.

A sixth assumption is that the decision making processes require that students engage in "higher order" cognitive levels of thought. In terms of Bloom's Cognitive Taxonomy (Bloom, Engelhart, Furst, Hill, and Krathwohl, 1956), the Application, Analysis, Synthesis, and Evaluation levels are the ones most often involved. Students are involved in selecting a framework, applying it to the case, citing evidence to support the application, generating courses of action consistent with the analysis (and some of these can be quite creative), and evaluating the possible courses of action to select the ones that might work best. Students engaged in applying a theory, model, or set of principles to a case engage in cognitive processing quite different from learning the same material to take an objective or essay exam.

Overview of Case Methodology

At the University of Florida cases have primarily been utilized with two groups of undergraduate students: teacher education majors and arts and sciences majors taking educational psychology and human growth and development courses in the College of Education. Cases are used as applicational tools during the later part of the course, not as the sole teaching method for teaching the entire course. The first part of the course is typically taught using the traditional lecture–discussion method. This is followed by "mini–case analyses," which introduce the students to the process of working in small groups and analyzing the case from the standpoint of the "theory of best fit," then defending their analysis by citing appropriate evidence from the case. At this point, they do not take the next step and try to generate courses of action that the teacher might try to solve the problem.

Depending on the course, the first complete case study is introduced anytime after the first third of the term. In some courses, two case studies of 2–3 weeks of class time each are done, while in others only one is done at the end. The rationale here is that the student should first be introduced to the theory and appropriate references before trying to apply it to a case.

Selection of Cases and Theories

We have used a variety of approaches for selecting cases for teaching in the classroom. In some courses we have let the students decide what case they want to work on. In others we allow them to pick from a small number that we choose. One of the more interesting procedures, especially with teacher education majors, is to give them 3 x 5 cards, ask them to skim the cases and rank order the three cases that they worry about most when they think about being a classroom teacher. The small groups of 4–6 students are then formed according to the student choices. I think it's fair to say that no one way works best all the time. It all depends on the instructor's objectives and feel for student abilities and dispositions.

We usually encourage each group to begin analyzing the case by discussing the situation from their own personal belief systems and then asking what frame of reference they have studied that comes closest to it. "Starter questions" help guide students in the process of finding an appropriate theory to use to analyze each case. When a group flounders, the instructor can often get the groups moving again by asking the right questions or reviewing material learned.

In some situations, however, we assign both the case and framework for analysis. For example, after studying operant conditioning and behavior modification, all the groups might be asked to do an operant analysis and resolution of the same case. Again, instructional objectives and knowledge of students are the determining factor; however, this is usually done when more than one case is used during the semester and the second case involves student choices.

Instructor Role

Once the groups are formed, the instructor informs them that his/her role is now changing from that of lecture/discussion leader to one of a resource person/group stimulator. The instructor first asks the students in each group to exchange certain information with one another (names, addresses, phone numbers, and times when they can meet outside class) and to select one reliable group member as group "recorder." It is the job of the recorder to keep attendance at group meetings, schedule formal group meetings with the instructor, keep the instructor informed as to where and when the group is meeting outside class, and make sure the group paper is turned in in proper form and on time.

The instructor usually begins the first meeting by indicating that the group product will be an approximately 10 page (typewritten, double–spaced) paper. Students are told that the case study activity has two purposes: (1) to learn to apply the material learned in the course, and (2) to learn to work with others in small groups. The latter is something that teachers have to do throughout their professional careers (curriculum committees, textbook adoption committees, report card committees, etc.). They are asked to work with their group for at least one week. If at some later point the groups subdivide or individual students wish to do their own paper, that will be their choice. However, part of the idea is learning to work with and relate to others.

A discussion is usually conducted regarding the importance of each person contributing to the group and talking through problems early if a student fails to attend group meetings and do their share. Each group member is told at the beginning that their contribution to the group will be evaluated by the other group members. This evaluation asks students to rate the contribution of each member of their group on a five–point scale.

A typical case study can take up to eight one–hour class periods. "Distributed practice" seems better than "massed practice" as far as the scheduling of group meetings is concerned. The instructor has to be sensitive to group needs as the process unfolds. Sometimes groups wish to work without the instructor and other times want the instructor to join them. I usually require the recorder to schedule a meeting with me when they feel they have finished analyzing the case and can cite evidence to support the analysis. If this goes well, we then begin to discuss what courses of action (or applicational techniques) might make sense for the teacher to use.

Knowing when to engage and disengage from a group is a skill that comes only with experience. This is especially true when disagreements appear in a group that threaten to split it or when the group is deciding what to do about a group member who isn't contributing. The instructor's first inclination might be to step in and tell the group what to do. We have found, however, that groups often work out solutions better than the one the instructor would have suggested. Just be available and ready to support and advise.

Evaluation

We generally evaluate group papers on six criteria: (1) applying accurately and fully a theory, model, or set of principles in analyzing the case; (2) supporting the analysis fully with objectively cited data from the case; (3) generating courses of action for the teacher to implement that are consistent with the analysis; (4) generating courses of action that are practical or feasible in the context of the case; (5) stating courses of action in a specific, operational form; and (6) organizing the paper into a coherent whole and following the rules of grammatical construction, footnoting, quoting, etc.

The students are told that there are no right or wrong answers in analyzing and resolving a case. Regardless of the theory they use or applications they derive, their paper is a good one if it meets the above criteria. We also tell the students not to concern themselves with convincing the teacher to execute the courses of action they recommend. Worrying about "teacher consultation" may be important for school psychology majors, but the intent here at the undergraduate level is to help students identify and develop specific context–based practices that flow from theories or models.

Unusual Uses

From time to time, we have experimented with student products other than the ten–page paper. For example, in other classes students have acted out the decision they have developed. Classroom teachers have staged cases and then the students, after working on the issue for some time and asking follow–up questions of the teacher, have developed and acted out a decision. The decision was then critiqued by the teacher. They were always preceded by the usual written process first, however, so that the strategies involved would become clear to the students.

There are other possibilities that we have not yet tried. Presentations could easily be videotaped, which would allow for an array of teaching and evaluation uses. Also, we have even conceptualized an experienced—based teacher preparation model utilizing case studies. Using a core of professional cases as recommended by Broudy (1990), students would experience preparatory classes in the manner previously described. They would then move into teaching situations where they could continue to blend theory and practice. While functioning first as tutors and teacher aids, they would continue to meet in groups to generate and share cases as well as strategies and possible solutions. Micro–teaching, complete with videotaping, would also be an excellent vehicle for analysis and decision–making. Finally, internship and the first year of teaching would serve as culminating experiences. Metacognitive decision–making strategies first learned in case study work would be applied in an increasing variety of experienced–based settings.

Sample of Case and Student Paper

One of the best ways to illustrate the type of cases used and the kind of student products that result is to present one of each. The case entitled "Shy Sally," taken from the *Case Studies for Teacher Decision Making* casebook, is especially illustrative. The paper is a product of a small group of five undergraduates enrolled in an undergraduate educational psychology course for various majors from the College of Liberal Arts and Sciences at the University of Florida. Following the case is a student paper and finally a brief critique of the students' analysis.

Shy Sally

Brooks Elementary School serves a primarily white (75 percent) K–6 student population in a rural area of a populous western state. The building was constructed in the 1950's but is well maintained and well equipped. Mary Powell is a veteran teacher of 21 years experience and is currently teaching 24 sixth graders. It is early in the school year (November), and Mary is moving from student to student as they work on math problems. Mary moves to the desk of Sally Gorman who is staring at a blank sheet of paper.

Mary [frowning]: **Are you have trouble, Sally?**
Sally [startled, whispers]: **No. I just don't know how to do it.**
Mary [bending down next to Sally's desk and pointing to a problem on her paper]: Don't you remember when we went over these yesterday?
Sally [staring at the paper]: Yes, but I forgot.
Mary: Don't you remember I called on you and you got the answer right?
Sally: Yes, but I really can't do them!

Mary [raising her voice slightly]: Can't or won't, Sally? Weren't you daydreaming just now?

Sally [barely audible]: I guess so.

Mary: You're a very smart girl, Sally, but you have to pay attention and do your work.

Sally: But I can't do these! I don't know how!

Mary: Go ahead and try, Sally, and I'll be back in a little while to check on your work.

❂

After school is over and Mary has finished supervising the loading of her students onto school buses, Mary goes back into the building to the office of Emma Buell, the school's guidance counselor.

Emma: Why, Mary, hello! Have you come to visit me?

Mary [smiling]: Hi, Emma. I wish I could say this is a social visit, but I'm afraid that I've really come to find out what you can tell me about one of my kids—Sally Gorman.

Emma [searches in a file cabinet and pulls out Sally's folder]: Well I can tell you several things about Sally. Are you having trouble with her?

Mary: Well she's very shy and is content to sit and do nothing. She doesn't contribute to class discussion and, when I try to draw her out, she speaks in a very low voice—almost a whisper—so I have a hard time understanding her. When I try to talk to her one on one, she keeps telling me that she doesn't understand and can't do the work, even though I know she can and does on occasion. It's very frustrating, Emma! Sally doesn't pay attention and seems to spend most of her time daydreaming.

Emma [opening Sally's folder]: I think you're right about her being able to do the work. Her I.Q. was 111 last time she was tested—a definite underachiever. I think that a lot of Sally's problem is her mother.

Mary: I've never met Mrs. Gorman. She didn't come to the open house in October.

Emma: That's an experience you can do without, believe me!

Mary: What do you mean?

Emma: She's a noisy, aggressive, thoroughly obnoxious woman! The most negative parent I've ever been around! It's no wonder that Sally's shy. I'm sure that her mother beats her down all the time!

Mary: Then, Mrs. Gorman works?

Emma: Yes, she works on the assembly line at Central Electric. I'll bet she can cuss with the best of them too! [Pause] Yes, I'd say that Sally's problem stems from home.

Mary: Any suggestions?

Emma: It's hard to try to compensate for that kind of a home disadvantage. You might begin by trying to get some kind of a self–concept measure on Sally and then try to use it to draw her out. Perhaps you could use that sentence completion inventory that you used a couple of years ago.

Mary: Good idea, Emma. I'll have all the kids do it along with that projective thing of having them draw a picture and tell a story about their home. Then Sally won't feel singled out. Great idea!

❂

It is two days later, and Mary is conducting a science discussion on animals as a precursor to an upcoming field trip to the zoo. She deliberately stands in front of Sally so Sally cannot daydream during the discussion.

Mary: And now, boys and girls, let's talk about what the book has to say about the cat family. What is the biggest cat? [All the students except Sally raise their hands.] Yes, Roger?

Roger :The lion.

Mary [smiling]: Ah, ha! I fooled you! You all thought it was the lion, didn't you?

Becky [without raising her hand]: I didn't!

Mary [with a twinkle in her eye]: You didn't, Becky? What is the right answer?

Becky: The tiger.

Mary: That's right! Now how many of you knew that? [All hands but Sally's go up.] Oh I don't think so! I think that some of you are trying to fool me! [Several children titter.] Now let's all look at the picture of the members of the cat family on page 43. As you look at the picture, which cat is the largest? Sally?

Sally [points to the tiger.]

Mary: That's right, Sally! What do we call that cat?

Sally [barely audible]: Tiger.

Mary: That's right! Say it louder, Sally, so we can hear you.

Sally [whispers]: Tiger.

Mary: That's better. Now class, let me ask you a very difficult question. What is the largest cat in the Western Hemisphere? [Pause—no hands are raised.] I'll give you a hint. It has spots, but it's not a leopard. Anyone know? Becky?

Becky: Is it the puma?

Mary : No. This cat has spots. [Sally very tentatively raises her hand and then takes it down.] Sally?

Sally [shakes her head]

Mary: I told you this was a tough one. Jerome?

Jerome: A bear. A black bear.

Mary: No, Jerome. The bear is neither a cat nor does it have spots. Okay, Becky, you want to try again?

Becky: A jaguar?

Mary: Right, Becky! You know the answer! [Looks at Sally] Did you know the answer too, Sally?

Sally [shakes her head "yes" but says nothing]

Jerome [without raising his hand]: Yeah, I'll bet! If she knew the answer, I knew it too! [Sally lowers her head and looks down at the floor.]

Mary: That's enough, Jerome! We can't read other peoples' minds, can we? I know Sally is a person who tells the truth, and I think she did know! [Pause] Now let's talk about some of the smaller cats. [Sally continues to stare at the floor]

❂

It is the next afternoon after school. Mary has asked Sally to stay after class and sits in front of her desk talking to her.

Mary: Don't worry, Sally, I'll get you to your bus on time. I just wanted to talk to you a minute. [Sally states down at the floor.] I was so pleased yesterday when you knew about the jaguar. [No response.] You studied that lesson, didn't you? [Sally nods her head "yes" but continues to stare at the floor.] Sally, I'm so pleased for you because I've been a little worried about your work. You haven't been doing your work and participating in class.

Sally [whispers]: I can't.

Mary: Sally, you're a very smart girl. I know you can if you try.

Sally [whispers]: I try, but it's too hard.

Mary [very gently]: Sally, why don't you talk more in class?

Sally [whispers]: I don't know.

Mary: I noticed you don't play with the other kids at recess. Why not?

Sally [whispers and looks at the floor]: They don't like me.

Mary: Do you mean the other children?

Sally [nods her head "yes."]

Mary: Well, Sally, I like you and want you to do well. Maybe I should talk to your mother to see if she can help. Would that be okay?

Sally [looking up at Mary for the first time with fear in her eyes.] I
guess so. [Pause] It doesn't matter.

Mary [sighs]: Okay, Sally. Run along and catch your bus.

✪

It is one week later, and Mary has arranged a conference with Sally's
mother in her room after school. Mrs. Gorman is in her middle thirties
and is overweight and somewhat disheveled in appearance. Her face
seems lined in a permanent scowl.

Mary [nervously]: Thanks so much for coming, Mrs. Gorman! I
know you're very busy, and I wouldn't have asked to see you if I
wasn't so concerned about Sally.

Mrs. Gorman [frowning]: What's the matter with Sally? I knew her
grades weren't too good, but that's because she's lazy. [Raising
her voice] If you'd give her a good whack or two she'd straighten
up and get to work.

Mary [hesitantly]: Well, Mrs. Gorman, Sally doesn't seem to believe in herself and doesn't try. She thinks she can't do the work
when she's really a very bright little girl.

Mrs. Gorman [with a glint in her eye]: I think she's got your number! I'm telling you, all you've got to do is give her a kick in the
pants. I'll tell you, she sure doesn't pull that stuff at home! I'll
guarantee you she does her work around the house! I just don't
put up with any crap! [Pause] Look, Mrs. Powell, I'm very busy
and I really don't have any more time for this! I expect teachers to
do their jobs just like I do mine! I would appreciate it if you would
not bother me about Sally unless it's really important! I've got
another, uh, appointment that I've got to go to. Good–bye.

✪

It is two days later, and Mary is speaking to her class as she passes
out papers.

Mary: Students, I think you're going to find what we're going to do
now is a lot of fun! Now first look at the sheet of paper that says
"Sentence Completion" at the top. We're not doing English when
we fill it out. You get to make up your own answers to complete
each sentence. There is no right answer—just tell how you really
feel. This will help me get to know each of you better and do a
better job of teaching. [Short pause] When you're through completing the sentences and turning your paper in, I want you to
draw me a picture and write me a story about it. Take two blank
sheets of paper from this pile [pointing] and first draw me a pic-

ture of your home. Then write me a story about what it's like to live at your house. Yes, Kevin?

Kevin: Are we supposed to color our picture?

Mary: You may if you like. It would be nice if you did, but do what you feel. [Pause] Okay, let's begin. [Mary stands next to Sally's desk to make sure she participates.]

❂

It is Monday of the following week, and Mary meets with Emma Buell, the guidance counselor, in Emma's office after school.

Emma: How did your conference with Mrs. Gorman go?

Mary: Just like you predicted. An aggressive, almost masculine, woman.

Emma [laughing]: One thing's sure—she's certainly no gentleman!

Mary [smiling]: Yes, I'll bet she more than holds her own with the other workers. [Short pause] What did you think of Sally's response on the sentence completion inventory and the picture and story she wrote.

Emma: Well I'm certainly no expert on projective techniques, but I didn't think the picture and story revealed much. They almost seemed to be more of an academic exercise than a revelation of Sally's view of her world. But the sentence completion responses were certainly interesting!

Mary: I thought so too. What do they tell you?

Emma: They reveal a girl who is very depressed and who has very little confidence in herself. I could call Sally in and give her a self–concept inventory, but I think we both know what it would tell us.

Mary [sighing]: Yes, it would tell us that Sally has a very negative self–concept. [Pause] Emma, what am I going to do? How do you help a child like Sally?!

Sentence Completion Interest Inventory

Name: *Sally Gorman*

1. My father likes me best *Don't know. Don't see him. (Hardly ever)*
2. My mother likes me best *When I do what she tells me. (If she's in a good mood.)*
3. I feel Proudest *Nothing, I can't think of anything. When I do right.*
4. When I finish school I want to be *Don't know. Maybe work at Central.*
5. My favorite hobby is *Reading and watching T.V.*
6. When I go home after school I like to *Have free time so I can do what I want to.*

7. My worst fear is *Doing bad. Making my mother mad.*

8. People are happiest *When they get to do what they want. When they are left alone.*

9. My friends *I like to be alone. Friends can get you in trouble and tell lies.*

10. My favorite school subject is *I like reading stories like fairy tales best of all.*

11. School is *Good when they let you do what you like to do. Bad when they make you talk in front of others.*

12. Home is *Working hard and doing what you are told.*

Student Paper

The following student paper was written by Rebecca Clarke, Michele Golden, Joy Martin, Crystal Mead, Jennifer Nelson, and Aaron Reid in an undergraduate educational psychology course taught by the author at the University of Florida and is printed with their permission.

Introduction

Presented in this case are two main subjects, "Shy Sally" and her mother Mrs. Gorman. Mrs. Gorman is a divorced, single mother who shows little to no interest in her child Sally's welfare. Sally, a sixth grader in Mary Powell's class, shows signs of insecurity and withdrawal as seen by her many instances of daydreaming in class. Mary Powell is an experienced teacher who hopes to have a positive influence on her students' lives. Mary has noticed Sally's insecurities and is attempting to help Sally overcome them. During Mary Powell's quest to assist Sally, she discovered evidence indicating that some of Sally's problems may stem from her homelife. It was found that Mrs. Gorman was quite neglectful of Sally's feelings due to her own lack of love and belonging.

Analysis

This case study attempts to pinpoint the levels within Maslow's Hierarchical Theory of Motivation that Sally and her mother have not yet fulfilled and to provide solutions that will attempt to assist each one to move on to the next level. Maslow developed a hierarchical order of needs required for a healthy, normal, and fully satisfying life. Within Maslow's theory, it is stated that there are five levels of needs to be met. A person's life is generally dominated by the need they are currently trying to satisfy. Until the lowest (most basic) level of needs are met, the higher needs cannot be fulfilled.

The most basic level of needs are the physiological needs. They include the needs of food, drink and shelter. The second level, safety and security needs refer to the person's need for an orderly, stable and safe world. In the next level, love and belonging, the individual seeks affectionate and intimate relationships with other people, needing to feel part of a group. The fourth stage of needs is the need for esteem which is the necessity for respect of oneself and the respect from others. The highest and least basic need is self–actualization. This final stage refers to the desire of a person to fulfill their highest potential. Self–actualization is the most difficult stage to reach (Engler, p. 373–374).

According to Maslow's hierarchy of needs, Sally seems to have fulfilled the first level which is almost always met. There is evidence that Sally is presently attempting to satisfy the next level of the hierarchy which is safety and security.

Throughout the case study, Sally displays numerous instances of shyness. Shyness indicates insecurity and lack of self–confidence. For instance, during a classroom discussion, even though Sally knew the answer, she was hesitant in speaking out.

> *Mary: ...which cat is the largest? Sally?*
> *Sally: [points to the tiger.]*
> *Mary: That's right, Sally! What do we call that cat?*
> *Sally: [barely audible] Tiger.*
> *Mary: That's right! Say it louder, Sally, so we can hear you.*
> *Sally: [whispers] Tiger.*

This conversation indicates that Sally seems to have no desire to be at the center of the class's attention because she lacks the confidence within herself to speak out. All of the above reasons indicate that Sally has not fulfilled the fourth level, self–esteem.

In response to a classmate's comment, "If she knew the answer, I knew it too!" Sally "lowers her head and looks down at the floor" (Greenwood and Parkay p. 183). When Ms. Powell notices that Sally is not playing with the other children at recess, Sally's response was "They don't like me" (Greenwood and Parkay, p. 184). These are two indications that the level of love and belonging, the third level, has not been fulfilled.

Maslow's second level, safety and security, can be characterized by a person who is seeking a safe, orderly, predictable and organized world (Maslow, p. 87). A safe environment is one that is free of fear. This study does not directly state that there is abuse of any kind taking place in the home, but evidence shows that there is fear within Sally of her mother. For example, when Mary mentions having a conference with her mother to Sally, Sally "looks up with fear in her eyes" (Greenwood and Parkay, p. 184). A sentence completion exercise done in the classroom tells of Sally's worst fear: "Doing bad. Making my mother mad" (Greenwood and Parkay, p. 186). Her desire to isolate herself, watch television, and read fairy tales demonstrates that Sally is placing herself in what she may feel is a safer and more predictable environment. Thus, Sally's life appears to be dominated by her need to fulfill the level of safety and security.

Mrs. Gorman has fulfilled her physiological and safety and security needs. She has achieved her safety and security need level through her monotonous work routine and controlled environment. She has no fear or instability in her world. "She works on the assembly line at Central," (Greenwood and Parkay, p. 182) proves the fact that her world is consistent and stable.

Mrs. Gorman appears to be stuck in the level of love and belonging. While in this stage, "The need for love entails the ability to receive love and to give it" (Engler, p. 339). There are two known ways that Mrs. Gorman could possibly receive love, through her husband and her daughter. "What about Mrs. Gorman's husband?" Ms. Powell asked. Emma, the guidance counselor, responded, "They're divorced, of course. Poor man probably couldn't take it!" (Greenwood and Parkay, p. 182). Because Mrs. Gorman's husband divorced her, any possibility of her receiving love from him was severed. What Mr. Gorman conceivably could not deal with was the fact that Mrs. Gorman was not capable of giving him the love he needed.

Due to the fact that Sally has not yet reached the level of love and belonging, as previously shown, she too is incapable of giving her mother love. On the other hand, Mrs. Gorman also does not display any love toward Sally. This is evident from her statement, "I would appreciate it if you would not bother me about Sally unless it's really important!" (Greenwood and Parkay, p. 184). Further evidence exhibits the lack of love that Mrs. Gorman conveys to her daughter Sally, "...all you've got to do is give her a kick in the pants...I just don't put up with any crap!" (Greenwood and Parkay, p. 184). Mrs. Gorman does not appear to have the ability to give or receive love.

Decision

Proposed Cooperative Learning Technique for Sally

Cooperative Learning is the method we propose to fulfill Sally's need for safety and security. The theory was developed in the 1970's and like Maslow's theory of motivation, it's roots lie in Humanistic Theory. Thus, cooperative learning focuses on affect and is child centered (Slavin, p. xi). The main goal of cooperative learning is getting students to work together rather than competing. This is done with the use of student groups.

There are many different techniques of cooperative learning which vary in group size from two to twenty and in homogeneity in ability, age, gender and race. Each of these techniques contains five components: group/individual incentives, group study, task specialization, equal opportunity testing, and between–group competition. Of these five, group incentives were found to have the most profound effect on motivation (Gage and Berliner, p. 442).

Cooperative learning was seen to be potentially beneficial for Sally due to its success in fostering "liking of class" without decreasing academic ability. In addition, this method provides needed structure in the classroom.

The two specific cooperative learning techniques that were chosen to fulfill Sally's needs are Cooperative Integrated Reading and Composition (CIRC) and Student Teams–Achievement Divisions (STAD).

CIRC – CIRC is designed to use pairs of students from different level reading groups. Pairs are given reading tasks which they must complete together. Each individual student is also a member of a reading group specific to his/her ability level (Slavin, p. 5).

The CIRC method was chosen based on Sally's interest in reading as shown on her sentence completion interest inventory. Sally states "My favorite subject in school is: *I like reading stories like fairy tales best of all*" (Greenwood and Parkay, p. 186). Thus, it was felt that Sally would feel most comfortable working with others in the subject of reading.

In addition, CIRC will provide a structured environment in the classroom. This structure will be dependent on each student's desired levels, due to the use of task sheets for each pair. This is important for Sally's insecurity need because it provides order on a daily basis.

STAD – The other method chosen is the evaluation aspect from STAD. This aspect takes the form of individual quizzes on the material, in this case reading books. Quizzes are scored in comparison with the part average of each individual student. Points are accumulated by scoring above or at the past average. The points of all group members are summed to form a team score which is compared to other team scores. Teams which meet a set goal, earn a reward for their achievement (Slavin, p. 4).

STAD was found to improve general self–esteem, increase motivation by internally attributing locus of control, increase number of friends named by students, and improving cooperation (Slavin, p. 44–49).

Based on this data, STAD's method of evaluation was thought to be beneficial for Sally because it, like CIRC, increases social interaction and interest in class activities.

In addition, STAD provides a structured evaluation which shows a direct relationship between student input and team achievement. The scoring method also reduced the risk of feelings of failure. These details are beneficial to Sally because she needs an ordered environment and needs to be appreciated for her reading ability to build her self confidence.

Based on the preceding analysis it is recommended that Mary Powell should implement the CIRC and STAD techniques in the following ways:

The class will first be divided into pairs of differing ability levels. Sally will be paired with someone of lower ability in order to encourage Sally to interact with her partner in completing the reading tasks.

Secondly, a book which is long enough to be used for three weeks will be assigned to every group. This book will need to be of median ability level, to allow each student to achieve up to their ability.

Pairs will then be given a list of reading tasks which revolve around the book. Activities may include such things as plot summaries, or character analysis. Pairs will meet three times a week to complete their list. In addition, each student will be in a separate ability level group for reading. Groups will separate to work with the teacher in discussing ability appropriate ideas.

Teams will be evaluated using individual quizzes on the material that the pairs cover. Sally and her partner's scores will be added together to form a team score. Sally will receive points for scoring above her own previous mean. The team will receive a certificate at the end of each week if they have reached the set reading task goal.

In conclusion, the use of this cooperative learning method should help to fulfill Sally's safety and security need by providing an ordered classroom environment. By creating a relationship based on achievement in Sally's favorite subject, a stability in Sally's emotional life and an improvement in her academic self–esteem will be created. Finally, cooperative learning should increase Sally's interest and participation within the class.

Proposed Interaction Plan for Mrs. Gorman

Parent involvement in school plays a critical role in the success of the student. Sally's answers to the interest inventory sentence completion exercise reveals that her mother, Mrs. Gorman, is not interested in her school activities. It is assumed, based on Sally's overall behavior and her responses to the class exercise, Mrs. Gorman's influence is not positive. Therefore, one of the goals of this stimulation is to increase positive interactions between Sally and her mother, and subsequently increase the positive influence that Mrs. Gorman has on Sally.

After taking into consideration Mrs. Gorman's harsh attitude towards Sally and her schoolwork, it was decided that the most successful plan would be one that took the emphasis off actual academics and implemented a fun activity. Another concern was that Mrs. Gorman would not respond to this plan. Therefore, this proposal also suggests an alternate plan for dealing with any rejections that Sally's mom might have to the proposed plan.

The devised plan incorporates a step–by–step cooperative effort among Sally, Mrs. Gorman, and an active, trained teaching assistant. The purpose of this plan is to make Mrs. Gorman feel that she is making an active contribution in the education of her daughter, and to give Sally the support and positive attention that she needs to receive from her mother.

The proposed plan is as follows:

Step 1 – A letter will be sent to the parent or parents of each child in Sally's class announcing a cookout party to be held at a local park on a Saturday afternoon. Lunch will be served free of charge and carpools will be arranged for any family in need of transportation.

The cookout will serve to honor all working parents. It will also kickoff a new bookmaking activity called "Bookmaking Fun with Parents." This activity will be constructed by the child and his/her parents. The activity will involve the child and the parent constructing a short book that describes a day at the parents' place of employment. The book will include drawings and a broad description of the events surrounding a day at work. The activity is to be completed by the child and parent during any after school hours spanning a three–week period. Children will not be assigned homework over this three–week time span. All materials for this project will be provided by the school.

The children will not be graded on this activity. However, during another planned cookout, the parent and child will present this book. Each parent and child will receive an award of recognition. The children and parents of the top three books will each receive a gift certificate donated by a local restaurant.

Step 2 – (The following plan is provided as a backup in the instance that Mrs. Gorman does not respond to the letter sent home.)

A teaching assistant (T.A.) trained to work with parents from varying socio-economic backgrounds will personally call Mrs. Gorman, or any parent that does not respond to the letter. The T.A. will attempt to make Mrs. Gorman feel welcome and accept her as an individual. The T.A. will also explain the "Bookmaking Fun with Parents" activity that is being implemented in Sally's classroom.

The T.A. will arrange for a home visit. One goal of a parent involvement program is to involve all parents. It might be necessary to directly contact parents who have not been responsive to written messages or invitations from the school (Olmsted, p. 221). The sponsors of one parent involvement program called Follow Through found that "...a home visit was the best direct–contact method" (Olmsted, p. 221). The home–visitor can discuss briefly how the child benefits when the home and school work together (Olmsted, p. 221).

By going to visit Mrs. Gorman, the T.A. will make her feel important and accepted by the school community. The T.A. will also praise Sally's good school-work. The visit also serves to explain to Mrs. Gorman the many benefits this bookmaking activity is offering to Sally. Finally, the T.A. will offer to come by and pick up Mrs. Gorman and Sally so they can all ride to the cookout together.

These proposed ideas should make Mrs. Gorman feel more important and involved. Subsequently, a portion of her need for esteem will be fulfilled.

After these proposed techniques for both Sally and Mrs. Gorman have been carried out, it would be hoped that each would move on to the next level of Maslow's Hierarchy of needs which are love and belonging and self–actualization, respectively.

References (Student Paper)

Engler, B. (1991). *Personality Theories an Introduction* (3rd edition). Boston, MA: Houghton Mifflin Company.

Gage, N.L. & Berliner, D.C. (1991). *Educational Psychology* (5th edition). Boston, MA: Houghton Mifflin Company.

Greenwood, G.E. & Parkay, F. W. (1989). *Case Studies for Teacher Decision Making*. New York, NY: Random House.

Maslow, A.H. (1954). *Motivation and Personality*. New York, NY: Harper Brothers.

Olmsted, P.P. (1991). Parent involvement in elementary education: Findings and suggestions from the follow through program. *The Elementary School Journal, 91*, 229.

Slavin, R.E. (1990). *Cooperative Learning: Theory, Research and Practice* . Englewood Cliffs, NJ: Prentice Hall.

Critique of student paper

The paper presented above received an "A," and is of good overall quality compared to other undergraduate papers. It meets all six criteria rather well. A motivational psychologist might complain about the lack of depth in applying Maslow's theory, for example, in defining Maslow's need levels. They might also note the fragile tie–in between Maslow's theory and cooperative learning techniques. However, the paper is a product of 9 fifty–minute class meetings plus time outside class and represents a good general grasp of Maslow's theory and stages on the part of five undergraduates who were introduced to the theory for the first time.

Likewise, it might be argued that the decision section of the paper shows a shallow understanding of cooperative learning techniques and fails to fully operationalize them. This criticism ignores an important point, however. The typical depth of understanding Maslow's or any other theory among under-graduates who take an educational psychology course rarely goes beyond the memorization or comprehension required by objective or short answer exams. This small group of six undergraduates will know at least one theory in some depth as a result of participating in the case study project.

Conclusion

All student papers aren't as good as the one presented. However, our students indicate that they generally not only enjoy the case work, but learn a strategy for approaching difficult teaching situations. I might add that a number of former students who are now teachers have told us that they "fell back" on the decision making strategies that they learned in the course when they were confronted with a teaching situation they didn't know how to handle. Such transfer of learning is a primary goal in our use of case studies.

It seems to me that Broudy is right when he argues that case studies have a contribution to make in helping preservice and inservice teachers, as well as other members of the educational community, develop strategies for dealing with the common core of professional problems. If that is true, then the use of case studies must be more than a clever and interesting set of discussions about a case. The students must have a professional knowledge base from which to draw theories, models, and sets of principles and have the opportunity to learn strategies for applying such content. In this way students can learn to see the applicational value of the materials they are learning and learn how to trans-late theory into practice. Such learning should be of great value to them when they enter the real world.

References

Bloom, B.S., Engelhart, M.D., Furst, E.J., Hill, W.H., & Krathwohl, D.R. (1956). *Taxonomy of educational objectives. The classification of educational goals: Hand-book 1. Cognitive Domain.* New York: Longmans Green.

Bloom, B.S. et al. (1956). *Taxonomy of educational objectives. The classification of educational goals: Handbook 1. Cognitive Domain.* New York: Longmans Green.

Broudy, H.S. (1990). Case studies—why and how. *Teachers College Board, 91,* 449–459.

Dunkin, M.J. & Barnes, J. (1986). Research on teaching in higher education in Wittrock, M.C. (Ed.). *Handbook of Research on Teaching.* New York: MacMillan, 3rd ed.

Gliessman, D. (1970). *Critical Moments in Teaching Film Series,* New York: Holt, Rinehart and Winston.

Sanford, N. Research and policy in higher education (1962). In Sanford, N. (Ed.), *The American College,* New York: John Wiley.

Shavelson, R.J. (1973). What is the basic teaching skill? *Journal of Teacher Education, 24,* 144–151.

Dr. Gordon E. Greenwood is professor of educational psychology in the College of Education at the University of Florida. He received his doctorate form Indiana University in 1967 and has conducted research in the area of parent involvement in education, teacher belief systems (including teacher locus of control, stress, and burnout), and the evaluation of college teaching methods.

Dr. Greenwood has numerous publications in journals such as the *Journal of Educational Psychology, the Journal of Research and Development in Education, Elementary School Journal, Research in Higher Education, Assessment and Evaluation in Higher Education, and Theory into Practice.* He has also authored two casebooks for teacher education for Harper and Row and Random House. His involvement with the case study method of college teaching extends back to 1965.

Our Hero Comes of Age:

What Students Learn From Case Writing in Student Teaching

Judith Kleinfeld

Learning from experience is neither automatic nor easy, especially when you have made professional mistakes you would just as soon forget all about. Writing a case compels students to think through the experience of learning to teach. Evaluating what students learned from writing cases about student teaching, I found substantial changes in their conceptual maps of the educational world. Students started out with educational maps that were simple, implicit, and formulaic. After writing a case, their conceptual maps became far more complex, contextual and sophisticated.

Introduction

Learning from experience is neither automatic nor easy—especially when you have made mistakes you would just as soon forget about. If you pause to recall a difficult professional experience of your own, you can appreciate how hard it is for education students to engage in reflective inquiry about their problems in learning how to teach. We often want to avoid thinking about troubling experiences. We can also think about troubling experiences and draw the wrong lessons. Many student teachers who try out a new teaching technique and draw the conclusion that it simply doesn't work remind me of Mark Twain's cat, who sat on a hot stove and learned never to sit again.

In this paper, I offer a specific instructional strategy for helping education students reflect on their teaching experience and learn from it. This strategy is case writing, especially writing a case about the student teaching experience. Case writing creates an occasion for reflective inquiry about student teaching. The story form of the case increases the chances that students will draw useful lessons from their experience.

I first describe how I came to use cases and case writing when I developed an innovative new teacher education program centered on multi–cultural teaching. In the appendix, I include the specific case writing assignment I used and invite other teacher educators to adapt it to their situations.

I next describe my efforts to evaluate what my students learned from this case writing assignment. I provide an extended example of the changes in one student's thinking. Case writing, I found, led to substantial changes in student teachers' conceptual maps of the social world. Students started out with conceptual maps that were simple, implicit, and formulaic. After writing a case about student teaching, their conceptual maps became contextual, explicit and conditional. Students did not simply change their ideas about the social world, replacing "false" ideas for "true." Rather, their world–views became more sophisticated, and they became more sensitive to the situation.

In my own evaluation of what students learned from case writing, I found valuable changes in students' world–views. In the conclusion to this paper, however, I do not argue that we need more evaluation of case method teaching and case writing. I point out the similarity of our evaluation efforts of case method teaching to the unfruitful efforts to evaluate discussion teaching or inquiry teaching. We would do better to consider case methods as one valuable strategy among others, a strategy useful in certain situations, such as in thinking through the student teaching experience.

❖

Cases and Stories: My First Effort to Use the Heroic Tale as a Metaphor for Learning to Teach

When I became director of an innovative teacher education program at the University of Alaska Fairbanks, I wondered if the classic heroic tale might be used to give point to the pain of students struggling to learn how to teach. Student teaching especially is an ordeal, a classic rite of passage. Students must make the transition from the student role to the teacher role, from dealing with authority to becoming that authority. Framing their experiences as a story—a heroic ordeal—I suspected, would give them the emotional distance they needed to analyze it.

I turned to one of the my favorite books, Shirley Park Lowry's *Familiar Mysteries: The Truth in Myth* (1982) to consider her description of the classic life pattern of the hero:

> *The essential heroic pattern is a simple one of four parts. The hero (1) enters the unknown, (2) struggles with what lies there, (3) finds something of value — a boon, and (4) returns with that boon to his community. Parts 3 and 4, of course, do not always occur in the story.*
>
> *Many an adventurer's bones lie bleaching in the wilderness, many a community locks its gates against the returning adventurer, many a prize, when unveiled before the throng, is found to have turned to dust, and many a hero is so transformed by his experiences in the forest that home is lost to him forever. Indeed, it is these tragic possibilities that keep the basic pattern meaningful, without real risk, that pattern would become a mere cliche."*

I could certainly name students whose bones lay bleaching in the wilderness as well as those who came back with a boon. The heroic story, I decided, had possibilities.

"What would you think about organizing our new teacher education program around the metaphor of a heroic quest and ordeal?" I asked a colleague. She hated the idea. She preferred more humility, I suspected, than heroes usually offer. But she had another reason, which I found compelling. Most of our students, she pointed out, were going to be teaching in culturally different communities, and the notion of coming in as a hero aroused the wrong associations.

✺

Reading Cases of Teaching Problems in Culturally Different Schools

I gave up the heroic tale and turned to the business of planning a new teacher education program. The "Teachers for Alaska" program was designed to help students learn how to teach in an especially complex setting — small Eskimo and Indian villages. Students had to grapple with problems for which traditional teacher education programs did not prepare them — the experience of entering a small village as a cultural outsider, the differences in values and expectations of children, the political sensitivities that arose from a troubled history of intercultural relationships.

We needed curriculum materials for our teacher education program that dealt with the specific problems of teaching in this cultural context. I turned to cases, stories about problems other teachers had experienced. The narrative form could render a problem with subtlety. Nor did stories mislead with formulaic solutions. A story only made the claim that conflicts like this one sometimes occurred and this was how one person dealt with it and this is what happened. Stories created sensitivities.

I sought out experienced rural teachers and asked them to write cases about troubling situations which prospective teachers should think about. (Kleinfeld, 1990). Counseling high school students was difficult, for example, in Eskimo villages where many parents did not want their children to leave them and go away to college — this dilemma became the basis for a case (Allen, 1990). Sexual teasing was another pitfall. Eager to be accepted in a culturally different community, young female teachers could unwittingly send "come hither" signals and engage in flirtation games where they did not know the cultural rules. These matters became a pivotal incident in another case (Carey, 1989). Such cases became a centerpiece of our teacher education program.

The cases served as cautionary tales. They offered students vicarious experience with the problems they would face and developed their abilities to analyze the situations and figure out alternative ways of handling them. Students also enjoyed the cases with their conflict, drama, and emotion, and we enjoyed teaching them.

Writing Cases as a Means of Learning from the Student Teaching Experience

Cases improved the first semester of the program. However, our final semester, accompanying the student teaching experience, was not going well. Since most of our students were teaching in remote communities, we could not have an after school seminar. Rather, we asked students to return to campus after their student teaching experience for a week–long seminar. We wanted to provide additional instruction in weak areas, help our students reflect on what they had learned from student teaching, and give them the benefit of other students' experiences in different settings.

After the initial excitement of meeting old friends and hearing what had happened to them, the seminar had taken the form of presentations by speakers invited to discussion educational topics students were concerned about. The seminar was disjointed and boring.

The student teaching seminar is difficult to make productive. Examining teacher education programs across the country, Edmundson (1990) found that students viewed these seminars as contributing little to their teaching. Students rated these seminars less interesting than any other education course, with the exception of foundation courses. The study team found little evidence that the seminars accompanying student teaching actually promoted reflective inquiry.

I began to think again about the possibility of the heroic tale. Several of our student teachers had come back with fascinating adventure stories and I had asked them to write up their experiences as cases for our curriculum. As I worked with these students in shaping their student teaching experience into a story, I realized that writing a case was a powerful way of helping the students learn from their experiences in student teaching.

The act of constructing a story imposes meaning on what would otherwise be mere chronology, event following upon event (Journet, 1990; White, 1981; Kermode, 1966). To create a story we must decide on the central conflict or dilemma. We must figure out what we will call the beginning, middle, and end. We must describe the characters and the setting. We must select the crucial incidents. We must reflect on the experience and what it means.

But the stories that the students came back with, I realized, only partially fit the genre of heroic tales. The students did go into the unknown and face ordeals, but these were not tales of conquering heroes. They were more "coming of age" tales. They were classic *bildungsroman:* stories about the naive youth who goes out into the world and gains an education. One of our students wrote a case that aptly showed the mixing of the two genres. His case was called "On a White Horse" with a cover picture of himself as Don Quixote with a pencil for a sword, a dunce cap for a helmet, and his eyes buried in a book rather than scanning the terrain (Anonymous, 1991). The theme of his case was his moral error in pridefully charging ahead with a Foxfire project that did not fit the school setting, instead of stepping carefully through the territory.

To see if case writing would improve the student teaching seminar, I asked all of the student teachers to write a case about their student teaching experience. Since students had read cases, they were familiar with the case form. A case, the assignment emphasized, was not a description of what had happened to them first, second and so on (See Appendix). A case was a story which centered around a problem or conflict and showed how the protagonist dealt with it. To help students turn their experience into a story, I gave them a version of the basic "story grammar" (Mandler, 1984).

When the students returned to the concluding seminar, each had two hours to present their draft case to the student group. The other students and professors were asked to help the student interpret the experience. The final case was due two weeks later.

As students presented their cases, the atmosphere became charged. Student sat at the edge of their chairs, leaning forward, their faces expressing sympathy and strong emotion. As students told their stories, the other students offered stories of their own, verifying the first story, amplifying it, modifying it, contradicting it. Each student's story was placed in a distribution of similar experiences—this was a common experience, an occasional one, an unrepresentative experience which required contextual explanation.

My own students' responses in this seminar were strikingly similar to Mattingly's (1991) account of the response when occupational therapists told stories about their practices. When the therapists were describing their clinical cases using biomedical discourse, a language Mattingly terms "chart talk," the audience was respectful but remote. When the therapist changed into the mode of telling stories:

> *The affect of the group changed dramatically. Several leaned forward and focused more directly on the speaker's face. The structure of conversation shifted. During the first half of her talk (a description of Parkinson's disease) the audience was quiet, respectful. During the second half, the audience paid increasingly close attention to the speaker, mirroring her facial expressions on their own faces in sympathetic accompaniment to the unfolding story. Talk changed from a strict monologue to an increasingly flowing, overlapping dialogue, with nearly all audience members participating in the end. The audience became a chorus, first in largely nonverbal expressions that marked their strongly felt participation in the story, quickly followed by storytelling of their own . . . (p. 247).*

For our teacher education students, telling their stories was therapeutic, as well as educative. The students provided emotional support for each other. There were moments of epiphany—as when one teacher described the way a group of Native students tested and teased her and a Native student teacher remembered his own participation in such hazing and tried to explain why it happened. Some students who had had relatively tame student teaching experiences expressed envy for those who had experienced more interesting and educative difficulties.

Evaluating Case Writing: Figuring Out What Students Had Learned

While the seminar had been exciting, I wanted to see what students had actually learned from writing cases about student teaching. What problems had they reflected upon? What had they come away with?

I began by categorizing the problems and conflicts the students wrote about. This analysis yielded nothing of interest. I found the usual beginning teacher problems — difficulties with time management, authority, overly ambitious projects. More important, this analytic approach, I realized, did not yield a good representation of the nature of the problems themselves.

One student, for example, indeed wrote about "time management"— how difficult it was for him to grade lengthy homework assignments he insisted on giving his students, how students resented his breaking the unwritten low homework code, how little time he had to spend with his wife and children, and how his Foxfire–style journalism project failed when he ran out of time. But this student titled his case The Judas Tree, quoted Matthew 27, and identified himself with the betrayer Judas. His case was not about "time management." His case was about a spiritual problem — his sense that he had betrayed his own teaching ideals. He had given such lengthy homework assignments and done the Foxfire project, he had come to believe, not from any genuine concern for his students but from ambition, his desire to make a showing in the district and get a teaching job.

As I again read through the cases, I began to notice common features:

- **The cases were drenched with emotion**. If the stock line for a mystery is "It was a dark and stormy night," then the stock line for a case about teaching would be "I waited till I got home to cry." The students wrote about their anguish when heroic efforts failed, when other teachers did not support them, when students resisted them. They wrote about their joy when teaching went well and when colleagues supported them.
- **Many dealt with spiritual and ethical concerns**. The students were writing about teaching but they were also writing about the kinds of people they saw themselves to be. The stories were filled with moral judgments about themselves and other people. Mattingly (1991) makes the same point in describing the stories told by the occupational therapists, "There is little or no effort to exhibit a value–neutral stance toward the events depicted . . . (the narrative) is strongly moralizing" (p. 248).

•**The cases were situated at the crossroads between an inner world of emotions and ethics and an outer world of people and events.** The students were not writing about technical teaching problems, the kinds of problems a supervisor and a student teacher might discuss after a classroom observation. Nor were they writing autobiographies. They were weaving stories at the intersection of their inner world and the outer world.

• **The starting point for the narrative was typically an intention, a desire to accomplish some good.** A case fundamentally traced what Bruner (1986, p.16) calls the essence of a story — the "vicissitudes of intention." The student teacher had an intention which led to action and experience. The student then interpreted the experience and this interpretation became the basis for new intentions and actions.

How Student Thinking Changed Through Writing Cases

What changed as intention led to experience, and experience led to new intention was students' **conceptual maps about the social world.** (See Figure 1). Students had beliefs about causality in the social world similar to their beliefs about causality in the physical world. These beliefs could be described in a series of "if/then" statements: "If I participate in community affairs and don't stay aloof from the Native village, Native people will like and respect me, or "If I teach American history by the textbook alone, then students will be bored and dislike history." The students' conceptual maps contained scripts of what they should say and do to produce effects. They also had images of the "Native community" or the "ideal social studies classroom." Their conceptual maps, in short, were composed of beliefs about causality in the social world, scripts, and images.

Each of the cases the students wrote, I realized, could be analyzed in terms of the changes that occurred in these conceptual maps of the world as they reflected upon their experience. People did not necessarily react as they expected. Their images were often inaccurate. As they tried to interpret their experience, to figure out why what they expected had not occurred, they developed much more sophisticated models of the social world.

In brief, their initial conceptual maps tended to be **simple, formulaic, and implicit.** Students' images of the "Native community," for example, or of the way students reacted to textbook teaching were based on the notions they had developed from education classes or from ideological rhetoric.

Students' revised conceptual maps tended to be much more **complex, conditional and explicit.** Students realized that they had to make distinctions, to

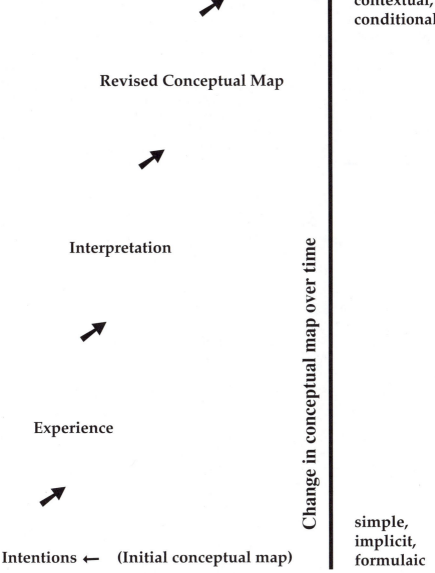

Questions

complex,
explicit,
contextual,
conditional

Revised Conceptual Map

Interpretation

Change in conceptual map over time

Experience

simple,
implicit,
formulaic

Intentions ← (Initial conceptual map)

Figure 1: Changes in Students' Thinking Through Writing a Case

consider the context, to think about the conditions under which their original beliefs did and did not hold true. They rarely decided that their initial ideas were simply wrong. Rather they developed more detailed conceptual maps contexts under which their original ideas did and did not hold true. Participating in Native community affairs, the student decided, might sometimes lead to greater respect in the village but might also get them into serious trouble. Teaching by non–textbook methods might develop enthusiasm for history among some students, but other students, conditioned to learn from textbooks, did not like challenging new approaches (especially during their last semester as high school seniors).

In sum, students were not simply substituting old ideas for new ones, false ideas for true. Their cases set forth enlarged conceptual maps which embraced both the old ideas and the new experience. In their cases, they created a more subtle and fuller vision of the world.

To explore what students had learned from writing a case about student teaching, I examined six elements:

1. **Initial Conceptual Map.** The content of this map was sometimes stated but usually needed to be partially inferred from students' intentions and actions.

2. **Intentions.** Students usually stated directly what they intended to accomplish and this intention formed the springboard of the case.

3. **Experience.** Students described the vicissitudes of their intentions, what actually happened.

4. **Interpretation.** Students offered an interpretation of their experience, an explanation of why their intentions were not realized.

5. **Revised Conceptual Map.** Based on the interpreted experience, students revised their initial views of the world.

6. **Questions.** Students often ended their cases with questions. To what extent had their experience resulted from their own inadequacies? How could they see this type of problem coming the next time?

❁

An Example of Learning from Case Writing

I offer the following case example to show how this analytic framework can be used to examine what students learn from writing a case. The example is actually a smaller story within the larger case, a microcosm of the case's themes and concerns. While I have abbreviated the story, most of the language is the student's and is taken directly from the case.

Case Example "The Easter Egg Hunt"

Shumayuk was just what Patsy had hoped for—a small Native village with a people and culture she held in high respect, science classes she wanted to teach, and even the possibility of a sled dog race coming through town.

"How could this get so thoroughly bad this soon?" Patsy asked herself. From the start, she had been in a war with the male high school students, who defied her authority. These boys had never before had a female high school teacher, let alone a female science teacher, and resisted all of the new science activities she tried to introduce. They taunted her by playing sexually explicit and vulgar music at top volume during the lunch hour.

Patsy's student teacher experience had been a series of confrontations with Native parents angry at how she disciplined their children, with the local school custodian who "accidentally" locked her out of her rooms and with the male high school students.

One time Patsy had yelled at the boys for refusing to chase a soccer ball during a physical education class. One boy exploded with his view of her situation.

"You're the one who just doesn't understand," he yelled at her. "You just won't understand. WE DON'T WANT YOU HERE!! YOU ARE NOT WANTED HERE! WE WON'T DO WHAT YOU SAY BECAUSE WE DON'T WANT YOU HERE!"

The Easter Egg Hunt, Patsy hoped, would allow her to improve her standing in this community.

On the Saturday before Easter, Claire, one of the women Patsy met at church and whose husband was on the school board, stopped by Patsy's room and asked her help in hiding eggs for the village's Easter Egg Hunt. Patsy was happy to help, thinking this would be a positive community activity to join and assist, and what fun it would be for the young children. Perhaps this could improve her relationship with the village and ease tensions.

Claire especially asked Patsy for help in hiding the "golden egg," wrapped in shiny gold foil and containing a note for $50. About 20 of the 200 eggs they would be hiding had notes for money rewards. Last year, Claire told Patsy, the egg hadn't been hidden well and people found the egg much too quickly.

Patsy was not pleased when she realized she would have to get up at 3:30 a.m. to hide the eggs but decided to go ahead.

As Patsy and another woman worked to hide the eggs around every home with children, she was surprised to find a house with adults gathered on the porch. She asked the young men if they wanted to help hide the eggs but they refused. As per instructions, she hid the golden egg in a remote spot, near some spruce trees by the airstrip.

Next morning Patsy was awakened at 6 a.m. by children begging for hints as to where she had hidden the golden egg. She was dismayed to find that the majority of the eggs had been retrieved not by the children of the village but by some of the adults. The young men who had been up at 3:30 in the morning watching her hide the eggs had gathered them up, including the ones with money notes.

The children kept coming to her begging for clues as to the location of the golden egg. Some had been searching in vain since 6 a.m. in the morning. Claire had disappeared leaving Patsy with the problem. Claire had gone fishing for the day.

The other teachers seemed to think it was a hilarious situation and said that's the reason why they didn't get involved in village affairs. The teachers said that Patsy was the perfect scapegoat, and maybe she would learn never to put herself in that type of situation again.

If the golden egg wasn't found by 8:00 p.m., the village council said, Patsy should retrieve it. At 8:00, Patsy, accompanied by a crowd of children, went to the airstrip and pulled the egg. Just then a 4–wheeler sped to the airstrip with the driver yelling, "Don't pull the egg! Don't pull the egg! The Council decided you shouldn't take the egg until 9:00."

Patsy stood there holding the golden egg in her palm. The crowd yelled their disapproval. Not only did she hide the golden egg so people couldn't find it, she had also disregarded the Council's directions in retrieving it. Who did she think she was, anyway?

Patsy made it back to her cubicle before the tears came. The past 24 hours seemed like a perfect set up to her. Instead of improving her relations with the village and doing something positive, she had succeeded in alienating more people and found herself condemned. She asked herself: How could this happen? Why can I try so hard and fail so miserably? How could I have foreseen this? What could I have done to prevent this entire situation.

This case shows Patsy acting from intentions based on a simple, formulaic view of the world (See Figure 2). She wanted to improve her relations with the village and believed that teachers created positive relations with Native communities when they took part in village affairs, rather than setting themselves apart in the school. Her case represented a continuation of personal concerns about winning the respect of Native people. This motive, while common among education students, was particularly intense for Patsy. In the Teachers for Alaska program, she distinguished herself by frequently directing her questions to the Native students in the class and keeping a close eye on them to see how they reacted to what was going on.

Implicit in Patsy's conceptual map were other concepts and assumptions. Village people, she thought, were always indulgent toward children. Sacrificing your own needs for the sake of others, she believed, brings approval and respect. Patsy had only one image of what an Easter Egg Hunt might be like, a model based on her own childhood experience.

After her disturbing experience with the Easter Egg Hunt in Shumayuk, Patsy's conceptual map became more complex. Easter Egg Hunts, she realized, might take several different forms. Her concept of "Easter Egg Hunt" had changed to an open, rather than a closed, category. When I asked her if she would participate in an Easter Egg Hunt in another Native community, she told me that she would wait and observe for a year or two.

Participating in community affairs, she realized, might bring respect under certain conditions but not others. Her conceptual map had developed branches with one path connecting community participation to good teacher/village relationships and another path connecting community participation to poor relationships. As she tried to understand what had happened to her, she reflected on important issues — the way a village with traditional gender roles respond to female authority, the undermining of male sources of power and prestige through recent economic changes, and the pressures on changing communities.

As the conclusion of the case, Patsy had not resolved these matters. She ended the case with questions: What cues had she missed? How could she have prevented this situation? Patsy had developed problems to reflect on. She was engaged in an inquiry.

To discuss Patsy's case in these analytic terms does not do justice to its emotional import or to her generosity in opening her experience to others. Every year, in the Teachers for Alaska program, we have two or three teachers, typically women, who undergo a variation of Patsy's experience. Through Patsy's case, we now have a cautionary tale. The case raises questions about culturally appropriate expressions of authority, as well male and female roles in Native communities, which our students would do well to consider.

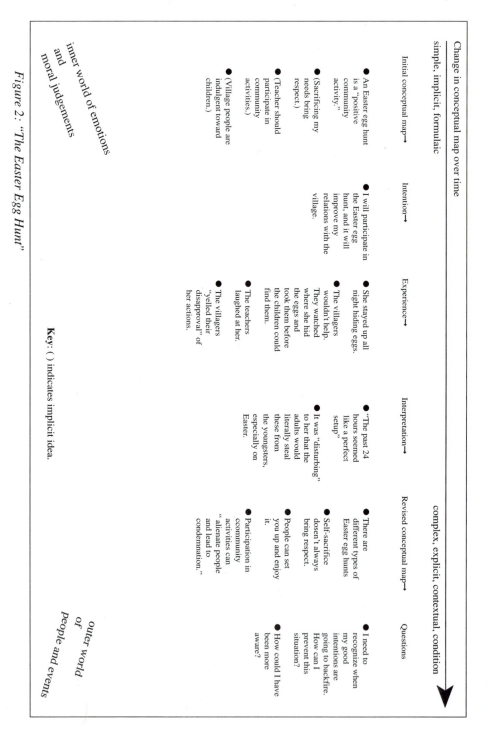

Figure 2: "The Easter Egg Hunt"

Conclusion

We can learn from experience without writing cases. The discipline of case writing, however, provides a valuable structure which helps us reflect on our experience. Case writing creates an emotional distance from events and encourages us to take an analytic stance. We see ourselves and others as characters in a complicated situation. Case writing encourages us to come to grips with our experience and ourselves.

Writing cases about student teaching produced important changes in teacher education students' social maps of the world. Students originally had quite simple concepts of teaching strategies, multicultural communities, and people's emotions and reactions. These simple formulas and naive images gave way to a much more contextualized and sophisticated maps of the social world.

As important as these cognitive changes can be to students' abilities to navigate through the world, especially in multicultural settings, I was also impressed by the emotional education that cases seemed to offer. Years later, teacher education students stop me, tell me about a difficult experience, and exclaim, "I said to myself — this is a case!" I know what they are getting at — sometimes I tell myself exactly the same thing.

Case writing can also be used to develop a localized curriculum which takes into account local priorities and concerns. In Alaska, we focused on preparing teachers for rural Alaska Native communities. Other teacher education programs will have different emphases, but case writing may be no less valuable as a source of highly relevant, localized curriculum materials.

As in the heroic tale, case writing enables education students to come back from their student teaching experience with a boon — cases that they can contribute to the teaching community.

References

Allen, T. (1990). *The guidance counselor and the reluctant seniors*. Fairbanks, Alaska: University of Alaska, Center for Cross–Cultural Studies.

Anonymous (1991). *On a white horse*. Fairbanks, Alaska: University of Alaska, Center for Cross–Cultural Studies.

Bruner, J. (1986). *Actual minds: Possible world*. Cambridge: Harvard University Press.

Carey, R. (1989). *Harassment in Lomevik*. Fairbanks, Alaska: University of Alaska, Center for Cross–Cultural Studies.

Edmundson, P.J. (1990). A normative look at the curriculum in teacher education. *Phi Delta Kappan*, May, 717–722.

Journet, D. (1990). Forms of discourse and the sciences of the mind. *Written Communication, 7*, 171–199.

Kermode, F. (1966). *The sense of an ending*. New York: Oxford University Press.

Kleinfeld, J.S. (1990). *Teaching cases in cross–cultural education*. Fairbanks, Alaska: University of Alaska, Center for Cross–Cultural Studies.

Lowry, S.P. (1982). *Familiar mysteries: The truth in myth*. New York: Oxford University Press.

Mandler, J.M. (1984). *Stories, scripts, and sciences: Aspects of schema theory*. Hillsdale, NJ: Erlbaum.

Mattingly, C. (1991). Narrative reflections on practical actions: Two learning experiments in reflective storytelling. In D. Schon (Ed.), *The reflective turn* (pp. 235–257). New York: Teachers College Press.

White, H. (1981). The value of narrativity in the representative of reality. In W.J.T. Mitchell (Ed.), *On narrative (pp.1–23)*. Chicago: University of Chicago Press.

Appendix

Writing a Case Study of Your Student Teaching Experience: What Have You Learned?

The purpose of this assignment is to help you think through and make sense of your own experience as a student teacher in a particular classroom, school and community setting. We want you to develop the habit of reflecting on your own teaching experience and considering the philosophical, ethical, political, interpersonal and pedagogical problems and dilemmas embedded in it.

Directions for Writing the Case Study of Your Student Teaching Experience

1. A case is essentially a story. However, it is NOT simply a chronology of what happened to you first, second, and so forth. A story centers around a problem or conflict and shows how the "hero" dealt with this situation. You could center your case on instructional problems, political problems, ethical problems, and so on. Think about your experience and consider what you have learned from it. Your first and most difficult problem will be thinking through the question, "What is my story about?" "What is the central problem or learning experience that organizes my story?"

To help you organize your case, you may find it helpful to look at the sample story grammar we provide below. This "story grammar" has been generated from cross–cultural research on stories and identifies a basic structure of stories across cultures.

2. You can write the story in the first person ("I") or the third person (giving your character a different name). DO DISGUISE THE NAMES AND PERSONAL CHARACTERISTICS OF THE STUDENTS, SCHOOL, AND COMMUNITY. THE PURPOSE OF DISGUISE IS SIMPLY TO PROTECT CONFIDENTIALITY AT YOUR SCHOOL.

3. After writing the base, add an epilogue to the case in which you discuss what you learned from the student teaching experience, both about yourself and about the problems of teaching. At this point, what do you see as the les–

sons of your story? How might these lessons influence your future teaching and your future learning about teaching? Keep in mind that you may view your own student teaching, its lessons and influence differently as time passes.

Come to the concluding seminar with a first draft of your case and a videotape of you in your student teaching setting.

You will be presenting your own student teaching case and videotape informally to other students and soliciting their help in making sense of your student teaching experience. The final case (approximately 15 pages) will be due two weeks after the concluding seminar.

Story Grammar

This is a story grammar—a basic story form that arises in stories across cultures. Many different researchers have come up with the same basic pattern, and we have adapted it here for your use.

1. **Main Character and Character Clues:** Who is the main character and what is the main character like? (Ordinarily you—the student teacher—will be the main character. Think about yourself the way you might think about a character in a story — your personality, appearance, reactions.)

2. **Events and Reactions:** What are the important events in the story and how does the main character react to and feel about these events?

3. **Problems:** Name the problems or conflicts that the main character is facing. These may be external problems in the setting or these may be internal problems, a conflict in the main character's mind, or some combination. Circle the main problem, the fundamental problem that you can use to organize your story.

4. **Attempts:** How do the characters try to solve the problems? These may be efforts of the main character or other people's efforts.

5. **Resolution:** How does the main problem get solved or managed? Sometimes a distinct resolution may occur and sometimes the problem or situation may be unresolved.

6. **Theme:** What is the underlying point of the story? What has the main character learned about himself or herself? What has been learned about teaching?

Judith Smilg Kleinfeld is Professor of Psychology at the University of Alaska, Fairbanks. Her most recent publication on case methods is *Gender Tales: Tensions in the Schools* (St. Martins Press), a textbook for college students which explores the ethical and policy dilemmas in achieving gender equity (with Suzanne Yerian). She also does research on fetal alcohol syndrome, recently reported in *Fantastic Antone Succeeds: Experiences in Educating Children with Fetal Alcohol Syndrome* (University of Alaska Press, with Siobhan Wescott).

Professor Kleinfeld developed a teacher education program, Teachers for Rural Alaska, which was designed to prepare secondary school teachers for Alaska's small village high schools. This program relied heavily on case methods, which brought to students attention the difficulties that other teachers like themselves were facing in these small, multi-cultural schools.

What's in a Case — and What Comes Out?

Greta Morine–Dershimer

This chapter begins by describing development of a videocase on classroom management problems experienced by a student teacher in a multiethnic, urban middle school. An examination of what prospective teachers learned from discussion of the case follows. Reactions of four class sections, noting the influence of instructional organization (small vs. large group discussion) and students' program area (elementary vs. secondary majors) are also included. Results are illustrated by details of the discussion and reactions in the two secondary sections. Questions are raised as to what types of outcomes might be considered most desirable.

Introduction

General interest in use of case methods for teacher education has grown rapidly since Shulman (1986) first proposed case knowledge as a critical component of teacher knowledge. My own interest was immediately piqued by Shulman's proposal, because my research interests focused on teacher cognitions, including practical knowledge and decision-making. My interest was supported by my work in the Virginia Commonwealth Center for the Education of Teachers. Since its inception in 1988, the Commonwealth Center has helped to host two national conferences on writing cases and teaching with cases, conducted a national survey to determine types of involvement with case-based instruction in teacher education (White & McNergney, 1991), and hosted an annual national invitational team case competition for preservice teachers (McNergney, 1993). The Center supported my initial efforts in 1989 to develop cases for use in the generic methods course that I taught and coordinated, as well as the evaluation study reported here.

Procedures in Use of Case Methodology

The cases I have developed are derived from a study of the decision-making of secondary student teachers at Syracuse University (Morine-Dershimer, 1991). In stimulated recall interviews over their videotaped lessons, eight student teachers in four subject areas discussed their observations of pupils and their reasoning related to lesson planning and interactive decisions. Additional data in this study included pupils' written responses to the lessons (statements of a "key idea" of the lesson, and reports of "two things you heard anybody saying" during the lesson), as well as interviews with the cooperating teachers and college supervisors as they viewed the videotaped lessons and commented on the interactive events they observed. These data provided a rich source for development of cases that focus on issues of classroom management, questioning procedures, and evaluation of instruction.

There are two features of these cases that I consider to be unique. First is the focus on student teachers. This focus is based on my belief that prospective teachers may identify with and learn more readily from the experiences and problems of novice teachers than from the smoother performance of experienced teachers. The second feature is the use of brief video segments of classroom events, supplemented by written materials presenting the various participants' (student teacher, cooperating teacher, college supervisor, and classroom pupils) reactions to these events.

The generic methods course that provided the site for my initial use of these cases, and for the evaluation study reported here, is a year-long course in which students are introduced to a series of alternative instructional strategies, which they practice in peer teaching and field settings. In the fall semester they plan and teach three lessons in a field setting, using at least two alternative strategies. In the spring they plan and teach a two-week unit in a field setting. Instructional planning, classroom management procedures, questioning and discussion skills, pupil participation, and classroom diversity are topics addressed in the fall semester.

The course instructors work as a team to plan class sessions and prepare course materials, then teach their individual sections. Case analysis is only one of the teaching techniques used in this course, and instructors use both small group and full class discussion of cases. In the fall semester video cases are used to explore issues related to classroom management, questioning and discussion skills, and classroom diversity. In the spring, written cases are used to raise issues related to evaluation of pupils.

Evaluation Procedures

There is little evidence to demonstrate the impact of case-based teaching. As I taught with cases, I began to wonder about what prospective teachers really learned from case methods, and what aspects of case-based teaching might influence what was learned. Unless we begin to address these questions, the case method approach to teacher education is unlikely to survive as a successful innovation. The evaluation study reported here focuses on the second of these two questions. Specifically, it examines the impact of instructional process on prospective teachers' perceptions of the messages emerging from class analysis of a case.

Participants

Participants in the study were three teacher educators teaching four sections of our generic methods course, and 112 prospective teachers who were their students. The prospective teachers were predominantly fourth-year students in the University of Virginia's five-year teacher education program, but approximately one-fourth of them were first-year students in the two-year postgraduate program. They included elementary education students, secondary education students, and special education students.

During the semester of data collection class size for the four sections varied from 23 to 39. Two class sections, one smaller and one larger, taught by two different instructors, included primarily elementary education students. Two sections, one smaller and one larger, were taught by a single instructor, and included primarily secondary education students. Special education students were scattered across the four sections. All class sessions were 100 minutes in length. All sections met twice a week for the first half of the semester and once a week during the six-week period of the students' associated field experience.

The case discussions examined in this study took place in October, just before students were scheduled to make their first visit to their assigned field settings. During their first visit they were expected to observe and report on the classroom management procedures followed by the cooperating teacher. All classes were given reading assignments on classroom management as preparation for the case discussions and the field visits. The textbook for elementary sections was *Elementary Classroom Management: Lessons from Research and Practice* (Weinstein & Mignano, 1992), and the textbook for secondary sections was *Teaching From a Research Knowledge Base* (Bellon, Bellon, & Blank, 1992).

The Case

The case explored in the classes observed in this study is entitled "Exploring the Meanings of Success and Failure: A Ninth Grade Urban English Class" (Morine-Dershimer, 1990). It includes videotaped segments of a lesson, together with comments on the lesson from interviews with the student teacher who taught it, her cooperating teacher, and her college supervisor. In addition, written statements from ninth graders identifying "a key idea of the lesson," and their reports of "two things you heard anybody saying during the lesson" are included to provide information on pupil reactions to the lesson.

Lisa, the student teacher, is teaching a class of multiethnic pupils of varying ability levels in an inner city school. She plans a unit on a play that is based on a theme of "success and failure." In her introductory lesson, she organizes pupils into "non-negotiable" groups and asks them to brainstorm a list of words that they associate first with success, then with failure. The transition into groups is lengthy and chaotic, but once the groups are organized, pupils get quickly to work generating ideas about success. Groups report on their ideas for success, then begin to generate terms they associate with failure. When they report on these lists, they start to name each other as examples of failure. Lisa initially laughs along with her pupils when pupil names are cited as examples of failure. Later, prompted by one pupil's objection, she admonishes, "No names. That's not very nice." At the end of the lesson, pupils' written reports of what they heard being said are heavily oriented toward disparaging comments about each other (*Steve's cheating; Tina's a stoner; Danielle is on drugs; Zak telling Derek to shut up; Cheech was yelling at someone who wrote his name down*).

Comments on the lesson events by Lisa and the cooperating teacher reveal that this is only the second time these pupils have worked independently in groups. It is the first time the cooperating teacher has worked with a student teacher, and she believes that you learn to teach by "trial and error," so she gives Lisa no advice before a lesson, although she does suggest possible improvements after the lesson. Comments by Lisa, the cooperating teacher, and the college supervisor all identify the transition into groups and the name-calling as problem areas, and all suggest possible ways to improve these as well as other elements of the lesson.

Teaching notes for the case suggest analyzing the case in two segments, the first focused on the process of organizing pupils into groups, and the second on pupil reporting of the "failure" lists. Within each segment the teaching notes recommend: viewing the videotaped lesson segment; discussing observations and reactions to the videotaped segment; reading the case participants' comments on the lesson events; and comparing participant observations/reactions to those of the students who are analyzing the case. For each case segment, the teaching notes provide some possible questions for discussion. These questions are displayed in Table 1. The case materials provide opportunities to discuss a variety of instructional issues, including effective classroom management procedures, classroom social climate, teacher expectations for pupils, and productive student teacher-cooperating teacher relationships. As the case was used in this course, discussions focused on classroom management procedures and social climate.

Table 1 — Questions Suggested in Teaching Notes for the Case

Possible questions for discussion of first segment

What management procedures do you see being used here?
Why do you suppose Lisa chose to use these procedures?
What procedures are working well?
What procedures might be improved?
What alternative procedures could you suggest?
Can you foresee any problems that might develop as this lesson progresses?

Possible questions for discussion of second segment

How does Lisa handle the transition to having groups describe failure?
What alternatives could you suggest?
Should Lisa have expected pupils to name each other as examples of failure? Why/Why not?
How do you think Cheech and Zak felt?

What management procedures does Lisa use for group reporting?
What are the potential benefits of these procedures?
What are the potential problems?
What alternatives could you suggest?
What might you have done in this situation?

Possible questions to be raised at end of discussion

When should a student teacher be allowed to "fail" in order to learn from experience?
What do you think Lisa learned from this lesson?

Data Collection and Analysis

Data collection procedures involved videotaping discussions of this case in each of the four sections of the course. All three instructors had taught the case at least once before, and two were teaching it for the third time. All discussions occurred within a two-day period in the fall of 1992. At the close of each class session students were given a 3x5 card and asked to "write on the front a key idea of this lesson (i.e., the case analysis discussion), and write on the back two things you heard anybody saying during the lesson."

Transcripts of the videotaped case discussions were prepared and used to develop a description of the instructional process used in each class section. Aspects of instructional process examined were:

- degree of teacher direction, as identified by ratio of teacher to student talk, predominant communication pattern (e.g., teacher-student-teacher), specificity of guidelines for discussion, and amount of time allotted to independent discussion in small groups;

- reliance on the teaching notes for the case, as determined by instructor use of the questions suggested in the teaching notes, and class exploration of the perspectives of the case participants (student teacher, cooperating teacher, college supervisor, and pupils) as revealed by the number of student comments reacting to participants' comments about lesson events;

- topical emphasis, as indicated by the length of time devoted to discussion of specific questions, and the number of students contributing to such discussions; and,

- key events in the case analysis discussion, as revealed by student tendency to focus on particular comments or interchanges in reports of what they heard being said.

Student responses to the case analysis discussions (key idea statements and reports of what was heard) were each analyzed in two ways. First, a content analysis of responses was conducted, focused on the substance of responses as related to the case discussed. Second, responses were categorized using category systems developed in two prior studies that identified relationships between pupils' responses to lessons and teachers' instructional process (Morine-Dershimer, 1991). Patterns of student responses were compared across the four class sections, using proportional frequencies, in order to identify possible relationships to patterns of instructional process used in the four sections.

Categories of Key Idea Statements

Four general categories emerged from the content analysis of students' key idea statements. These were:

- Classroom Management Procedures - statements in this category were simple references to the broad topic of the lesson (e.g., classroom management, classroom management techniques as witnessed through a case study);

- Relation of Management to Instruction or Learning - statements in this category made general reference to the importance of good management for effective teaching (e.g., carefully planned classroom management techniques are very helpful in establishing a positive classroom environment, classroom management is essential for effective teaching);

- Analyzing/Evaluating Management Procedures - statements in this category emphasized the case analysis process (e.g., watching a teaching segment to decide what worked and what didn't and why, to view a teacher's form of classroom management and then to discuss pros and cons and any possible ways to change or make it better); and

- Generalizations About Classroom Management - statements in this category drew conclusions or specified beliefs or principles (e.g., it is very important for the teacher to gain control of the class and make their rules clear at the start of the lesson, make sure directions are clear before you have students begin the activity).

In earlier studies, three types of key idea statements were distinguished by phraseology. Student statements in this study exhibited the same three types of phrasing:

- Teacher-Oriented statements emphasized teacher role or influence in the lesson (e.g., *to get us familiar with* ways of implementing structure in a classroom, *to have us be exposed to* a classroom management situation);

- Pupil-Oriented statements emphasized student role or activity in the lesson (e.g., *to generate thought* about classroom management and how we are going to approach it, *to discuss* class management in small groups *to see what others thought*); and,

- Topic-Oriented statements focused solely on the topic (e.g., clear directions and goals are vital elements of a lesson, situation of classroom behavior problem – solution/possibilities of prevention).

Prior studies indicated that secondary school pupils tended to use more pupil-oriented key idea statements in lessons that were student-centered, compared with lessons that were teacher-directed (Morine-Dershimer, 1991). Key idea statements in this study were analyzed to determine whether similar patterns of relationship existed for the four case discussions.

Categories of Reports of What Was Heard

Content analysis of student reports of what they heard being said in the case discussions resulted in identification of ten categories, differentiated by substance of the comments reported. Table 2 presents the labels for these ten categories, together with examples of comments reported in each category.

In earlier studies, pupil reports of what was heard were categorized by source of the comment and degree of focus on content of the lesson. For this study a similar category system was used, with four types of reports identified:

- Student Talk on Lesson Content (e.g., Amy made a good point about using the board to write up the 5 examples of failure.);

- Student Talk on Other Than Lesson Content (e.g., Is this a good time to ask questions about next week's assignment?);

- Teacher Talk on Lesson Content (e.g., Instructor: So how do you think the rest of Lisa's lesson will go?); and,

- Teacher Talk on Other Than Lesson Content (e.g., I can't tell you how much time to spend to spend on the next assignment - 2 hours is an estimate.).

Table 2 — Substantive Categories for Comments Reported As Heard

Categories	Examples of Reported Comments
Specifying/Clarifying Events in Case	I just want to know what or who Cheech is - Adam. Tammy thought Cheech was from Cheech and Chong.
Identifying Problems in the Case	It took too long to divide into groups. Lisa should have stopped the name-calling sooner.
Stating Ideas for Improving Procedures	Make the purpose of the assignment clear so students have a goal. Amy – I would have them write their list of failures on the board.
Delaying Judgment About Lisa's Decisions	Many people would not foresee kids' names coming up. Sometimes teachers let the teasing go on because they know the kid can take it.
Predicting Failure of Lisa's Lesson	Lisa will lose control of the class. This will be a "who talks the loudest" lesson.
Reacting to Perspectives of Case Participants	The professor was unfair in his/her judgment of the class - too low of expectations. I think Lisa was too positive and the cooperating teacher had the best ideas.
Noting Peers' Feelings About Case Events	Mike is "hard-line" on discipline. I wouldn't initially have tried to brainstorm because I find it intimidating – Kate
Stating Beliefs/Principles About Management	It is important that teachers really listen to what students are saying. Alex - It's important to establish consistency in routines so that the teacher and students know what's expected.
Instructors' Questions/ Summaries	What I'm hearing is that we're more optimistic than pessimistic. Don't you think Lisa had goals in mind?
Conversation Off–Topic	Ms. "C" telling Sally that she couldn't ask a question about the assignment.

Prior studies indicated that secondary school pupils reported hearing more pupil talk on lesson content in lessons that were student-centered, compared to lessons that were teacher-directed (Morine-Dershimer, 1991). Student reports of what was heard in this study were analyzed to determine whether similar patterns of relationship were exhibited for the case discussions.

Reports of what was heard were also used to identify "key events" in the case discussions. A key event was defined as an incident (individual comment or interchange between individuals) that drew the attention of a number of students (at least 25% of the class). Such a prevalence of reports of hearing a given event was taken to indicate that it was a salient event for participants in the case discussion.

Organization of Results

The case discussions in the two secondary sections are described separately here, with information on both the instructional process used and the student responses to the discussion. Then these two lessons are compared in terms of both instructional process and patterns of student response, and similar comparisons are made with the patterns in the two elementary sections. Conclusions are drawn about factors that apparently influenced instructors' decisions about instructional process, and about aspects of instructional process that apparently influenced student perceptions of the messages communicated in the case discussions.

Results

The two secondary class sections were both taught by the same instructor, called "Caroline" here, but the discussions differed in degree of teacher direction. A comparison of these two lessons identifies an apparent relationship between instructional process and student response to the discussion, as well as pointing to class size as an important factor in the teacher's selection of instructional process.

Caroline's Smaller Class

Twenty-three students were present for the case discussion in the smaller secondary section that Caroline taught. The lesson was conducted entirely as a large group discussion. Interaction in the discussion was mainly teacher-student-teacher-student-teacher, but there were several instances of student-student-student interactive sequences, and in many cases the teacher reaction intervening between two student comments was a simple "Um-hum."

An interesting feature of the interaction in this lesson was that students disagreed with each other's interpretations of the lesson events in several instances, and also (without any prompting from Caroline) acknowledged that they did not have all the facts in the case available to them. The following slice of the discussion, focused on the first segment of the case, illustrates this feature:

> Carl: *The focus (of Lisa's lesson) doesn't seem to be clear enough yet. They've kind of wandered over to their groups, and they've got a piece of paper, and they've got the word, "success," but why? What's the point? Just another busywork exercise.*

> Caroline: *They don't know the purpose of the lesson. Do you think that could cause a problem with the lesson?*

> Carl: *It would for me.*

> Debbie: *I agree with Carl. She should talk about the play first, to give them some background about the meaning of success and failure in the play.*

> Esther: *Well, what if she wants to let them get their own ideas out first, before they get ideas from the play about what success is?*

> Fran: *We didn't see the beginning of the lesson. Maybe she did explain to them what would be in the play.*

> George: *Yeah. I would have liked to see how the "drama" thing went. How did the brainstorming work? Were they just throwing out random ideas, or was she making them think?...We don't know, because we didn't see the "drama" part.*

Caroline had taught this case twice before, and she followed some suggestions from the teaching notes, while skipping over others. She specifically asked many of the discussion questions suggested in the teaching notes (What management procedures did you see? What could Lisa have done to improve the lesson? Can you anticipate any problems Lisa might have with this lesson?). She had students read the case participants' comments about lesson events, and invited their reactions, saying, "Tell me if there's anything you're surprised about here." This invitation was met with silence, so Caroline offered her own conclusion, "I would say we were pretty much on track in our discussion - we saw the same things that Lisa and her classroom teacher and college supervisor saw."

The topic that received the most emphasis in this class, based on the time allotted to discussion, and the number of students commenting, was the name-calling that accompanied pupils' reports of terms for failure. Student comments included:

> *With that group of kids, I think she should have expected that. That kind of playing around goes on all the time....Of course, it's easy to say you expected it after you've seen it. (laughter)*

> *Well, she shouldn't have let the student go on, she shouldn't have thanked him, she should have stopped him immediately. She should have said it was incorrect to use names.*

> *I don't think she even heard it. I don't think she was really listening to them.*

> *Well, when you're teaching, like in our peer teaching lessons, sometimes you're so busy thinking about your next question, you're not really tuned in to what students are saying.*

> *I thought maybe she was just trying to ignore the behavior, but I thought that behavior shouldn't be ignored.*

> *Well, maybe Zak just laughs it off, because this is a friend of his, and they're always talking like that to each other. Or maybe he's really upset and thinking, "That's really a crappy thing to say."*

> *Maybe she saw that he wasn't bothered, and thought "There's no response on his face, so maybe he didn't hear it, so if I don't bring attention to it..."*

> *In my high school classes there was always stuff like that going on. If you think a student can handle it, you might let it go. If you think a student would be really bothered by it, I don't know that the appropriate thing would be to make a big deal out of it in class.*

There was one key event in this case discussion, based on student reports of what they heard being said. Eight of the twenty-three students reported on the personal reaction of a peer, Kate, who said that she wouldn't have asked student groups to do brainstorming, because she found it to be an intimidating process, and it took her a long time to get warmed up to generating ideas. This was not a major point in the overall substance of the case discussion. Caroline attributed the high frequency of reports of hearing this comment to the fact that Kate was typically an infrequent participant in class discussions.

Student statements of key ideas subsequent to this case discussion were primarily topic-oriented, but close to one-third were pupil-oriented. Substantively, statements of nine students were simple references to the broad topic of classroom management techniques. Six students emphasized the case analysis process (e.g., to discuss class management/discipline to see what others thought and to watch a student teacher's situation and how she used management and discipline). Key idea statements of four students referred to the importance of good management for teaching or learning (e.g., the importance of classroom management in producing a positive learning environment). Another four students stated beliefs or principles about classroom management (e.g., classroom management requires attention to what is going on by both teacher and students, as well as clear directions and responsiveness by the teacher).

Student reports of what was heard in this case discussion were predominantly student talk on content. Reports of teacher talk on lesson content were quite infrequent, but there were a few reports of both teacher and student talk on other than lesson content. These instances of non-content-related talk all involved reports of a student question about an impending assignment, and Caroline's response to that question. These reports suggest a slight lack of attentiveness to the case discussion on the part of some students.

The substantive category reported as heard most frequently in this lesson was Stating Ideas for Improving Procedures (10 of the 23 students). A close second were comments Noting Peers' Feelings About Case Events (9 students). Four students reported hearing comments Identifying Problems in Lisa's Lesson, while another four reported hearing comments Indicating Possible Reasons for Lisa's Decisions.

Caroline's Larger Class

Thirty-five students participated in the case discussion in Caroline's larger secondary section. After watching each video segment of the case, students discussed their observations and reactions in small groups for an extended period of time, then groups reported on their perceptions to the full class. Student comments in this discussion were fairly lengthy and complex, and students frequently referred to each other's comments. These features of the interaction are illustrated in the following sequence:

> *David: With the brainstorming, it didn't seem like they knew what to do... .*

> *Ernie: Like David says, they didn't know what to do. I don't think she ever conmnected the idea of drama with the idea of success, so the kids were asked to brainstorm on the idea of success without ever knowing how it fit into her overall plan. They don't really know what they're doing. So I think after one or two minutes, they might run out of ideas on success, and that could lead to more disruptions.*

As in her other case discussion, Caroline used the suggestions in the teaching notes selectively. To guide discussion in the small groups she displayed all of the suggested questions from the teaching notes on an overhead transparency, and said, "Here are the questions I would like you to focus on." When one student asked if they should appoint a group recorder, she responded, "You don't need a recorder, you're just discussing." For the group reports on the first segment of the case, Caroline concentrated on just one question from the set of suggested discussion questions, saying, "Tell me what alternative procedures you would suggest to Lisa after having seen her lesson." At the close of discussion on the second segment of the case, she had students read pupil responses to the lesson, then, rather than asking directly for reactions to the pupils' perspective, she asked, "What do you think Lisa learned from this lesson?" David responded:

> *I think she learned that people weren't hearing what she thought they were hearing...As far as people remembering what was heard, none of them were at all related to the lesson, and I think that had to do with the lack of control and discipline as far as getting students to listen to each other. And like Frank said, if you'd had the groups write down what the other groups had said, that might be what they'd remember.*

The topic that received most emphasis in this case discussion, in terms of allotted time and number of students contributing comments during the group reports back to the full class, were ideas about how to improve the lesson. To begin the group reporting after the second case segment, Caroline said, "Tell me what you might have done if you were Lisa." Student comments included:

> *Give better directions.*

> *I thought one thing that contributed to her starting to lose control was telling students to list 5 things off their list, when they've got long lists. I think I might have said, "Give us one thing off your list."*

> *Also you want to make some provisions so that people are listening to each other...some evaluation procedure that forces them to listen.*

> *If she had written down what was said, then she could actually go back to that to tease out some kind of generalization about what they had said.*

One key event in this case discussion involved student concerns about the name-calling during pupil reports about failure. Twelve of the thirty-five students in this class reported hearing comments on this aspect of Lisa's lesson. The interesting facet of this reporting was the fact that this issue was not raised during the public, large–class discussion. Students were reporting on what they heard being said in their small group discussions, which suggests that they were fairly task-oriented in these discussion groups. From the public discussion, one other key event emerged. Nine students commented on Ernie's statements that Lisa's pupils did not understand the goal or purpose of the lesson. Students' statements of key ideas following this case discussion included a high rate of pupil-oriented statements, though the majority were topic-oriented. Substantively, key idea statements focused mainly on the case analysis process and beliefs or principles related to classroom management. Thirteen students made statements about the case analysis process (e.g., analyzing a case study for classroom management procedures and discussing with our peers the problems and ways to improve certain procedures we observed). Nine students stated beliefs or principles (e.g., we need to give clear directions and let students know why they are participating in an activity in order for them to want to be involved, and to get the things you want them to learn out of the lesson). Seven students referred to the importance of good management for effective learning (e.g., the importance of proactive management procedures in the classroom and how they affect the amount and effectiveness of content the students attain). Six students referred simply to the broad topic of classroom management.

Student reports of what was heard in this case discussion were predominantly about pupil talk on content. Teacher talk on content was reported very infrequently, and there were very few instances of reports of teacher talk on other than content. The substantive category reported most frequently in this case discussion was Stating Ideas for Improving Procedures (16 of the 35 students), followed closely by comments Identifying Problems in Lisa's Lesson (15 of the 35 students).

Comparing the Secondary Class Discussions

There were clear differences between Caroline's two lessons in terms of both process and outcome. In terms of process, the case analysis in her smaller class was more highly structured or more teacher-directed than the discussion in her larger class. In the smaller class the discussion was all teacher-led, while in the larger class a considerable portion of time was devoted to independent discussion in small groups. Thus, in the larger class, students had greater control over what questions were discussed, and the balance between teacher and student talk was more heavily weighted toward student talk.

As in the elementary sections, student responses to these two case discussions reflected the differences in degree of teacher structuring of the discussions. There were proportionately more pupil-oriented key idea statements made by students who participated in the less structured case analysis, compared to those in the more structured discussion. Students also reported hearing proportionately more student talk in the more student-centered (small discussion groups) case discussion.

With regard to use of the teaching notes for the case, Caroline's more structured discussion involved more explicit attention to the questions and issues suggested in the teaching notes. In the more student-centered discussion, while all questions were listed on the overhead and available for students, each small discussion group was actually free to choose the questions they would focus on, and in the public discussion Caroline asked a very limited number of quite open-ended questions (tell me what alternative procedures you would suggest to Lisa after seeing her lesson, tell me what you might have done if you were Lisa).

There were clear substantive differences in student responses to Caroline's two case discussions. For students in the more teacher-directed discussion, the key idea statements were primarily simple references to the broad category of classroom management procedures, followed by statements emphasizing the case analysis process. For students in the more student-centered discussion, the key idea statements primarily emphasized the case analysis process, followed by statements of beliefs or principles related to classroom management.

The possible explanations for differences in instructional process exhibited in the two secondary case discussions are greatly limited by the fact that both lessons were taught by the same instructor. Thus, preferred instructional style and familiarity with the case, and case methods, are not reasonable explanations. Caroline's own explanation focussed on class size. In the smaller class (n=23) she felt that students had ample opportunity to participate in a large group discussion, but she did not consider that to be true in the larger class (n=35). While class size was an important factor in her decision to use small discussion groups in the larger class, Caroline also noted that her smaller class did not work particularly well in groups, and she felt that group work generally was harder to manage.

Comparison Across Four Cases

Similar differences in instructional process and student responses were evident in the two elementary class sections. "Angela" taught the smaller class of twenty-one students, and led a fairly teacher-directed full-class discussion. "Barbara" taught the larger class of thirty-three students and organized small student-led discussion groups.

Tables 3, 4, 5, and 6 provide data on the proportional frequencies for the four classes in each of the four category sets for student responses to the case discussions: types of key idea statements; focus of key idea statements; types of comments reported as heard; and substance of comments reported as heard.

Table 3 – Types of Key Idea Statement (proportional frequencies)

| | Elementary Classes | | Secondary Classes | |
| | Angela's Class | Barbara's Class | Caroline's Small Class | Caroline's Large Class |
Statement Phraseology	(n=21)	(n=33)	(n=23)	(n=35)
Teacher-Oriented	.095	——	——	.029
Topic-Oriented	.810	.697	.696	.571
Pupil-Oriented	.095	.303	.304	.400

Table 4 – Focus of Key Idea Statements (proportional frequencies)

| | Elementary Classes | | Secondary Classes | |
| | Angela's Class | Barbara's Class | Caroline's Small Class | Caroline's Large Class |
Statement Substance	(n=21)	(n=33)	(n=23)	(n=35)
"Classroom Management Procedures"	.48	——	.39	.17
Relating Management to Instruction/Learning	.19	——	.17	.20
Analyzing/Evaluating Management Procedures in This Case	.14	.03	.26	.37
Generalizing About Management Procedures	.19	.97	.17	.26

Overall, the patterns of student response in these case discussions replicated the patterns identified in earlier studies with secondary school pupils (Morine-Dershimer, 1991). There was a clear relationship between instructional process and student outcome. In lessons that were more student-centered, key idea statements tended to be phrased more in terms that emphasized the pupil role as contributor and learner in the lesson (see Table 3). Substantively, the key idea statements tended to be fairly complex and more specific with regard to substantive content of the lesson (see Table 4). Further, in these lessons, students tended to report hearing considerably more student talk on lesson content than teacher talk (see Table 5). Conversely, in lessons that were more teacher-directed, key idea statements tended to be phrased more neutrally, focusing primarily on the lesson topic, and providing fewer references to either teacher or pupil role in the lesson. Substantively, the key idea statements tended to involve more simple references to the broad topic of the discussion. Students still reported hearing more student talk than teacher talk, but the relative proportion of teacher talk reported was high (over 25%). Taken together, these patterns of student response provide evidence to support the view that there was more active student involvement, more sustained student attention, and more complex processing of information by students in the more student-centered case discussions.

Class size was an important contributor to instructors' consciously-stated decisions to conduct the case discussions with the full class or to organize small groups for analysis of the case. The small group discussions were less structured, or more student-centered, than the teacher-led discussions with the full class in both elementary and secondary class sections. So class size was a factor that influenced degree of structure in the case discussions in this study.

Table 5 – Who/What Was Heard (proportional frequencies)

	Elementary Classes		Secondary Classes	
	Angela's Class	Barbara's Class	Caroline's Small Class	Caroline's Large Class
Type *of Comments*	*(n=42)**	*(n=66)**	*(n=23)**	*(n=66)**
Teacher Talk - Content	.214	.152	.068	.091
Teacher Talk - Other	.071	——	.159	.030
Student Talk - Content	.714	.848	.727	.879
Student Talk - Other	——	——	.045	——

*Each student was asked to report two things they heard anybody saying; some reported only one comment. Frequencies based on number of comments reported.

Another factor related to degree of structure exhibited in these case discussions was the program area of students in the class. The discussions in the elementary sections were more highly structured than those in the secondary sections in each of the two organizational settings (full class or small group discussion). This is most readily illustrated by comparing Barbara's case discussion with the discussion in Caroline's larger class. There were clear differences in: length of time allotted to independent small group discussion (two 5-minute periods for Barbara, two 15-minute periods for Caroline); guidelines for discussion topics (discuss each of 3 questions for Barbara, "focus" on questions in list of 6-9 questions for Caroline); and accountability for task completion (group recorder assigned to take notes to be handed in to Barbara, no written record of groups' productivity for Caroline).

While the differences in degree of structure in elementary compared with secondary sections of the couse were less marked than the differences in the full class discussions compared with the small group discussions, the variation in structure was evident in the student responses to the lessons. In each of the two organizational settings, there were proportionately more pupil-oriented key idea statements in secondary sections than in elementary sections (see Table 3).

Another interesting difference between the elementary and secondary sections was the tone of the discussion. Students in the elementary sections were more judgmental and more negative in their reactions to Lisa's lesson than students in the secondary sections. This was true even though both Angela and Barbara specifically encouraged their students to withhold judgment or to identify positive features of the lesson. In introducing the public discussion, Barbara said, "It's really easy to pass judgment on somebody else, but it's probably more fair to admit that we don't know everything that's going on, and to raise questions." Toward the end of Angela's discussion, following several critical student comments, she asked, "Is there somebody who'd like to state a case for the other side - do you think that she did gain some success from working with these pupils?"

In contrast, Caroline's questions in both her classes were more neutral. In the more structured discussion she asked: What management procedures do you see here? Why do you think she chose these procedures? What could she have done to improve the lesson? In the more student-centered discussion, she said: tell me what alternative procedures you would suggest to Lisa, tell me what you would have done if you were Lisa. Without specific prompting by the instructor, students in these discussions acknowledged that they did not know everything about Lisa's situation, and offered possible reasons in support of her interactive decisions.

One explanation for this difference in the tone of the discussions could be that the secondary students felt more empathy for Lisa, because she was a secondary education major teaching a class in a middle school. Perhaps they could identify with her, as they themselves were about to begin a field experience in a secondary school setting. Whatever the reason, the difference in tone was reflected in student reports of what they heard being said in the lesson. This was particularly evident in reports of hearing comments in two relevant categories: Identifying Problems and Stating Ideas for Improvement. Attention of students in the elementary sections was more focused on problems in Lisa's lesson, while attention of students in the secondary sections was more focused on possible solutions to those problems.

The four case discussions also differed in the degree to which instructors followed the suggestions in the teaching notes for the case. Factors that seemed to be influential in this regard were instructor familiarity with this case and familiarity with case methods in general. Angela, who was least familiar with the case, followed the teaching notes most specifically. Barbara, who was more familiar with the case, and was also a developer of cases, diverged the most from the suggestions in the teaching notes. Caroline, who was familiar with Lisa's case, but not a developer of cases, followed the suggestions of the teaching notes more closely in her large group discussion than in her small group discussion. One apparent consequence of this variation was that the perspectives of the case participants (as revealed by their comments on the events in Lisa's lesson) were explored most fully in Angela's class, and addressed least in Barbara's class.

This variation was reflected in the variety of student reports of what was heard during the case discussions (see Table 6). In Angela's class eight different categories of comments were reported as heard by at least 10% of the class. In Barbara's class only three different categories of comments received this degree of student attention. In Caroline's large group discussion six different categories of comments were reported as heard by at least 10% of the class, and in her small group discussion only three categories of comments received this much attention.

Finally, the four case discussions varied with regard to the specific topics stressed within the discussion, as measured by the length of time devoted to the topic, and the number of students contributing to the discussion of the topic. In Angela's class the discussion emphasized student predictions about how Lisa's lesson would work out, based on what they observed happening in the first case segment. In Barbara's class and Caroline's large group case discussion, the emphasis was on concerns about the name-calling during pupil reports of terms for failure. In Caroline's small group discussion the topic emphasized was suggestions for how Lisa's lesson might be improved. These various emphases were reflected in student reports of what they heard being said in the case discussions. In Angela's class nine of the twenty-one students (43%) reported hearing comments on predictions for the success of Lisa's lesson. In Barbara's class twenty-five of the thirty-three students (76%) reported comments from the discussion on name-calling (mainly criticisms of Lisa's behavior). In Caroline's large group discussion eleven of the twenty-three students (48%) reported hearing comments from the discussion on name-calling (mainly suggestions about how to change the interaction). In Caroline's small group discussion nineteen of the thirty-five students (54%) reported hearing comments from the discussion on ways to improve Lisa's lesson (responses to Caroline's question, "Tell me what you might have done if you were Lisa.").

Table 6 – Substance of Comments Reported As Heard (proportional frequencies)

Substance of Comments	Elementary Classes		Secondary Classes	
	Angela's Class (*n=21*)	Barbara's Class (*n=33*)	Caroline's Small Class (*n=23*)	Caroline's Large Class (*n=35*)
Specifying/Clarifying Events in a Case	.10	——	.13	——
Identifying Problems in Lisa's Lesson	.29	.79	.17	.43
Stating Ideas for Improving Procedures	.24	.21	.39	.46
Delaying Judgement about Lisa's Decisions	.14	.03	.22	.03
Predicting Failure of Lisa's Lesson	.14	——	——	——
Reacting to Perspectives of Case Participants	.24	——	——	——
Noting Peer's Feelings About Case Events	——	.03	.39	.03
Stating Beliefs/Principles About Management	——	.33	.04	.11
Instructor's Questions or Summaries	.38	——	.04	——
Conversation Off-Topic	.10	——	.22	——

Key Issues

The results of this exploration of four class discussions of a single case raise several interesting points worth further discussion and consideration by teacher educators interested in case-based teaching. First of all, it seems clear that "a case is a case is a case is a case" is NOT the case. The variation in treatment of the case of Lisa in these four classes, and the associated variation in the messages that students took away with them, demonstrates that teacher educators' decisions about procedures to be used in a case analysis are critical in determining what may be learned from the case. It is particularly worth noting that the instructors in these four classes had a long history of working together in team planning for the course they taught, and shared the same general goals for student learning in the course as a whole, and in this particular segment of the course. While they did plan to use different organizations for discussion, they did not consciously plan to achieve diverse student outcomes in their four case discussions.

Two aspects of the decisions made by these four instructors were especially influential with regard to the variation in student reponses to the case discussions in this study. The degree of structure or teacher direction of the discussion had an apparent impact on the complexity of student processing of information from the case. In addition, the selection of specific aspects of the case to be emphasized (phrasing of questions, time allotments to particular questions) had an apparent impact on the messages that students identified as important (key ideas) or salient (what was heard). For these four lessons, that selection also impacted the type of thinking that students practiced in their analysis of the case. Angela's class practiced predicting consequences of the opening minutes of Lisa's lesson. Barbara's class practiced critiquing or evaluating Lisa's planning and interactive decisions. Caroline's two classes practiced generating alternative managerial and instructional procedures to solve the problems Lisa encountered.

While the results of this study are limited to a particular case taught in a particular teacher education program, the differences in what prospective teacher participants learned from the different approaches to discussion of the particular case are not trivial. Neither were they readily apparent to the teacher educators who planned and taught the case-based lessons. Careful analysis of classroom interaction and student response was necessary to reveal the patterns discussed here. We need a great deal of further research examining relationships between instructional process and student outcomes if we are to provide useful advice and support for teacher educators attempting to improve their instruction through case-based teaching.

The results of this study raise one additional question with regard to student outcome. Is there agreement among teacher educators using case-based teaching about what might be the most desirable outcomes from prospective teachers' analyses of cases? Should there be such agreement? For example, of the three types of thinking noted above that were practiced in these four case discussions, is one more desirable than another, or are all equally desirable? With regard to the various substantive foci of the key idea statements produced by students in this study, are statements referring to the case analysis process more or less desirable than statements referring to generalizations or principles related to the topic discussed? Do we want students to form generalizations on the basis of one case? Can we expect such generalizations to be refined as additional cases are discussed and analyzed? These are questions that need to be addressed within and across teacher education programs, but they are also questions that should be informed by further research.

Interest in use of case methods in teacher education continues to expand. If this innovation is to be more than one more fad, here today and fading fast tomorrow, we need sytematic research into the effects of case-based teaching. The study reported here is one small drop in a very small puddle. I earnestly hope that the puddle may grow to be a reservoir that can sustain the further development of case methods for teacher education.

Notes

1. This chapter is based on a paper presented at the annual meeting of the American Educational Research Association, Atlanta, April, 1993. This study was supported in part by the Virginia Commonwealth Center for the Education of Teachers.

References

Bellon, J.J., Bellon, E.C., & Blank, M.A. (1992). *Teaching from a research knowledge base*. New York: Macmillan.

McNergney, R. (1993) *Case-based, campus-based instruction: The first national competition in retrospect*. Paper presented at annual meeting of the American Colleges for Teacher Education, San Diego.

Morine-Dershimer, G. (1990) *Exploring the meanings of success and failure: A 9th grade urban English class*. Case presented at conference on the Role of Case Methods in Teacher Education, Charlottesville, VA.

Morine-Dershimer, G. (1991). Learning to think like a teacher. *Teaching and Teacher Education*, 7:2, 159-168.

Shulman, L.S. (1986). Those who understand: Knowledge growth in teaching. *Educational Researcher*, **15**:2, 4-14.

Weinstein, C.S. & Mignano, A.J. (1992). *Elementary classroom management: Lessons from research and practice*. New York: McGraw-Hill.

White, B. & McNergney, R. (1991) *Case-based teacher education: The state of the art*. Paper presented at the working conference on The Case Method in Teacher Education, James Madison University, Harrisonburg, VA.

Greta Morine-Dershimer is a Professor in the Curriculum and Instruction Graduate Program of the Curry School of Education, University of Virginia Teacher Education Program and Senior Researcher in the Curry School's Commonwealth Center for the Education of Teachers. Her research focuses on teacher and pupil cognitions associated with classroom interaction. Recent publications include "Student Teaching and Field Experiences"(with K. Leighfield), a chapter in *The International Encyclopedia of Education* and "Studying Teachers' Thinking About Instruction: Issues Related to Analysis of Metaphoric Language"(with P.T. Reeve), a chapter in *Teachers' Minds and Actions: Research on Teachers Thinking and Practice.*

Creating the "Multiple I – Search" Case Study

Greta Nagel

The Multiple I–Search Case Study is a field–based assignment that prepares teacher education students to examine the strengths and needs of individuals from a variety of perspectives. The format involves each student in personal research, requiring in–the–field observations, gathering information from multiple sources and informants about a child who is identified by the classroom teacher as being a "problem" student. The "Multiple I" has been an effective learning tool in Educational Psychology and Literacy classes that credential students take. It results in a five–page paper that concludes with a detailed action plan. Each writer's suggestions are grounded in the multiple "I" perspectives of the teacher, of the student him/herself, and of the teacher–education researcher.

Novice teachers often speak of feeling helpless in the face of problems (Martin, 1991). The "problem child" is an inevitable member of every classroom, and new teachers are frequently baffled by their behaviors, whether they are related to discipline or to learning. Beginning teachers are normally beset by self–images that proclaim "I'm no expert." Experts, to them, are people who hold advanced degrees. The Educational Psychology class that I teach is intended to provide new teachers with a tool, the Multiple I–Search Case Study, that can guide their professional thinking as they deal with the complexities of classroom life. The Multiple I–Search strategy also can serve experienced teachers in their work as teacher–researchers.

For teachers to find success within the complex realities of today's classrooms, they must be able to adopt multiple perspectives. It is also critical for classroom teachers to possess the expertise to look at their students as individuals and assess their strengths and needs as they analyze the strengths and needs of their program. Because realities in our K–12 schools include huge backlogs for special testing, timelines that are long, and human resources that are stretched, experts are seldom readily available for consultation. On–site psychologists and reading specialists are rare, and are becoming more scarce in the face of the ongoing budget problems in most states. At the same time, schools are participating in greater inclusion of students who were once segregated into special classes and programs.

The Multiple I–Search Case Study is a field–based class assignment that involves a guided observation process and results in a five–page paper. The assignment is made in the Educational Psychology and Literacy classes students take as part of their credential program. The Educational Psychology class deals with how students learn, and includes such topics as motivation, theories of intelligence, cognition, human development, implications of language and culture, group dynamics, brain research, and classroom management. The Literacy class deals with language arts methods for teaching children in kindergarten through middle school. By participating in active and reflective projects, university students explore concepts and pedagogies that relate to instruction in reading, writing, speaking, and listening.

The Multiple I–Search Case Study assignment guides teacher education students to look carefully at individual students' strengths and needs from a variety of perspectives. It involves a study process in order to make specific recommendations based upon an analysis of the circumstances and actions that affect a child who is identified by the classroom teacher as being a "problem" student. Each student's action plan is grounded in careful observations that are written from the multiple perspectives of the teacher, of the student him/herself, and of the teacher education researcher.

The Multiple I–Search Case Study is intended to help preservice and inservice teachers to: (a) Adopt the attitude that classroom teachers are "experts." (b) Experience a case study rather than depend upon deductions from complex testing procedures and statistics. Ethnographic approaches (watching, listening, talking, writing, and analyzing) can support intelligent inductive conclusions and recommendations, and teachers learn through their own construction of knowledge. (c) Examine situations from multiple, not singular, perspectives, a trait that must be present in good teachers. There are few schools where teachers do not face the dynamics of a pluralistic society. (d) See that discussing and defending cases can help everyone to see the many issues and concerns that confront teachers. Reasoned discussion (not just complaining) helps to build a repertoire of wise actions and practices.

Background

The I–Search format for personal research and writing originated with Ken Macrorie. His work advocated the writing of research papers that bypass the conventional "stack of notecards" and library approach in order to involve the student in the formulation of a personal research question requiring in–the–field observations and analysis (Macrorie, 1980, 1988). The I–Search involves the physical participation of the credential student–writer in gathering of information from multiple sources and informants.

In creating this class assignment, I went beyond the Macrorie search to devise the use of the "Multiple–I" after thinking about hundreds of discussions that I have engaged in during school study sessions and in personal conferences with teachers. I am always struck by a tenacious viewpoint, even in experienced teachers, of "That kid has a problem and I have done everything I can." Common is a lack of "walking in another's moccasins." When I ask about a student's strong points it is startling to hear responses such as "He has none," or "What strong points?"

When teachers get into frustrating situations, they retreat into monocular perspectives. Any I–Search is a useful gathering of multiple perspectives, but I believe that when students go a step further to write from the first–person points of view of the involved individuals, they consider each person's feelings and they examine the dynamic contexts of classroom problems. After initially assigning the case as an I–Search with third–person writing, I soon concluded that writing from the "Multiple–I" evokes far richer detail and deeper thinking. Such narrative writing is also a means for helping teachers to be empathetic multicultural educators.

Initial Procedure

At the beginning of each academic quarter, I provide the following written assignments for students in teacher preparation courses for Language Arts Methods (Literacy) and Educational Psychology at the state university. We discuss some the implications of various techniques to use for communicating with kids. The explanations that follow also include some of the typical comments and questions that arise as students strike out on their own.

The Assignment for Educational Psychology

Students are asked to identify a classroom that is convenient for them to visit on two or three different occasions. They ask the cooperating teacher to help identify a child who presents a "problem" of some sort and to use a pseudonym for this individual child in their writing. Also, if he or she has already been identified as a special education student, they may want to select another child.

They observe the child as he or she participates in class. Students are instructed to take notes, working to be descriptive (of the setting and the events), rather than interpretive (making generalizations or judgments). They arrange to talk with the teacher about the child and what seems to be the problem, and to get a sense of what has already been done, both with and without success. They collect direct quotes, when possible, and chat informally with the student, making clear that they are interested in what the student thinks about school, and that the students are helping the university students to learn about schools and teaching and learning.

The paper that ultimately is written should have the following sections:

Page 1: Background. Describe the community, the school, and the classroom context from an "objective" point of view. Use a narrative style with rich description. "Show," don't "Tell." Use double spacing.

Write about the child's situation from three additional points of view:

Page 2: The situation as the teacher perceives it. What does the student do? What are the child's positive attributes? What seems to be the problem(s)? What has the teacher already tried to do? Use the pronoun I.

Page 3: The way the child sees his or her situation at school. Interests, likes, and dislikes. Use the pronoun I.

Page 4: The way you see the problem; your analysis as a participant observer. Do not confuse your analysis with the recommendations that follow.

Page 5: Write this page as a letter to the cooperating teacher. Make specific recommendations for further work in the regular classroom and at home; seek to provide at least eight well–explained pieces of advice. Remember that it is important to build upon the student's strengths. Use correct letter format and single spacing. Deliver the letter if you are comfortable in doing so.

Page 6: List your resources, using bibliographic format. Possible resources: cooperating teachers, mentor teachers, colleagues, principals, reading specialists, resource specialist teachers, professors, as well as online library resources, periodicals, ERIC. Ask the reference librarian for assistance.

The most frequent questions about the Educational Psychology case work are related to "How do I interview a child?" I leave the techniques up to the university students, all college graduates. Nevertheless, because some class members have limited experiences in classrooms, they lack confidence at first. The overriding message is that the they must NOT indicate that the young student has a problem; they are to convey that the K–12 student is HELPING a teacher–to–be to learn about students in schools. In class, we develop possible scenarios in which we could have younger children play a game, read a book, or take a tour of the school. Talks with junior high or high school students could take place in a classroom corner or at break times. A visit to the school library is also possible. Case study writers are reminded that confidentiality is critical, and that only pseudonyms are to be used.

Another question that arises is "What if the *teacher* is the one who is making mistakes?" Many of our Ed Psych discussions relate to treating students with respect and finding ways to empower students and form classroom communities. When observers realize that these, or other learned principles, are not enacted in the classroom, they are often hesitant to criticize the practicing teacher. When practice can be improved, a good analysis deals with it. We discuss how important it is, once again, to retain confidentiality. Students know that they are guests in their respective observation classrooms and they are encouraged to look for positive attributes. We also stress ways to make suggestions in tactful ways ("Have you ever...? I was wondering...? Some teachers try..."), and we explore how reflection is so very important as teachers bind practice to theory in the heat of day–to–day classroom dynamics. Many of my students comment that they are asked to return to the classroom; the individual attention shown to the "problem" child results in a welcome break for both teacher and student.

The Assignment for the Literacy Class

The case study assigned for the Literacy class is preceded by the guided tasks of a fieldwork log, a collection of observations and reflections about a language arts classroom in the field. Each student spends time in a selected classroom at any grade level, first through sixth. Their initial fieldwork tasks include the following: (a) a detailed annotated map of the classroom; (b) getting acquainted with two different students by designing and administering an interest inventory to two children, one student identified by the classroom teacher as being a strong reader, the other being identified as a weak reader in that class; (c) an analysis of each student's reading miscues, done to see if errors impact meaning; and, (d) quotes and descriptions of student teacher exchanges during language arts time. The Multiple I–Search Case Study is intended to further the work that is begun with the student identified as a "weak" reader.

The format for the case study in this class is virtually identical to that of the paper assigned to the Educational Psychology students. The difference is in the specific emphasis upon the student's difficulties with reading and writing.

Things to watch out for include the ways in which students use their own critical thinking skills. I witness frequent confusion between the elements of the analysis and the specific recommendations, so it is important to give examples of each. I have learned to explain that the analysis is actually a summary of hypotheses based upon evidence gathered during the course of the classroom observations and work. The recommendations should be linked as closely as possible to the hypotheses in "if–then" logic. Recommendations deal with possible causes for conditions explained in the analysis. Recommendations also build upon the positive points that are highlighted in the analysis. The relationship between each analysis and a recommendation is not always a one–to–one correspondence, for one hypothesis may relate to several recommended actions, and one action may correspond with several hypotheses.

I expect students to make multiple recommendations in order to stress the complexity of all "problems." The idea of finding one solution is not in keeping with reality. Rather, a web of conditions is almost always needed to support change.

Rubric and Samples of Student Writing

Over the course of several quarters, using the Multiple–I Search Case Study format, several qualities have emerged that excellent papers seem to share.

- This paper shows evidence of a rigorous and thorough investigation. Careful observations have been made. The first page is descriptive and objective.

Jaime Ruiz is a student in Miss Victoria Grosz's Algebra I class at La Mancha High School. This school has approximately 1,000 students and is located in Los Angeles County. With its heavy chains, the front of the school looks more like a prison gate than a school entrance, but according to the security personnel, it is a necessary prevention measure. They have had many problems with outside kids coming in to sell drugs or cause trouble.

Inside the fence are some trees and grass, but no flowers. The school has no air conditioning, except for in the library and in the principal's office, both of which are in new buildings. The rest of the school suffers during the hot California days during the fall. This school has many ESL students, which makes it difficult for some teachers who do not speak Spanish. Some of the ESL students are placed in special programs, but the school tries to mainstream them as much as possible.

The community is composed of low income families. The majority of the population is Hispanic. Houses are in bad condition with paint peeling and graffiti that mark the gang territories. Kids say that they do not feel safe going to school in this environment.

Jaime's classroom, like many California classrooms, is very diversified. There are many Hispanic students, some Asian students, and a few White students. It seems obvious that even though most of the Hispanic students are fluent in English, they form a clique and they do not interact with the rest of the class. Most students participate during the class sessions. However, a couple students, including Jaime, show little interest in the class. He puts his head on the desk and pretends he's sleeping. When he speaks, it's to ask about his friend's date or the football game, but nothing to do with algebra. Sometimes he interrupts and says that the work is too difficult. "Ms. G., do problem #10 again. I don't understand! . . ."

- The use of "I" reflects views of multiple individuals. Their various perspectives are fully developed and written in appropriate voices. The reader can "hear" the various individuals. Significant details are fully described.

A Student:

Hello, my name is Jack. I'm really glad to be going to high school in September. I think it will be a lot better for me there. I don't know why, it just will be better. Maybe the teachers won't always be looking for me to screw around. Other kids mess around, but it's always me who gets caught.

I don't think I'm a bad kid. I mean, I never steal or do drugs or things like that. Neither do my friends. I don't have a lot of friends. I just have two friends that I do stuff with. I have a lot of friends at school I can talk to and stuff like that. I get in trouble mostly for talking and clowning around in class. I guess I shouldn't goof off in class but I just do. My parents have gone to school to talk with my teachers and principal lots of times. They come home, they give me the riot act, my dad then says the case is closed. That means I don't get to tell them my side of the story. Sometimes I listen, sometimes I leave the room or just tune them out. Then my parent start fighting and I'm off the hook.

I'd like to help mentally handicapped kids when I grow up. I did that in one of my classes this year and it was neat. I found out they don't like to be called retarded. I guess I never thought about what I would do with my life before.

I guess I dress and act normal for a kid my age. I like to wear baggy shirts and shorts. I just got all my hair cut off. Isn't it neat?

A Teacher:

I knew Brandon was going to be a handful even before he came to class. Brandon's third grade teacher had already briefed me. One of Brandon's problems is that he is a very good looking and popular student. He thinks it's his clowning around in class that makes him popular. He always wants to be the center of attention and he usually is. Probably the most frustrating thing about Brandon is that he is so intelligent, yet refuses to put any effort into his classwork. He hardly ever finishes his homework, and if he does, it's sloppy and done incorrectly. Part of the blame for this is that after school, he goes directly to the after–school program, Options. He stays there until after six. Most likely, he rushes through his homework so he can go out and play. I've tried talking to the women in charge at Options. I'll notice a change for a few days, but he eventually slips back into his old routine. His mother has acknowledged the problem with homework but says that by the time she gets home from work, picks Brandon up from Options and his little brother from the baby–sitter, she barely has time to get them fed, bathed, and ready for bed. She did say she would try. I figure that Brandon's classroom antics occupy 1/8 of our school day. That includes the time he spends disrupting the class and the time I spend disciplining him. It usually ends up with me removing him from the classroom.

Brandon has a very explicit knowledge and curiosity about sex. At the beginning of the year he went around the room asking all the girls if they were virgins or not. From time to time he blurts out some very sexual remark and earlier in the year he was suspended for three days after bringing a sexually explicit magazine to school and sharing it with other boys in the bathroom at recess. These are just fourth graders, still just children. Sometimes it scares me.

I did have one successful experience with Brandon. He was often very critical of students who were, let's say, "slow learners." Back in November I decided to seat Brandon next to a boy name Ryan who was very quiet and whose family was very poor and lived out of a car. I told him about Ryan's situation and I explained that I felt he could help Ryan....Sure enough my instincts were right. He got Ryan involved with other kids and actually became very fond of him. But when the kids returned to class after Christmas vacation, Ryan wasn't among them. We could only assume he moved again. Brandon quickly slipped back to his old behavior… It's now June and I haven't found any other effective way to *deal with him. I've gotten to the point where I just say, "Thank God it's almost summer."*

• The analysis reflects careful thinking. The paper refers to concepts and theories related to the coursework and reflects WHY observed phenomena seem to be true.

John is moving 50 miles per hour ahead of the rest of his class and the teacher. He is a bundle of energy and sometimes it is geared toward positive activities and sometime in negative activities. I think the biggest problems for John are his personality clashes with the teacher. They believe in very different styles for learning. Mrs. Getty is at her best with extreme structure. She enjoys the same format every day, with a special form for Fridays. She likes quiet, John like to talk. She likes to remain seated, John likes to move around. She likes to choose the topics for creative writing. John has a very hard time conforming to her regulations. He, in turn, becomes a behavior problem. He is quite capable of learning, even when you think he is off daydreaming somewhere. It's hard to figure out how he grasps any concepts. She is just continually in high gear. He is very artistic and has a wonderful imagination that has not been taken full advantage of due to the structure of the class.

• Recommendations are written as specific actions that indicate *who* is to do *what*. Actions are feasible to implement and will work together well.

. . .In talking with Ramon I learned that he is interested in computers. I suggest that you use the classroom computer as an incentive to get Ramon to finish his work. He could write his stories, letters to a friend or to the teacher directly on the computer, and at the same time he could be reading and responding to the letters.

The reading period lasts almost two and a half hours and it seems too long for Ramon. I recommend that you organize a rotation system of the two heterogeneous groups, whereby the children can spend time with you and then have independent seatwork, or go to the activity center with art projects and games to be used by the students.

I also recommend that you reorganize the math groups into a mixture of both high and low students. By mixing the high and low students, you will have more time to assist the students that need more help, while those who catch on quickly will proceed on their own. Both groups would also rotate between you and the instructional aide. You could instruct one group and have the aide do the follow–up or monitor the independent seatwork. The computer could be used to supplement math lessons.

I think that if Ramon keeps a small notebook taped to his desk, he will be able to record the page numbers of his assignments and describe what he is expected to do. Also, I would call Ramon's parents each time he is late. The parents need to know that the baby–sitter isn't doing her job of getting the children to school on time and feeding them breakfast.

I would like to see Ramon watch less television and get out to participate in some extracurricular activity, such as a sport. Finally, I recommend that he spend time in the public library now that summer is approaching. . . .

In addition, excellent papers should reflect that:

• Resources, both human and library, have been consulted.
• Conventions of written English are followed. The paper is edited and polished. The audience will be other educators. The letter and reference list are written with appropriate formats.

Sharing Cases

After I taught my first class at the university, I went from a procedure of collecting and turning back cases to having small groups share their cases during class. My students helped me to see the importance of discussing cases. Students talk in self–selected groups of four and nominate some cases to explore with the whole class. Because individual students investigate one situation deeply, they often do not take the opportunity to think about other grade levels until the group sharing times. Not only do students learn from one another, but individuals have commented that they appreciate the opportunity to talk about their work. Ideas come to them in the process of chatting about their children. I have come to view their collaborations as part of the writing process. Cases brought to discussion groups are considered drafts, and further additions and corrections are permitted before turning in final versions. When cases come up before the whole class, we enjoy some lively discussions that bring a sense of mission and unity to the whole group. I have realized some of my best moments as a teacher in the role of "guide–by–the–side" during these times.

Conclusions

Multiple I–Search Case writing has become an important part of the teaching–learning process for me. Using this assignment consecutively for four quarters has meant gradual refinement of my own expectations, and yet I have never been displeased with the process, nor with the work of my students.

They have always generated good suggestions, and many students have gone beyond the class task to create plans that shine with creativity and insight. Some students have had problems with conventions of written English, or with using imprecise language and nonstandard usage, but many of those same individuals have worked in schools for years and they present outstanding ideas in their work. A few students have presented ideas that were suggested by the classroom teacher without engaging in a rigorous examination of their own ideas, and they tend to be students who have had the fewest experiences with kids in schools.

Another drawback to this case process for preservice teachers is that the perspective of the parent is not usually directly available. Among my Ed Psych classes, one complete section was a cohort group of teacher's aides. I discovered that their writing and analyses were greatly enhanced by the extra information they had access to because of their intimacy with the classrooms and the homes. The political complexity of mandating a parental point of view for this class assignment has, however, eliminated this angle from most writings. I point out that regular classroom teachers certainly must consider this additional view. Aside from the few hitches, I am pleased with the results and my students consistently report that they find it to be a helpful assignment.

The I–Search strategy is one way to help teachers to reflect about a variety of classroom phenomena. In looking at alternative views of the "players" in school settings, it can shed light upon actions that seem reasonable from some perspectives but not others. It can also lead to solutions that are both reasonable and possible for everyone. The child who wants a kind word and a sense of responsibility does not see caring in the behavior of an inflexible and critical teacher. The teacher who wants an active, involved student does not see caring in the ways of a student who ignores the assigned task and merely socializes. A teacher who needs a learner who is fed and well–rested does not see caring in the behavior of a parent who sleeps through the breakfast hour and works through the evening hours, leaving a child to do his or her own parenting.

Therefore, although the Multiple I–Search is created as an academic class paper in the preservice university context, its components are adaptable to on–the–job use for inservice professionals. Classroom teachers do not have time to write polished papers, but they must take the time to reflect on their "problem" children if they are to be effective in dealing with them. Classroom teachers *do* have time to write in journals, if they write when their students write in *their* journals.

When a teacher jots down ideas about a case, he or she goes beyond the trial–and–error methods or the broken–record approaches that characterize too many teachers. The case technique can be used in the classroom where pages penciled in a journal can easily substitute for double–spaced typing and proper academic format. The important factor is the *process* of probing for viewpoints, careful thinking, and creative problem solving. The teacher who constructs her or his own project will own it and will grow.

References

Macrorie, K. (1988). *The I–search paper — revised edition of second writing.* Portsmouth, NH: Heinemann.

Martin, G. (1991). *Teacher's perceptions of their first year of teaching.* Unpublished doctoral dissertation, The Claremont Graduate School, Claremont, CA.

Greta K. Nagel works at California State Polytechnic University, Pomona, as part of the faculty in the Department of Teacher Education within the new School of Education and Integrative Studies. She also directs "Teach for Pomona," the alternative certification program at Cal Poly. Her most recent publications include *The Tao of Teaching* (Donald Fine, 1994), " I Never Knew I Was Needed Until You Called!: Promoting Parent Involvement in Schools" *(The Reading Teacher, April, 1995)* and "Advice to a Dialogue Journalist" *(Claremont Reading Conference 59th Yearbook, 1995).* Her current research interests include the dynamics of classroom groupings, the discourse of dialogue journals, and alternative pedagogies for working with diverse student populations, particularly in literacy development.

Tender Feelings, Hidden Thoughts:

Confronting Bias, Innocence, and Racism Through Case Discussions

Judith H. Shulman

This analysis of a pilot study provides insight into the potential of case–based methods in multicultural education. Rather than passively listening to generalized knowledge on multiculturalism through lectures, teachers have an opportunity to explore key issues in the context of real classrooms. They can make explicit their beliefs about teaching and learners; they can test out their assumptions about practice; they can confront their personal biases through a shared, socially constructed and deeper understanding of issues related to race, class, gender, and culture; and they can transform what they learn into effective instructional practices. The intensity of participants' contributions during the discussions, while at times difficult for both the participants and the facilitator, indicates how important this vehicle is for discussing these sensitive topics.

While there is much controversy over how to best prepare teachers for a culturally diverse society, there appears to be strong agreement that improving teacher education and professional development programs is necessary (Gomez & Tabachnick, 1991). Conventional approaches to multicultural education, typically in the form of separate courses that offer lectures and readings on different ethnic groups, are inadequate (for detailed reviews of the literature of these programs, see Grant and Secada, 1990, and Villegas, 1991). Most student teachers and teachers — predominantly white, middle–class females whose life experiences are different from their increasingly diverse students — neither change their understandings and beliefs about teaching minority children nor adapt what they learned to their instructional practices (McDiarmid, 1990; McDiarmid & Price, 1990).

Using evidence from cognitive research (e.g., Resnick, 1983), McDiarmid and Price (1990) argued that most of these programs fail to provide opportunities for teachers to reflect on both what they believe and what they are learning. According to these teacher educators, teachers need to make explicit their beliefs and assumptions about teaching, learning, and learners as they *take in* the new information; they must be given opportunities to discuss how to transform what they learned into tactics they can use in their classrooms; and they must confront their personal beliefs on issues of race, class, gender, and bias, even as they learn to teach (Nelson–Barber & Meier, 1990; Gomez & Tabachnick, 1991). In short, teachers are not likely to reconsider their deeply held beliefs and assumptions — many of which are held unconsciously — unless these are deliberately surfaced, examined, and in many cases, challenged.

But how do you engage individuals in such reflection? In most social and academic settings, it is awkward to discuss issues of race, class, and bias, particularly in groups that are themselves diverse. Instructors and students often shy away from making their views on these issues public for fear of unwittingly offending someone or saying something considered racist, insensitive, or prejudiced. And with few exceptions (e.g., Kleinfeld, 1990; Paley, 1979), materials designed to support such deliberations are not available.

I propose that case–based teaching is a uniquely powerful vehicle for dealing with these delicate issues.[2] Case discussions — rich with contextualized detail and verisimilitude about the challenges of teaching diverse students — can provide a context for teachers to confront their own assumptions and feelings about teaching diverse students. By collaboratively exploring and debating critical moments in the cases, teachers both develop the analytic skills to frame problems from different perspectives and expand their repertoire of effective instructional practices (Kleinfeld, 1992). They can also test their generalized knowledge about different cultural groups.

In this chapter, I present an example of what case–based teaching looks like in this context. Next, I discuss a small pilot study that used a case–based approach to multicultural education in order to address two questions: In what ways might case–based instruction about cultural diversity provide special opportunities for cross–cultural learning? What are some of the difficulties that accompany this approach, for both the discussion leader and the participants? I conclude with a discussion of potential implications of this work for teacher education and professional development. But first, a word about the background of this project.

Case Methods in Multicultural Education: Background

The Case Methods in Multicultural Education project, developed at Far West Laboratory, was conceived two years ago as a supplement to existing multicultural education programs. Using the prototype of the mentor and intern casebooks (J. Shulman & Colbert, 1987; 1988), which consists of teacher–written cases with commentaries by other teachers and scholars, we collaborated with the San Francisco Unified School District to produce a casebook on the challenges of teaching diverse students.

The Casebook

During the first year of the project, my school–based collaborator, Amalia Mesa–Bains,[3] and I worked with a group of ethnically diverse teacher–authors and commentators to develop the cases. The result of this effort was a draft of the volume, *Diversity in the Classroom: A Casebook for Teachers and Teacher Educators* (Shulman & Mesa–Bains, 1993).

More than just narratives, the cases in this book were meant to be "teaching cases," stories of classroom life that represent recurring challenges for teachers in diverse settings. Layers of commentaries follow each case, written by educators who represent different points of view — teachers, administrators, staff developers, and scholars.

The cases deal with several themes. Some describe the problems of a teacher from one ethnic group providing instruction to children from different ethnic groups or children whose knowledge of English is limited or nonexistent. Others deal with the challenges of working with parents and communities from different cultural groups. Most often, however, the cases focus on a teacher's difficulties with individuals or groups of children. Issues of racism, bias, class, culture, gender, and inexperience with other ethnic groups permeate the accounts. The casebook is designed to be used in teacher education and professional development settings. Our goal was that they would serve as stimuli for the type of case discussions I described earlier. In the casebook, we wanted to both model and provoke conversations and we used commentaries as one tool for doing so. Written by individuals from multiple perspectives, they are intended to raise significant questions about each story, and, hopefully, invite readers to do the same.[4]

The Field Test

In the second year of our project, we piloted the cases using discussion methods in a 10–week seminar with a group of 15 new teachers in San Francisco — 10 European–Americans, 3 African–Americans, and 2 Chinese–Americans. We had several purposes. One was to gather data to inform the development of a facilitator's guide to the casebook (Mesa–Bains & Shulman, 1994). Another was to study the impact of the seminar on participants attitudes toward diversity, their ability to frame problems from multiple perspectives, and any reported changes in teaching practices. We were also interested in the extent to which the case discussions engaged participants in confronting their own biases and contributed to collegial learning.

The seminar was held at the Laboratory, once a month for two hours after school. Since the time was short, teachers opted to read each assigned case and complete a brief questionnaire before coming to the session. Thus they usually came with questions, eager to dig into what they felt were the main issues of the case. As facilitators, we challenged assertions, probed for evidence and encouraged multiple perspectives. Occasionally, we called attention to a commentary if it presented information or a position that the group had not raised. Often we varied the typical, whole–group discussion with small–group activities or role plays. Our goal was to get everyone involved in the deliberations, particularly those who were more hesitant to talk in front of the larger group. At the end of each session, participants responded to another questionnaire during which they described both what new insights they gained from the discussion and how their classroom practices might change as a result. Comparing the pre– and post–questionnaires helped us trace how the discussions influenced the teachers' independent analyses. Mesa–Bains and I rotated roles during each discussion; while one facilitated, the other took detailed notes. We debriefed as soon as possible after each session, comparing our respective thoughts and feelings about the tone of the general discussion as well as examining individual components. These sessions proved to be invaluable as we independently planned subsequent discussions.

Our analysis of the project draws from several kinds of data: documentation of successive drafts of the 15 cases and interactions with case writers; documentation of similar drafts of the 33 commentaries and interactions with their authors; protocols of nine case discussions; questionnaires and writings of teachers before and after each discussion; and interviews conducted during the seminar. In addition, we used several of the cases with other groups of teachers to test both our style of discussion leadership and the range of participant reactions.

These data are limited because of an increase in absenteeism after the district pink–slipped all new teachers midway into the seminar. Many participants reported a need to attend district hearings in lieu of the seminar to save their jobs. By the last two sessions, only eight of the original 15 teachers attended. We cannot account for all those who quit, but many reported that the combination of fighting for their job at hearings and general low morale contributed to their absence.

Confronting Bias, Innocence and Racism: A Case in Point

In my experience, some of the most difficult case discussions to facilitate are those that deal with a case author's naivete and misperceptions about issues of race, class, culture and gender. These cases explore a special kind of misperception, such as when a teacher — usually a white, middle–class woman who had little experience in diverse settings — recounts a problem encountered in practice and concludes that, through the experience, she has learned something important about her own racism and has overcome her biases. The authors of the commentaries that follow, however, often assert that the author is still biased or has substituted one set of misconceptions for another.

Discussions about these cases are difficult to facilitate because they evoke strong emotions. Sometimes, minority discussants are offended by the teacher's perceptions and have little patience with her struggles. Middle–class whites may identify with the teacher's experiences and feel hurt if she is labeled a racist. Tender feelings and hidden thoughts often arise during these sessions, and facilitators must be prepared to handle them sensitively. A case in point is "Fighting for Life in Third Period" (Shulman & Mesa–Bains, 1993), perhaps our most emotionally provocative account.

Fighting for Life in Third Period

This case vividly portrays the struggles of an inexperienced, idealistic, white, middle–class teacher who taught in an experimental, ethnically diverse high school. After staying home for several years to raise children, she looked forward to returning to teaching and working with "other kinds of people" in an experimental high school. But nothing in her orientation prepared her for third

period. Students made fun of her idealistic speech about increased opportunities for minorities in the new high school. In the midst of the jokes, Veronica,
described by the case author as "stout, black, stuffed in a flame red dress,"
sauntered in slowly and asked in a "loud, husky voice, 'Who are you, some
kind of preacher lady?" Meanwhile, three large black boys began dancing
around the room rapping, "Yea Sister." At the end of the class, Veronica gave
the author a note that said, "I can see right now you never going to make it as
a teacher. This class is going to walk right over you."

During the "nightmarish" days that followed, the author confronted her
own bias:

> *I felt that I had run into the worst of everything I had heard about in the
> ghetto: crude, foul language, rudeness, low achievement, blatant sexuality, con-
> tinual talk of violence, guns, drugs — the works. These students would have
> been a fearsome group in any color, but their blackness seemed at first to be a
> barrier. I was not sure what **really** to expect from them. Were they truly capable
> of decent behavior? Did they need some other kind of schooling?*

The rest of the narrative recounts the teacher's struggle to gain control of
the class: She confronts her own black stereotypes; she asks for help from school
counselors and administrators; she tries a variety of discipline techniques before finding one that is constructive; she learns that each of the four students
has a stake in passing her course; and that Veronica is a single mother. At the
conclusion of the case, the teacher reflects on how much she learned during the
past year. She believes she has conquered her bias because she has lost all sense
of color. "I find that in the malls, on the streets, I hardly notice that people are
'different', because in fact they actually don't look different to me." In the end,
she concludes that poverty, not race, is the real issue:

> *Many of our African–American and Hispanic students come from good
> homes, where there is fine support. These students are doing very well. It is
> poverty that is the real enemy . . . the 'poverty mentality' — the apathy, lazi-
> ness, hopelessness that will surely doom them to perpetual poverty if they can't
> see beyond it.*

Four commentators interpret the case — a black scholar, a white veteran
teacher, and two intern teachers, one black and the other Latina. From their
different perspectives, they all commend the teacher on her perseverance and
her attempts to confront her biases. But they also notice some misperceptions
or misunderstandings in the case.

I have used this case on several occasions — with three groups of new teachers, including those in our pilot; with two groups of staff developers and administrators; and with five groups of teacher educators. In general, when I open

the discussion with the question, "What is this case about?," I have received dramatically different responses depending on the ethnic composition of the group. Often, predominantly white teachers say that it is a case of teacher versus student control, and do not consider other alternatives until I ask, "Can you think of any reason why the students might have responded like they did?" After analyzing the text, they can begin to reframe the problem from the student's perspective and examine the problem with new understandings.

My experience during these discussions also suggests that most middle–class, white teachers with limited experience in diverse settings admire the teacher's "growth" in combating her racism. Were it not for either minority participation or my intervention and challenge to their assumptions, particularly on the issue of color–blindness, they are not apt to consider other alternatives. Often, I hold the commentaries until after the group has had an opportunity to analyze the case first. When I hand out the commentaries and ask if they have learned anything new, they are frequently surprised by both the new information and unanticipated perspectives. The analysis then takes on new dimensions, both personally and professionally. Examining what "racist" means can be tense but ultimately constructive if skillfully facilitated. For some new teachers, these discussions may be the first opportunity to confront the view that what they had considered "racially sensitive" was not uniformly accepted as correct. As one teacher said with tears in her eyes, "I come from a suburban background and have never encountered these feelings before. I'm afraid to teach because I may say something wrong and hurt someone's feelings."

Others, particularly teachers of color, may become impatient with the naivete of innocent whites. For example, one young, African–American woman, Laurinda, who had been quiet during the beginning of the discussion, countered passionately:

> *I feel that racism and white supremacy is the issue, and that is what shapes everyone's belief and permeates all areas of life whether you realize it or not, and we're bombarded with it every minute in the media. Who's beautiful? White, blonde and blue–eyed. It [racism] is the real enemy, and it is an issue I deal with all the time . . . This woman [in the case] went into the situation as 'the great white hope' to save the darkies. What is the American dream?*

Another teacher, a black man, said,

> "I don't give this teacher any points. She's still color blind and does not want to deal with race."

Such moments during a discussion can be tense, especially for the facilitator. Yet these episodes can enable group members to better understand one another and, perhaps, themselves. They can also be powerful occasions for learning by the facilitators as well.

Findings: Impact on Participants

What did we learn during our pilot seminar with new teachers? Analysis of data from interviews, questionnaires, and transcripts of case discussions from the seminar suggest that this case–based seminar can influence teachers' awareness and sensitivity to cultural diversity.

Several teachers reported that they had a greater understanding of their students and of their own cultural biases and limitations. Some teachers also described new ways of communicating with students and their parents and of novel approaches to planning instruction. Finally, all of the teachers who were interviewed and/or filled out a final questionnaire valued this approach to multicultural education and recommended that the district bring the model to other teachers.

The data, reported through representative comments of a sample of teachers from questionnaires, interviews, and transcripts of case discussions, are grouped in three sections: (1) Changes in Attitudes; (2) Changes in Behavior; and (3) Responses to the Case–based Model of Professional Development.

Changes in Attitudes

Most teachers showed increased sensitivity and awareness of issues of cultural diversity and of personal limitations and bias. This was no small feat. From the very first case discussion on "Home Visits," it was clear how naively and narrowly many of the participants viewed their students' perspectives and home situations. The case begins with an impending disaster for an outdoor performance sponsored by community volunteers, because the third grade students who had been rehearsing for weeks had not arrived and the performance was due to begin in an hour.

When we initially began to discuss this case and asked, "Why didn't the kids show up?," many teachers saw this situation as simply one more signal that "these parents" are not interested in their children's education. As they saw it, the performance should have been a highlight in their students" lives. It was not until we began discussing the situation from the students' and parents' perspectives that these teachers began to consider other possibilities.

Awareness of Diverse Perspectives

Most of the teachers reported an increase in their awareness of diverse perspectives. Pauline's[5] comment below is representative of middle–class white teachers who had little experience in inner–city settings before their current assignment:

> *The discussions helped me gain some perspectives about the different ethnic groups, though I have also learned a lot just from teaching. I learned that these kids weren't just trying to be troublesome and difficult for me. They were just acting the way they usually did, and I had to learn that. (interview, 6/17/91)*

But those with limited experience were not the only ones who increased their awareness. For example, Anna, another white teacher who raises her family in a culturally diverse neighborhood, was affected:

> *I need to be aware of the ways my ESL students might perceive me, and perhaps modify some of my exuberance that might cause them embarrassment and discomfort in my classroom. (interview, 5/24/91)*

And William, a black teacher in his mid–forties who came to this seminar with a variety of experience in diverse settings, said,

> *"I will be more open to consider the environment from which the student comes to me" (questionnaire, 5/28/91).*

Some teachers found that they paid more attention to the difficulties of certain groups. Eloise, a young black woman, pointed to greater sensitivity to the concerns of her interracial third graders:

> *We've talked about some of the kinds of culture clash that occur with children who have a dominant home culture that is substantially different from the American mainstream culture. Some of those things I find happening with my interracial kids. The mainstream culture at my school is black and biased in that direction. Some of the kids look as black as the other kids, but in truth their home lives are different, and it's very confusing to the children where they're supposed to fit in. (interview, 6/5/91)*

David, a white teacher in his mid–forties who had previously taught in Harlem, spoke about his need to learn more about his African–American and Latino students:

> *It's hard to say what influenced me in this direction — my students or the project — but I've become aware of the need to learn more about AfricanAmerican and Latino youth cultures. (questionnaire, 5/28/91)*

Awareness of the Importance of Outreach to Parents

Other teachers reported that the seminar forced them to reevaluate the importance of going beyond the classroom and reaching out to parents. For example, when asked what they might do differently next year as a result of participating in this project, Pauline and Anna appeared more open to pursuing parents by phone:

> *The big thing that I learned is that I have to spend more time on the phone talking with parents. I felt frustrated this year with parents who I thought didn't support me, but I learned from the discussions, the cases, [and another teacher] that I should be more patient and stick with it… and that it's important to have more contact with families and the community. (interview, Pauline, 6/17/91)*

> *I'd make an extra effort to communicate with parents. The cases were an extra reminder that it was worth the effort… "Home Visits" reminded me of the importance of happy calls at the outset of the year. "An Unanswered Dilemma" warns of the importance of explaining curriculum and techniques to parents while retaining a firm sense of teacher authority. (Anna, final questionnaire, 5/ 2891)*

Awareness of Limitations and Bias

Regardless of their ethnicity, many teachers reported that they became more aware of their limitations and biases as a result of this seminar. Some teachers like Eloise were surprised to discover their biases. Before the seminar, Eloise thought she was quite open, but as she noted at the end of the year:

> *It's made me more sensitive to looking at biases that I know I have and biases that I don't recognize because they are part of the cultural norm. And, we don't see our society as biased, but it is. (interview, 6/5/91)*

Anna was also surprised at her limitations. As she reflected on the impact of the seminar, she said:

I think it made me aware of the limitations in my own thinking, especially from the written case studies that we read. I recognize myself through the foibles of many of the first year teachers [in our seminar] and in the Delpit articles. Especially, I realize the importance of cultural cues in teaching and the need to give very precise, definite statements of my expectations and behaviors, rather than just suggestive, cultural cue–type statements. (interview, 5/24/91)

Patrick, a white teacher who quit after the 7th session (see below), was particularly affected by the seminar. Though he had previously taught at a predominantly African–American school, he acknowledged his limitations during the third case discussion while we were analyzing our most emotionally provocative case, "Fighting for Life in Third Period":

I need this project. I don't know how to work with these [black] kids . . . I'm learning a lot by reading this [case] and thinking about how I've reacted [in similar situations] and how my kids react ... At the end of the discussion, he directed a question to the black participants:] "How do you teach these kids?" (case discussion, 2/12/91)

We discover why Patrick was particularly vulnerable at this time two months later, because he refers to this case discussion during our interview. He described similar problems with particular black students in his own classroom:

You know how meaningful that case was for me. It seemed like the teacher was backing down at the beginning, and she had to learn that she needed to be strong. I was in a similar situation at the time, and realized [after the case discussion] that I had to be more firm with those kids. At the beginning of the year, my kids told me things like I was prejudiced, and I used to back down, like that teacher in the case. I used to feel like, well, if I'm really strong with them they're going to think that I'm prejudiced. (interview, 4/23/91)

As he analyzed his situation, he pointed to his previous, more positive experience at a predominantly black school, where parents knew that he tried to treat all students the same regardless of color. But this "attitude" caused him to reevaluate, so he checked his perceptions with parents at conferences:

"Am I prejudiced because I'm being strong with your child? Should I treat your child any differently than I would treat any child that's misbehaving because your child is black?" They said "No! You should be treating my child just like you would treat any child and you should be as strong with them as you would with any kid." (interview, 5/23/91)

After the same discussion, Matthew, another inexperienced white teacher, referred to the importance of our discourse about racism and stereotyping:

I appreciated the honesty of the discussion about this teacher's racism and stereotyping ... I realize that I must alter/explore my own teaching styles instead of forcing the students to capitulate to me and my way of presenting things. (post discussion questionnaire, 2/12/91)

The seminar had a particularly profound effect on Robert, a Chinese–American, first–year high school math teacher who was having a rough time with his classes. Robert was raised in Chinatown and never thought about being "different" until he went to UC Berkeley, where he was constantly challenged about his racial identity. While contrasting his math instruction to Chinese students and Latinos in terms of effectiveness and comfort, he noted that there may be some cultural stereotyping involved in his perceptions of the latter. The seminar made him "more aware of his cultural biases ... and issues that he had never before considered cultural." Perhaps more important, however, was the challenge to his conception of teaching. Before the seminar, he felt that "if teachers want to get involved with the personal lives of their students, that's fine. But teaching is our main responsibility." Now Robert is not so sure; maybe teachers should take social issues into account:

There is a role that teachers have which is something like a social worker. I realized that I don't do so much of that in my classes, and I'm not sure how much I want to do because it's hard for me to talk to strangers. But it's an issue that I'll be addressing next year. We didn't get into these issues until the second semester, so it was kind of late to put some of these lessons into my classes. I had already developed some routines, and the kids had already developed a rhythm of how I teach. (interview, 6/10/91)

When asked what he may do differently next year, he responded:

I think I'll spend more time and effort on communicating with individual students... I think it [the seminar] made me easier to talk to. Perhaps these meetings have also modified my expectations of some students. It helped me to remember that not all students do poorly because of lack of effort. (questionnaire, 5/28/91)

In summary, Robert epitomizes the change that many teachers experienced as they went through the seminar. When they are encouraged to examine problems from various perspectives, collaborative analysis of the cases and commentaries enabled these teachers to think about their teaching and their students differently through increased awareness and sensitivity to multiculturalism.

Changes in Behavior

Not only did many teachers demonstrate their increased sensitivity to diversity, the data suggest that some teachers altered their behavior as a result of their participation in the seminar. They report a change in their interactional practices with students and parents. They listen more to students_ concerns, spend more time communicating with individual students and parents, and interact differently during instruction. A few teachers also report that the seminar influenced the way they planned certain lessons.

Change in Communication Patterns

When asked how this project affected their communication patterns, several teachers described specific modifications. Some teachers noted changes in their interaction patterns with students, while others described differences talking with parents.

Changes with Students

For example, Robert reported not only a change in the way he communicates with students but also alluded to why these discussions may have made him a more sensitive teacher:

> *[What I have gained from this project is improved communication skills.] Whenever I talk to a student about matters other than school, I always remember some of the ground rules we've used at the meetings. For example, I'd never demand an answer, or I'd always wait for the person to answer fully.*

While Robert's depiction is a change in communicating to students on "matters other than school," Anna reports a shift during instructional episodes. As a result of reading an article by Lisa Delpit (1988) distributed during the seminar, and participating in the case discussions, Anna reported a change in the way she gives directions and interacts with her students:

> *My third period class has a number of at–risk black males. From Eloise I learned to give very precise, very specific directions, and it made phenomenal differences in the behavior of the students…I have changed my classroom management to avoid indirect statements like, "It would be nice if it were quiet in here" and replaced them with direct instructions like, "Stop talking. You need to be quiet in order to concentrate on your work now." … As a result of a more*

quiet, orderly class, management has improved, and, I believe, their learning has increased. (interview, 5/24/91)

Changes with parents

Several teachers reported changes in communication patterns with parents, whose norms of communication were different from those of the teacher. Eloise, for example, maintained that a teacher should "be herself" in all situations (case discussion, 5/14/91). However, our interview at the end of the seminar suggests that she changed her mind and had begun to use cultural cues when interacting with parents.

More than anything, the case discussions have made me more sensitive to talking with parents, not trying to put my personality out as much as trying to keep our talks kind of professional and yet open. Basically I've come to the conclusion that I should follow the parent's lead, especially when I'm dealing with a parent and child at the same time. My job is not to be a parental force for the child but rather another adult that the parent can use for support and information. (interview, 6/5/91)

Altering Instructional Strategies

Anna and Eloise were the only teachers who described specific changes in their instructional strategies as a result of this project. Anna attributed her students' increased math test scores to three factors: (1) providing short–term goals rather than the "long–term, nebulous, middle–class goals" that she originally used, which were similar to the teacher in "Fighting for Life in Third Period;" (2) providing direct rather than indirect directions during instruction (described above); and (3) providing very specific instructions and record–keeping systems for how to obtain the goals, an idea she developed during one of our case discussions.

Eloise described several reading and social studies lessons that she linked to the seminar. In one particular reading lesson, she traced the development of a pre–reading activity to one of our case discussions:

We had a case discussion about a child from a Spanish–speaking background who was living and going to school in the United States. She was still having difficulty speaking English in class even though she could read and write. I have a child in this same situation right now and I think before I had this program I might have just taught it without thinking about the effect the story might have on this student. (interview, 6/5/91)

Another discussion prompted her to seek outside resources when she was uncertain of her approach and teaching methods with immigrant children. With the help of resource specialists, Eloise was able to provide more appropriate instruction and materials to these children, and linked her students' productivity, initial academic success, and comfort in the classroom to these efforts.

In summary, while we were pleased to see the kinds of changes that many teachers attributed to the case discussions, we were disappointed that only two described altering specific instructional strategies. Analysis of the case discussions suggests that perhaps we spent too much time examining the issues in the case and not enough on exploring alternate teaching methods. In the future, we will both allocate more time to this part of the discussion and provide small–group opportunities for teachers to examine their own related curricular concerns.

Responses to the Case Approach

Interviews and questionnaires conducted during the field test suggest enthusiastic support for the goals of the case–based model of professional development. Participants appear to value these aspects: their reduced isolation; the importance of having a support group where they could learn from one another; the opportunity for continuous learning through collegial analysis and reflection; and their enhanced sense of professionalism. The comments below are typical of the teachers' responses:

> *This program involves, quite often, self discovery. While personally challenging, such discoveries, I feel, are worth the effort.*

> *More than ever before I see teaching as ongoing problem–solving. You have to continue to work on your instructional strategies to fit the kids you have. And you have to keep what works and get rid of what doesn't.*

> *I was motivated to examine teaching strategies, cultural perceptions, and educational policies that affect our lives and careers as teachers. The project allowed me to problem–solve in crucial educational situations, free from concern of damaging students' well–being.*

Our reactions to the above enthusiastic remarks from the participants in this report are tempered by our concern for two of the participants who quit the seminar, an issue I discuss in the following section. It appears that these two individuals found it difficult to deal with the emotions they felt during some of the case discussions. Their departure reveals how deeply the case discussions can provoke personal reactions. As facilitators, we must be cognizant of the ramifications of such honest deliberations and be prepared for the possibility of personal discomfort. These episodes underscore the need for skilled facilitation and sensitivity.

The Challenges of Case–Based Teaching

Conducting case discussions that lead to attitudinal and behavioral change is a complex activity.[6] Skillful facilitating requires deep understanding of the issues embedded in the cases and numerous experiences experimenting with and reflecting on a variety of approaches with discussion techniques. In general, the more experience a teacher has using a particular case, the easier it is to facilitate the discussion because he or she will be able to anticipate the variety of responses each case evokes.

I came to this project as an experienced teacher educator and thought I knew something about leading case discussions. During the past several years, I had used cases from the mentor and intern casebooks in a variety of settings and had received generally high marks. But because of my limited background and experience in multicultural settings, I was not prepared for some of the challenges of facilitating these particular cases. What were some of the lessons that we learned?

Provide a Safe Environment

Of particular importance were the lessons about creating a safe environment for such discussions. In my previous experience with the mentor and intern cases, this had never been a problem. I had never encountered hostility or rude behavior between participants. But working with these cases was a different story. For example, on a few occasions participants intentionally or unintentionally trivialized colleagues' remarks as naive or uninformed.

A representative incident occurred during the first session of the pilot seminar, when the teachers were considering why a group of black children from a particular housing development did not show up at a class performance of their play. In the midst of this debate, Matthew, a young white male teacher innocently suggested that certain topics of conversation — such as the lack of field trip forms — were "irrelevant" and "off track," and went on to substantiate his position with data in the case. At one point, Wayne, an older black teacher who had raised the issue of field trip forms, retorted, "I don't think we're off track at all. . .It's just your opinion." And Matthew responded angrily, "OK, that's what I said. . .This is me speaking. It is my opinion. Excuse me!"

This was a tense moment for me as facilitator; I knew that something had occurred between Wayne and Matthew that I had neither anticipated nor prepared for. In response, I said that each person's opinion should be respected and valued. But by this time the damage was done and Matthew remained silent during the rest of the discussion. After the session was over he told me that he was angry at Wayne's "put down" and insinuation that he was naive, and he hoped that these kinds of occurrences would not happen again.

What we learned from this incident and others like it was the importance of continued attention to the elements of a safe environment throughout the seminar. In the future, we will involve participants in establishing clear ground rules for discussions, emphasizing the values of mutual respect and divergent points of view.

Monitor Participants' Emotions

We also learned that it is crucial to attend to individual feelings as they come up during each case discussion. Facilitators must be prepared for participants to unveil strong emotions. They must respond to verbal and nonverbal cues and have some ready strategies for dealing with tense moments. Though most of our participants reported that they valued the case discussions, two participants in our field test apparently quit because they felt too vulnerable. Laurinda, a black teacher, dropped the project after spontaneously revealing to her naive white colleagues the extent to which she felt the impact of racism and white supremacy (see previous section in "Changes in Attitudes"). As she told Mesa–Bains on the phone after the discussion, she was uncomfortable exposing her feelings to a group of strangers and tired of telling white folks how it feels to be black. This incident highlights the potential dilemma for minority participants who are frequently cast in the role of expert witness and feel polarized and marginalized as a result.

Patrick had other problems. As a white male who frequently identified with the teacher in the cases, he felt his perspective was not valued in our diverse group and felt growing discomfort in the discussions. He quit after the eighth session when he inferred that another participant was hostile to his remarks. As it happened, the precipitating incident occurred prior to the formal discussion and out of our hearing range. When we reflected on Patrick's departure, we realized that we must attend to interactions before and after the formal discussions to ensure that all members feel safe in the group.

Balance Personal and Participants' Agendas

Both facilitators found the discussions challenging to plan and to lead. We realized quickly, however, that it is one thing to promote an active and dynamic discussion, which inevitably happened, but it is another to establish whether participants learned something (Sykes & Bird, 1992). We wanted to focus on certain key issues in the cases, but had to balance our agenda with the concerns, questions, and experiences of the participants. We wanted to create an ethos of inquiry during the discussions, but realized that some participants identified so strongly with the teacher in the case that they were reluctant to "bash the teacher."

One of our biggest challenges involved learning how to use the diversity of our group to teach about diversity. For many white teachers, especially those with limited backgrounds and experiences in multicultural settings, these sessions provided an unusual opportunity to explore issues of race and culture from multiple perspectives and to get instructional insights from teachers of color. Yet, while some minority teachers enjoyed the role of informant, others did not. And some were simply tired of talking about racism and want to "get on with the business of learning how to teach." We are still looking for solutions to these dilemmas.

Limitations of Case–Based Teaching

Can case discussions ever be harmful? I think the answer is yes. Let me give an example: While Mesa–Bains and I were conducting our own field test, often spending hours debriefing one another after each discussion, we were also engaged in helping some local teacher educators use selected cases with their own first–year teachers. One teacher educator wrote a paper about the various misconceptions that her predominantly white teachers exhibited during one of the case discussions. When asked if she had ever challenged their misconceptions, she said, "No!" She had been so surprised by their naivete that she didn't know how to challenge them, though next time she will be more prepared.

After deliberating with my colleagues, I have concluded that this kind of case discussion can cause more harm than good. Without being challenged to confront their misconceptions, these teachers were able to leave the discussion reaffirming their biases and stereotypes. It's as if the discussion process legitimized their preconceptions and they may never seek an opportunity to challenge them. Confronting persons in constructive ways is difficult, especially when dealing with issues of race and class. Yet if our goal is to stimulate learning, discussion leaders must be prepared to assume these uncomfortable roles.

Implications

Although this study was small in scope, it provides insight into the potential of case–based methods in multicultural education. Rather than passively listening to generalized knowledge on multiculturalism through lectures, teachers have an opportunity to explore key issues in the context of real classrooms. During the case discussions, they can make explicit their beliefs about teaching and learners; they can test out their assumptions about practice; they can confront their personal biases through a shared, socially constructed and deeper understanding of issues related to race, gender, and culture; and they can transform what they learn into instructional practices that are tailored to their students. The intensity of participants' contributions during the discussions, while at times difficult, also indicates how important this vehicle is for discussing these sensitive topics.

Yet cases, even with commentaries, do not teach themselves. Discussion leaders must not only be sensitive to the issues represented in the cases, but also acutely aware of their own biases and intercultural blindness. They must understand the problems portrayed from multiple perspectives. And they must be able to anticipate in detail the variety of responses each case evokes, both emotionally and intellectually.

During the past two years I have undergone my own cultural education through co–editing and teaching these cases with a collaborator whose life experiences and cultural background differed dramatically from my own. While analyzing these cases together and soliciting commentaries, I gained knowledge about other ethnic groups and a lens into my own ignorance and blindness. My sensitivity and awareness continue to grow as I gain experience facilitating and debriefing case discussions. This experience suggests that the need for multicultural learning is not limited to teachers; it is a goal worth pursuing for today's teacher educators and staff developers as well. Studying and teaching with cases may prove a powerful vehicle for the needed continuing multicultural education of all educators.

References

Christensen, C. R., & Hansen, A. J. (Eds.). (1987). *Teaching and the case method.* Boston: Harvard Business School.

Christensen, C. R., Garvin, D. A., & Sweet, A. (Eds.). (1991). *Education for judgment: The artistry of discussion leadership.* Boston: Harvard Business School.

Delpit, L. (1988). The silenced dialogue: Power and pedagogy in educating other peoples' children. *Harvard Educational Review, 58*(3), 280–298.

Gomez, M. L., & Tabachnick, B. R. (1991). *We are the answer: Preparing preservice teachers to teach diverse learners.* Paper presented at the annual meeting of the American Educational Research Association, Chicago, IL.

Grant, C. A., & Secada, W. G. (1990). Preparing teachers for diversity. In W. R. Houston, M. Haberman & J. Sikula (Eds.), *Handbook of research on teacher education* (pp. 403–422). New York: MacMillan.

Kleinfeld, J. (1992). Learning to think like a teacher: The study of cases. In J. H. Shulman (Ed.), *Case methods in teacher education* (pp. 33–49). New York: Teachers College Press.

Kleinfeld, J. (1990). *Case series in cross–cultural education.* Fairbanks, AK: University of Alaska. Center for Cross–Cultural Studies (Separate cases available).

McDiarmid, G. W. (1990). *What to do about differences? A study of multicultural education for teacher trainees in the Los Angeles Unified School District.* (Research Report No. 90–11). East Lansing: Michigan State University, National Center for Research on Teacher Education.

McDiarmid, G. W., & Price, J. (1990). *Prospective teachers' views of diverse learners: A study of the participants in the ABCD project* (Research Report No. 90–6). East Lansing: Michigan State University, National Center for Research on Teacher Education.

Merseth, K. (1990). *The case for cases.* Washington, DC: American Association for Higher Education and American Association of Colleges for Teacher Education.

Mesa–Bains, A., & Shulman, J. (1994). *Facilitator's guide to diversity in the class-room: A casebook for teachers and teacher educators.* Hillsdale, NJ: Lawrence Erlbaum.

Nelson–Barber, S., & Meier, T. (1990, Spring). Multicultural context a key factor in teaching. *Academic Connections,* 1–11.

Paley, V. G. (1979). *White teacher.* Cambridge, MA: Harvard University Press.

Resnick, L. B. (1983). Toward a cognitive theory of instruction. In S. Paris, G. Olson, and H. Stevenson (Eds.), *Learning and motivation in the classroom* (pp. 5–38). Hillsdale, NJ: Erlbaum.

Shulman, J. H. (1991). Revealing the mysteries of teacher–written cases: Opening the black box. *Journal of Teacher Education,* 42(4), 250–262.

Shulman, J. H., & Colbert, J. A. (Eds.) (1987). *The mentor teacher casebook.* San Francisco: Far West Laboratory for Educational Research and Development.

Shulman, J. H., & Colbert, J. A. (Eds.) (1988). *The intern teacher casebook.* San Francisco: Far West Laboratory for Educational Research and Development.

Shulman, J. H., & Mesa–Bains (Eds.) (1993). *Diversity in the classroom: A casebook for teachers and teacher educators.* Hillsdale, NJ: Lawrence Erlbaum.

Shulman, L. S. (1992). Toward a pedagogy of cases. In J. S. Shulman (Ed.), *Cases methods in teacher education* (pp. 1–30). New York: Teacher's College Press.

Silverman, R., Welty, W. M., & Lyon, S. (1991). *Instructor's manual* for *Case studies for teacher problem solving.* New York: McGraw–Hill, Inc.

Sykes, G., & Bird, T. (1992). Teacher education and the case idea. *Review of Research in Education,* 18. Washington, DC: American Educational Research Association.

Villegas, A. M. (1991). *Culturally responsive pedagogy for the 1990's and beyond.* Princeton, NJ: Educational Testing Service, 793–801.

Wassermann, S. (1992). A case for social studies. *Kappan,* 73(10), 793–801.

Notes

[1] I would like to thank Susan Sather for her help analyzing data and Suzanne Wilson and Lee Shulman for their contributions to previous drafts.

[2] See L. Shulman, 1992; Sykes & Bird, 1992, and Wassermann, 1992 for discussions of purposes, rationale and uses of case methods in teacher education.

[3] At the time of the case development, Mesa–Bains worked in the district's Office of Integration as a specialist in multicultural education. Since then, she joined Far West Laboratory as a Senior Research Associate.

[4] See Shulman, 1991, for an analysis of the collaborative process we used to develop cases.

[5] To maintain privacy, all of the participants' names have been changed to pseudonyms.

[6] For an analysis of effective discussion techniques, see Christensen & Hansen, 1987; and Christensen, Garvin, & Sweet, 1991; Silverman, Welty & Lyon, 1991; Mesa–Bains & Shulman, 1994.

Work on this paper was supported by the San Francisco Foundation and the Office of Educational Research and Improvement, Department of Education, under Contract No. RP91–00–2006 to the Far West Laboratory for Educational Research and Development. The contents of this paper do not necessarily reflect the position or policies of the Department of Education.

Judith H. Shulman is the Director of the Institute for Case Development at the Far West Laboratory for Educational Research and Development. Her publications include *Case Methods in Teacher Education* (1992), three co–edited casebooks written by teachers, and numerous articles in such journals as *Education Researcher, Journal of Teacher Education* and *Educational Leadership* . Shulman's work focuses on the study of case discussions and case development and on the establishment of a case literature for teacher education. During the past few years, Shulman has worked with several groups of teachers and university faculty to analyze the challenges of teaching in diverse classrooms. Narratives from *Diversity in the Classroom: A Casebook for Teachers and Teacher Educators* (1993) served as the basis for this inquiry. Currently, she is working with teachers to develop new cases on the challenges of using groupwork. Before joining the Laboratory, she spent nearly 20 years in Michigan, where she taught in elementary school, community college, and the teacher education department of Michigan State University.

Teaching Without a Net: Using Cases in Teacher Education

Rita Silverman
William M. Welty

In this chapter, Silverman and Welty tell the story of Silverman's shift from lecturing to teaching with cases. She and Welty, who guided the change in her teaching, document the decisions they made as they prepared to introduce cases into a preservice teacher education curriculum and what transpired. As they chronicled this process, they came to understand that the learning goals they had originally established for the perspective teachers they were preparing by using cased-based instruction were not nearly as complex as they might have been, enabling them to extend and elaborate their goals for future students.

Prologue

We believe that each teaching experience is a potential story, and since cases often develop from stories it seems fitting that our experiences using cases in teacher education begin with Rita Silverman's story. Because Bill Welty is a key player in the second "Chapter" of Rita's story, her story is eventually Bill's story as well.

"And now," I said, as I concluded the lecture on motivation, a lecture I was particularly proud of, given its pithy connections between theory and practice and the anecdotes I used to make some important points, "are there any questions?"

I gazed at the thirty–four students in my undergraduate Educational Psychology class, practicing the wait–time that I had lectured about two weeks earlier. My patience was rewarded as first one, then two hands went up.

"Jamie?" I nodded at a young woman sitting toward the front of the second row who had raised her hand first.

"Will we need to know this for the final?" Jamie asked.

I controlled the desire to raise my voice dramatically and intone, "No, you will need to know this to be an effective teacher!" and instead replied calmly, "There will be some items about motivation on the final exam."

Turning to the other student who had raised his hand, I said, "Cary?"

"Yeah, it's OK, that was my question too."

There were no other questions. I dismissed the class and walked across the campus to my office, wondering if it were too late to begin a new career. "When the best lectures don't work," I thought, "it may be time to change jobs."

At the time that I began to think seriously about a career change, in my tenth year of college teaching, I was practiced in the art of what I have come to call the basket method of teaching. At the beginning of each semester, I would fill my metaphoric basket with the information I found most relevant to the subject I would be teaching, and in the course of the fifteen weeks of the semester I would empty this basket over (and, I hoped, into) the heads of the students. For years, this method had been paying off in positive student evaluations, even when it seemed to me that the class was charged more with torpor than electricity. But even before the motivation lecture that pushed me to think about studying for a real estate license, it had become clear that my witty lectures and clever vignettes were not helping my students become more effective classroom teachers. Anecdotal information from novice teachers confirmed that most new teachers felt they had learned little of use in their teacher preparation programs; instead, they believed they would learn to teach by teaching. And my observations in public schools corroborated that former students did not seem to be practicing the theories we in teacher education had presented to them at the university. Students who had earned high grades in my courses, whose papers and exam essays documented their commitment to improved classroom teaching were, a year after graduation, indistinguishable from their mediocre peers. Something was wrong, and as a professor who professed teacher responsibility for student learning, I found myself reflecting on my own teaching methodology.

Fortuitously, Pace University had just created a Center for Faculty Development, directed by William M. Welty, a management professor from the business school who was an experienced case teacher. Bill's teaching had been influenced most strongly by C. Roland Christensen, Robert Walmsley University Professor at Harvard Business School, who had developed a workshop first for beginning Harvard Business School faculty and later for Harvard faculty across the university using case studies about teaching. Christensen's work led to two very important books for anyone interested in case pedagogy (Christensen and Hansen, 1986; Christensen, Garvin, & Sweet, 1991).

The Center that Bill directed was holding a two–day faculty development workshop, and I eagerly signed up to attend. That workshop had a dramatic impact on my life as a teacher. During the course of the workshop, Bill Welty engaged a group of twenty–five disparate faculty in discussions of college teaching by using cases. I was impressed with Bill's facilitation of the discussions and with the power of the cases he used to generate lively, thoughtful exchanges about college teaching, exchanges that caused me to consider new ideas. It occurred to me that such discussions and exchanges of ideas might have a similar impact on my students. I shared my feelings with Bill, asking him if he thought this pedagogy would be effective in preparing teachers. His response was so encouraging that we joined forces to search for examples of cases in teacher education and to think about how we might use this method in a field other than business. (As an aside, Bill remembers that he encouraged me because I was the first person in one of his workshops to see the application of cases to her own teaching.)

Within a year of my attendance at Bill's workshop, he and I had discovered that there was little useful case literature for teacher education, but that there were a number of thoughtful people in education speculating on how cases and case pedagogy might have a positive impact on teacher education programs. (See especially Carnegie Forum on Education and the Economy, 1986; Lee Shulman, 1986, 1988.) We set at work to develop a handful of cases to use in an undergraduate mainstreaming course. I threw away my basket and began to think of myself as a case teacher.

❂

"And now," I said, as I surveyed the chalkboard covered with the ideas the students had generated as they analyzed a case on motivation, "are there any questions or comments about today's discussion?"

I gazed at the thirty–one students in my undergraduate Educational Psychology class, but I did not have to practice the wait–time that we had discussed in a case about questioning two weeks earlier. Several hands shot up immediately.

"Yes," I said to Julia, who was sitting about half–way up the left leg of the U that the tables in the classroom had been moved to form.

She posed a "What if . . . ?" question, and I looked out at the group. Several hands went up and I nodded to one of the students. A fresh dialogue had begun in the room. As the third speaker was responding to Julia's question, I glanced at my watch. Since this new discussion threatened to run away with the rest of the class time, when the speaker finished I held up my hand and turned to Julia. "Was this any help?"

"Some . . . but I'm still unsure. What would you have done?" she asked me.

The class started to laugh as I shook my head. "Sorry. You know the rules. I don't give answers. I get to ask the questions." Hands went up again. I smiled at the students. "Obviously, lots of people have more to say and I'm sorry to cut off the discussion, but I want you to have a chance to write. We have fifteen minutes left. Use your post–discussion paper to say the things you didn't get to say, now or earlier."

Almost immediately, every student was bent over his or her work. As they wrote, I sat at the desk in the front of the room and began making notes about my reactions to the discussion. Several minutes later, I was interrupted by some of the students who had a class in the room during the next hour, trying to come in. I waved them out and said to my group, "Sorry, it's time. Try to finish your most pressing thought and then hand in your paper."

I had to suppress a laugh as I saw students struggling into their coats with one arm while finishing their writing with the other. Some were walking toward me, still writing. I marvelled once again that the students in this class never signalled when the time was up by gathering their books or putting on their coats. Although the class met for two and a half hours, time was always short.

The students and I pushed our way past the group waiting outside the doorway, and the conversation about the case we had just discussed continued into the hall. Several students were trying to get me to answer Julia's question. I told them that Bill Welty would take away my case teaching license if I gave "right" answers. The crowd eventually disbursed, and I walked across the campus to my office, enjoying the late afternoon sunshine. No new career for me!

❂

Since this telling of the story juxtaposes the extremes of Rita's experience, we want to try to describe what happened to cause this change. As we wrote our first cases and then taught with them, two observations stood out: 1) Once students in case teaching classes understand and become comfortable with the new pedagogy, they do not ask if they need to know something for the final exam; and 2) Developing usable cases and learning to teach with them is incredibly time consuming. Because the outcome from the first insight provided immediate psychic payoffs — the students in our initial case courses were having as good a time learning as we were having teaching — we became committed to expanding our use of cases in teacher preparation courses. In order to continue our work and to deal with the time demands of case development, we sought support from the Fund for the Improvement of Postsecondary Education (FIPSE) and were awarded a three–year grant to develop cases based on the experiences of classroom teachers and to experiment with using them in selected teacher preparation courses. At the end of the granting period, we had developed nearly thirty cases, tested them in our graduate and undergraduate preservice core courses (Foundations of Education, Educational Psychology, Effective Teaching Methods, and Teaching Diverse Students), revised them, and written teaching notes to accompany them. We had also developed workshop models to help other faculty learn to teach with and to develop their own cases. (See Silverman, Welty and Lyon, 1992a, 1992b and Note 1.)

Once we had enough cases for a course in educational psychology, we needed to rethink the design of the course itself and the teaching methodology. It was clear that we could not abandon the established content — not only because that content presented the what and the how of the teaching–learning process, but because our program at Pace University is a traditional teacher preparation program, and professors who saw our students in later courses would expect them to be familiar with that established content. So we chose a textbook that presented the what and the how of the teaching–learning process in a clear and thoughtful way, and we tried to match the topics of the text to our cases. As we taught the cases and as the discussions evolved in ways we had not anticipated, we rearranged the cases and topics, discovering that a case could generate discussion on more than one topic and that we could revisit cases as the course developed and students gained familiarity with a variety of theories. A syllabus was developed which identified the weekly topics, the reading assignments from the text and ancillary sources, and the cases. Questions related to the readings and questions about the cases were included.

We anticipated that the cases would be effective "carriers" of the teaching/learning theories, providing contextual particulars that would allow students to see the application of the how and what in actual practice. But, we still needed a way for the students to gain familiarity with the theory presented with each topic. We agreed at the outset that case method teaching was unlikely to work if the students spent half of the class being lectured to, since the lecture method teaches students to expect the professors to provide the right answers, a lesson antithetical to case teaching. Therefore, all lecture notes and overhead transparencies were abandoned, and we moved exclusively to discussion–method teaching.

Early in the semester, the course was organized so that the theories related to the weekly topic were discussed in class first, followed by a case discussion in which the theory was applied. The discussion of the theory usually took one of two forms. One way was to conduct a whole–class discussion, based on a discussion–question outline we developed for each topic. The questions required students to think about issues rather than give "right answers." Often, we would preface the discussion with a brief writing activity. Students would be asked to jot down some thoughts about the first question we were going to ask. Their notes provided the basis for the initial discussion. When the discussion dragged (and it often did, particularly early in our undergraduate classes), we would again ask the students to write a response to a question. That way, we could call on students who were not actively volunteering, or we could poll the group and ask them to compare the responses and hypothesize about the variety (or lack of) in the responses.

Our other method was small group activities. We would break the class into groups of four to six students to solve a problem, or to interpret dense text, or to apply newly presented theories to earlier cases, and then the groups would report out, sharing their solutions or findings with the entire class. We tried cooperative learning groups, sometimes using a form of jigsaw; we allowed the students to form their own groups; we had the students count off to form groups; sometimes we kept groups together for more than one week, extending the initial activity over several topics. And, every week, a case.

Changing the teaching methodology for our course meant that we needed to rethink the way we measured student learning. As lectures were antithetical to the purposes of case teaching, so too were traditional paper and pencil tests. Cases gave students practice in solving problems and applying theories; we couldn't then test them by asking for right answers. As a result, the course became a writing intensive one. Students prepared an analysis each week of the case to be discussed, which we graded. (Each time we taught a case course, the analysis assignment was redesigned, in part because our understanding of what was possible in these papers changed and in part because our goals for case teaching were modified as we did more of it and reflected on our experiences.) The graded assignment included a post–discussion paper. After each case discussion, time was left for students to write a response to the discussion. Students were able to choose what to focus on in this free write. One option was to include "unheard" ideas. We acknowledged early in the course that one of the "rules" of thoughtful participation was to stay with the movement of the discussion. We explained to the students that some of their best ideas might not get heard at the point in the discussion when they were pertinent, and by the time the student could get the floor the discussion might have moved on. Rather than take the discussion "backwards," our suggestion was for them to make a note of their "unheard" ideas and include them in the post–discussion paper. We also suggested that this paper offered an opportunity to correct or amend an idea they had put forward in their pre–class analysis paper. Because we were grading their analyses, students would get frustrated when something they hadn't thought of surfaced or, worse, when their solution got "shot down" in the discussion. That frustration was alleviated if they could "correct" an idea, demonstrating the learning that resulted from the discussion, in the post–discussion paper. Students also used the paper to make a more fully formed argument for an idea, to make theory–practice connections they had not made in their papers, to continue a discussion that had ended prematurely for them, and so on.

The other writing assignment in the course was a journal, in which we asked students to record their thoughts, their reactions to class discussions, and, most particularly, their responses to the readings. Journals have the advantage of allowing students to consider ideas without having to come to conclusions. Rather, they can record their ideas, ask their own questions (and try to answer them), explore contradictions, and change their minds. The journal also provided an opportunity for students to describe significant educational experiences (current or remembered) and to reflect on them to see both what they had learned and what connections they could make from those experiences to the materials and ideas in the course. In a sense, the journal assignment encouraged students to integrate their personal educational experiences with the experiences of the cases and with educational principles and theories.

Our "final exam" required students to analyze a new case by applying theories studied throughout the semester. Over time, we tried this as an in–class final and as a take–home. Sometimes students worked alone; other times we made the final a group assignment. Once, following a student vote, we even tried it as an oral exam. (But only once — the competition for air time worked against our efforts to turn the classroom into a cooperative, learning community.)

Finally, we graded students on their participation. Class participation was worth 25% of the course grade. We used a participation grade both as a way to encourage students to become actively engaged in the discussion and to confirm that we would not do the talking in the class, the students would.

And so the process began. Because we worked together, we were able to think together about what was happening and what was and wasn't working. We began using cases in our teaching because we felt they would meet two important educational goals. The first was that cases could provide the theory–practice link that our students seemed to miss when the theory was presented in isolation. Believing that students who understood and could use educational theories and principles would be more effective teachers, we felt that cases offered a way for students to become active consumers of the theory. By analyzing the case and being asked to demonstrate the specific connections between theoretical principles (or absence of them) and the events of the case, we hypothesized that theory would come alive for students.

Parallel to this goal, we felt strongly that students who were active participants in their own learning would be more likely to use that learning in their own practice. Consistently, the research in learning theory has demonstrated that active learning has more long–term meaning than passive learning (Brophy, & Good, 1986). Furthermore, current research in cognitive development suggests that the social context in which learning occurs has a significant impact on the meaningfulness of the learning (Rogoff, 1991). Creating classrooms where discussion is the primary mode of learning (both discussion of the cases and discussion of the theoretical constructs of the content) would develop communities of learners who were active participants in a supportive learning environment.

Early in our work it became clear that both of those goals were being met. Anecdotal and observational evidence coupled with content analyses of students' writing supported our early hypotheses that case teaching would engage students in learning and would make theory applicable (Welty, & Silverman, 1991). But our reflection on the events and experiences in our first course suggested to us that our goals might have been too narrow. Case teaching holds the promise to do more than create active learning environments and enable students to understand and use relevant educational theories.

We began to understand the potential of this methodology as we observed our students — both during case discussions and through their written work. The easiest part of the analysis for most of the students was coming up with answers. During case discussions, they turned into fountains of ideas, spewing solutions to what they thought were the problems in the case. Almost any opening question in a case discussion stimulated students to produce responses to a different question: what to do about the problems they saw. It would not be unusual, as an example, for an opening question of, "Does the student in this case have a legitimate complaint?" to be answered, "Yes, and therefore the teacher should do . . . ." As we looked for ways to delay the solution part of the discussion until the students had delved more deeply into the case, we began to understand that the most difficult piece for them was the analysis itself — getting beneath the surface to understand the complexities and layers of the case. What we came to understand was that the students offered solutions before they understood the problems. Typically, they treated the problem in the case as if it were the only problem (or even the real problem). They had difficulty distinguishing between symptoms and problems, they were impatient with analysis, they wanted answers.

On reflection, this was not a surprising finding. Students spend most of their lives in school being told the answers and/or being asked for the answers. Answers are what they understand. And while it is possible to teach with cases by searching for answers (while meeting the goals of applying theory and engaging students in discussion), cases can do much more, and our teaching began to reflect our desire to move students to stretch their problem–solving capabilities.

We began by encouraging students to understand and analyze cases from more than one perspective. Since all of our cases are written from the teacher's perspective, that meant first understanding how the teacher saw the situation. Often, students would identify with the teacher, accept his or her point of view, and move on to solve the problems as the teacher presented them. Pushed by us to look at the situation in another way (sometimes from the perspective of other key players in the case, but more often using the theories we were studying to explain what might be going on), students began to get beyond their initial (and surface) understandings of the events in the case. This led us to see that with practice in case analysis, students could begin to develop and eventually inculcate a problem–solving heuristic, one that would "kick in" whenever they were faced with a classroom problem.

They practiced this heuristic by first taking different perspectives, then identifying a range of problems, distinguishing between symptoms and problems, and ordering problems (while separating those within the teacher's control from those not), and finally offering solutions and evaluating them. This problem–solving practice occurred both in the class discussions (large and small group) and in their case analysis assignments. We did not lecture to them about our problem–solving heuristic, nor did we present them with an overhead of our neatly crafted model; instead, they discovered the heuristic in the discussions, the small group activities, and the writing experiences we designed for them.

While working on these problem–solving skills, students began to see that if the teacher in the case had taken a different perspective, and if the problems within his or her control could be identified, then it was possible to develop long–term, detailed, and specific solutions to use in the classroom. The most important outcome from this experience was that our students came to understand that the teacher is responsible for solving the problems in the classroom. Students who early in the course saw the problems as outside the teacher's charge (the fault was with the students, or their parents or their home life, or the curriculum, or the principal) came to understand that they, the teachers, must assume responsibility and not attribute blame or fault elsewhere.

A clear lesson from our story is that we have learned a great deal about our own teaching in general and case teaching in particular by developing our own cases, using them in courses with education students, assessing what happened, and then reflecting ultimately on the process. We were interested in increasing the student learning that took place in these classes, student learning defined in terms of understanding, wisdom, and applicability to their future professional lives. And, just as our former students, now professional educators report to us, this learning process continues beyond our classrooms reinvigorated by the excitement about and reflection upon the craft of teaching that case method engenders.

Our story would not be complete without including the influence our colleagues across the country have had on our work. Five years ago, when we were just beginning, we participated in a small working conference on cases in teacher education cosponsored by the President's Forum of the American Association of Higher Education (AAHE) and Far West Laboratory for Educational Research and Development. There we met a remarkable group of people also beginning to think about cases in teacher education whose work has had an enormous influence on us and from whom we continue to learn. We could use that conference as a starting point for a new story about our experiences with cases, since it was Helen Harrington who got us thinking about perspective taking (1993); Lee Shulman about how cases are related to a long history of pedagogical thinking and practice (1992); Katherine Merseth about important history and research issues (1991); Pat Hutchings about reflective practice, (1993); Judy Shulman about how we craft our cases (1992); and Judy Kleinfeld about meaningful discussion (1992), among others.

After seven years of this work, our teaching continues to generate stories, and our students' teaching experiences are now becoming the raw material upon which we develop new cases for our collection. In Rita's previous life described above, a former student, now a first or second–year teacher, would occasionally appear in her office with a problem seeking advice, actually looking for answers, from her baskets of wisdom. They would talk a while and Rita would empty a basket or two. Now instead of dispensing answers, Rita asks questions that help the new teacher find appropriate paths of thinking about the situation for him or herself. At the same time, Rita begins to collect information which will serve as the beginning of a new case. The process recreates itself.

Notes

1. The instructor's manual which accompanies our cases contains an introductory essay on case method pedagogy which has served as the basis for our case method teaching training workshops. It also contains teaching notes which provide beginning case teachers with a road map for using these cases in class. This work has continued beyond the FIPSE grant and now all of our cases are published by McGraw–Hill's new custom publishing venture Primis. Each of the now sixty cases we have developed is described and cross–indexed by key words, subject matter, and course applicability in the Primis Education catalog so that faculty may build their own case books to fit the specific needs of the particular class in which they are to be used.

References

_____(1986). A nation prepared: Teachers for the 21st century. *The Report of the Task Force on Teaching as a Profession.* New York: The Carnegie Forum on Education and the Economy.

Brophy, J., & Good, T. (1986). Teacher behavior and student achievement. In M.C. Wittrock (Ed.), *Handbook of research on teaching (3rd ed.).* New York: Macmillan.

Christensen, C.R., & Hansen, A.J. (1986). *Teaching and the case method.* Boston: Harvard Business School Publishing Division.

Christensen, C.R., Garvin, D.A., & Sweet, A. (Eds.) (1991). *Education for judgment. The artistry of discussion leadership.* Boston: Harvard Business School Press.

Harrington, H.L., & Garrison, J.W. (1992). Cases as shared inquiry: A dialogical model of teacher preparation. *American Educational Research Journal, 29,* 4, 715–735.

Hutchings, P. (1993). *Using cases to improve college teaching: A guide to more reflective practice.* Washington, DC: American Association for Higher Education.

Kleinfeld, J. (1991). *Changes in problem–solving abilities of students taught through case methods.* Paper presented at the annual meeting of the American Educational Research Association, Chicago.

Merseth, K. (1991). *The cases for cases in teacher education.* Washington, DC: American Association for Higher Education.

Rogoff, B. (1991). *Apprenticeship in thinking. Cognitive development in social context.* New York: Oxford University Press.

Shulman, J.H. (Ed.) (1992). *Case methods in teacher education.* New York: Teachers College Press.

Shulman, L.S. (1986). Those who understand: Knowledge growth in teaching. *Educational Researcher, 15,* 4–14.

Shulman, L. (1988). Teaching alone, learning together: Needed agendas for the new reforms. In T.J. Sergiovanni & J.H. Moore (Eds.). *Schooling for tomorrow: Directing reform to issues that count.* Boston: Allyn & Bacon.

Shulman, L.S. (1992). Toward a pedagogy of cases. In J. Shulman (Ed.), *Case methods in teacher education.* New York: Teachers College Press.

Silverman, R., Welty, W.M., & Lyon, S. (1992a). *Case studies for teacher problem solving.* New York: McGraw–Hill.

Silverman, R., Welty, W.M., & Lyon, S. (1992b). *Instructor's manual: Case studies for teacher problem solving.* New York: McGraw–Hill.

Welty, W.M., & Silverman, R. (1991). *Student outcomes from teaching with cases.* Paper presented at the annual meeting of the American Educational Research Association, Chicago.

Rita Silverman is Professor of Education and Co-Director of the Center for Case Studies in Education at Pace University. She has written in the areas of mainstreaming, assessment, and most recently, case studies and case methods teaching.

William M. Welty is professor of Management at Pace University's Graduate School of business, Director of the Pforzheimer Center for Faculty Development, and Co-Director of the Center for Case Studies in Education. He has written case studies in business and education and writes on discussion and case method teaching.

Silverman and Welty were awarded two successive grants from the Fund for the Improvement of Postsecondary Education (FIPSE) in 1988 and 1991. The first grant was to develop cases in teacher education, which led to the book *Case Studies for Teacher Problem Solving*, the second edition of which will be published in 1996. The second FIPSE grant focused on cases about diversity issues in college teaching for use in university faculty development. The cases and teaching notes developed during this grant have been published by the Center for Case Studies in Education at Pace University. Professors Silverman and Welty have been featured presenters on case teaching and case writing at a number of national conferences and at more than sixty colleges and universities.

Dear Steve: The Case for a Video Case Evaluation

Kimberly D. Trimble

Within the emerging field of case studies in teacher education, there has been a great deal of discussion about what students learn from interacting with cases. Little, however, has been written about the use if cases to assess learning. This chapter discusses the use of video cases to assess what students learned in a methods course in a secondary credential program. Written in the form of a case, the chapter documents the development of the video case that was used as a final examination for a classroom management class. It elaborates upon the impetus for developing the video, as well as issues related to the writing and taping of it. Using written student evaluations of the activity, critical issues associated with case studies as evaluative tools are also outlined and analyzed.

Scene 1

"Can everybody see the screen?" I asked. I waited until the sound of scraping chairs had stopped, and most people had settled into their chairs. "Okay, you'll probably want to take notes on this to use in your letter. Remember, you should be as specific as possible in describing the problems Steve is having and what he should do about them." I moved over to the VCR. "Alright, here we go," I pushed the Start button and waited for the video to begin.

The tardy bell rings. Four or five students are crowded around the teacher, talking loudly to one another and to Steve, the teacher, who is seated at his desk. Several other students wander around the room. The rest of the class is talking loudly. One student, who has walked to the front of the room, turns on the overhead projector, makes a comment that elicits laughter from several other students, and sits down.

Standing near the door, two students are spinning a Frisbee, and passing it from one to the other. While Steve continues talking with the students crowded around his desk, five students enter the classroom and find their seats.

After another minute or two, Steve gets up from his seat at the desk. "Shutup. That means everybody," he says in a voice that shows mild irritation. "You guys need to do what needs to be done, or it's just...or that's it. OK."

He directs each of the three people standing around his desk to go to their seats. "Sit down in your seats. Everybody. Put your butt in the plastic. Cesar," he says to one of the several students still out of their seats. After walking over to one corner of the room and instructing a group of students to sit down, Steve returns to the podium, where he begins to take roll.

"You guys quiet down. You guys," Steve is almost shouting now to be heard above the noise of the class. "Sit down, sit down. Jennifer, sit down."

Miguel walks across the front of the room. "Miguel, what are you doing? Sit down. No, over there. Sit down."

"Can we sing happy birthday to Andrea?" a female student calls out. "No, no, no. You just got here. Miguel," he motions again for him to sit down. "Happy birthday to you. Happy birthday to you," sings the girl, waiting expectantly for others to join in.

"Hold on. Let me take roll and I will get to your questions." "Happy birthday, happy birthday, happy birthday to you," continues the girl in the front row. "No. We'll sing Happy Birthday to Andrea at the end of the class." says Steve. He turns back to the roll book on the podium and continues to take roll...

That evening, lounging in a chair, I began to read the exams that the students had written.

Dear Steve,
After viewing the video of your social studies class, I can understand your need in wanting some advice....

Another began,

Dear Steve,
You seem to have a handful in your last period....

"Dear Steve," began a third,

I understand that you are having difficulty handling your classes. Believe me, I know how you feel. Nobody said teaching was going to be easy — at least nobody said it to me!...

Five and a half hours and eighty–one papers later, I had read all of the final examinations. The class is one of several required courses in the teacher credential program at my university. The students are either individuals presently completing a semester of student teaching or interns teaching on an emergency credential in schools throughout the Los Angeles area. These letters were in response to a writing prompt that they received before viewing a fifteen minute video of a class.

"Now in your third year of teaching," the prompt began, you are well–known in your school as someone who excels in your ability to manage your classes. Steve, a new social studies teacher from down the hall, has been having a great deal of trouble with his classes. Though he says that he works hard to plan interesting lessons, they rarely come off well. He is becoming desperate and has come to you for help. As your conference period is the same as Steve's, it is difficult for you to observe any of his classes. You and he decide to tape the class that he is having the most trouble with, so that you might be able to watch the tape and give him some ideas on how he might improve his classroom management.

After watching the video, these students in my two secondary classroom management classes had had an hour and a half to complete the letter. I watched them write the final with a certain amount of relief edged with anxiety. This was the first time I had used the video, which had been shot only two days before at a local high school. I was relieved that the VCR and tape had worked without any problems.

✪

Setting up the Props

The video, however, was the culmination of three years of using cases in my own classes. In the spring of 1991, I had read an article that featured beginning teachers who were writing descriptive accounts of their experiences. Within two weeks I had introduced one of the cases that had appeared in the article to my social studies methods class, and given them the task of writing about their own experiences as struggling, beginning teachers. The assignment had enormous appeal for me. Here, I thought, would be an excellent opportunity for these teacher–students to step back from the details of their lives and reflect on their own practices. By writing their own experiences, they could gain an authorial voice, constructing their own meaning within the contextual realities of classrooms and transforming themselves from passive recipients of knowledge into empowered members of the teaching profession.

They hated it. But as well–trained college graduates, they marched through the assignment, turning in cases that adhered to my unimaginative guidelines.

Over the summer I changed jobs, moving to a university that prepared teachers for urban schools. Never one to be deterred by the evidence, I eagerly scanned my teaching schedule to see where I might insert my case–writing assignments. My hapless subjects this time were members of a student teachers' seminar. As part of the class, they were asked to write two case studies of incidents from their teaching experiences. They too dutifully completed the task, but suggested in the course evaluations that these assignments were a burdensome addition to their already heavy work load as new teachers. The following semester my teaching responsibilities changed, and I reluctantly stashed my case assignments into a folder in my file cabinet.

A couple of semesters later I was asked to assume major teaching responsibility for the secondary classroom management classes in our program. As I soon found out, this course posed special challenges for the instructor. The class is reserved for uncredentialed teachers who are working on their certification while teaching full time under an emergency waiver. Most of these interns teach in very challenging schools. Like many beginning teachers, they are often given the most difficult and unruly classes. While some interns in these classes occasionally enter our program after a few years of teaching, most are new to the classroom, with many having had no prior experience working with adolescents.

Following a full day of teaching in their schools, each Wednesday they spend five and a half hours on our campus, taking courses as part of the certification program. Students regularly arrive late to my 4:30 class, often with hair–raising stories. That semester, one teacher apologetically told the class that he had been delayed after tackling a student who had stabbed a classmate on the athletic field. Another related his near–fatal confrontation with gang members who had driven their car onto campus. Others came into class with more mundane explanations for their delays — filling out child abuse reports, parole officer visits, and parent conferences — that nevertheless suggested the staggering demands placed on these novice teachers.

These factors create high levels of anxiety among our students. Many feel that they are continuously asked to perform tasks for which they have had little or no training. Further, there is often only minimal levels of support within the school or district. Faced with the daunting task of orchestrating classrooms of up to forty–three adolescents, planning lessons to engage student interest, and dealing with sundry personal problems, our students are often frustrated, almost desperate, for concrete ideas to help them cope in the classroom.

The first few semesters of teaching this course, I stuck closely to the way it had been taught by the previous instructor. I emphasized a practical approach to classroom management, with a heavy emphasis upon organizational skills and arranging the classroom environment to reinforce learning and clarity of expectations. I also taught low–stress management techniques that encouraged students to work together collaboratively and take responsibility for their actions.

I had an uneasy sense, however, that while addressing some of the immediate, practical needs of the beginning teachers to survive, I was providing few skills that would allow them to continue to grow and refine their teaching. While I sensed the importance of equipping them with utilitarian tools for managing their classrooms, I was concerned that I was helping to create teachers who might be unable to think beyond canned responses to classroom problems. I wondered how well our students would be able to identify and apply effective practices when confronted by a new situation (Sykes and Bird, 1990). Though at the time I was far too occupied with the details of teaching to express it, I sensed that I was providing few opportunities for these struggling beginners to be "thinking like a teacher" (Shulman, 1992).

While pondering these questions, I had also been moving towards other ways of evaluating students' performance in the class. I dramatically reworked course assignments, removing those that seemed to be merely academic exercises and connecting others to activities to be done in the students' own classrooms. I dropped from the course the comprehensive, multiple–choice midterm. I also revised and adjusted the final to reflect more closely what I saw as the important objectives of the course. Still, I was aware that my evaluation procedures fell short of gauging whether students either understood or could apply tenets of classroom management to their own classroom situations.

In a discussion following a classroom observation in the fall of 1992, Steve, a student teacher, asked whether I might help him tape his students' presentations the following week. By the end of the discussion, he had volunteered to have his class taped to demonstrate some of the management problems that beginning teachers often face. Steve was in two of my methods classes that fall, and I had also served as his university supervisor, observing his classroom six times over the course of the semester. We agreed to talk about this further, and tentatively set the month of January for the time when we might do the taping.

It was not until April, however, that I got back to Steve about the taping. He had finished his student teaching assignment two months before and was working as a daily substitute teacher in several school districts in the area. Steve was quite enthusiastic about the project, and contacted his former master teacher and arranged to do the filming during the first week of May. I told Steve that I had written the broad outlines of a script, highlighting a few key events that I thought might be interesting to get on tape. We briefly discussed the issues I had identified for the video, and Steve made additional suggestions that I included in my notes.

The master teacher had alerted the class that both Steve and I would be there that day. I explained to the class that we were making this tape to use with other beginning teachers to help them learn how to teach better, and stressed the importance of their cooperation. We had, I reminded them, only 55 minutes in which to make the tape, which made it imperative for them to listen and follow directions. With Steve's help, I chose a few students to play major roles in the first key incident, and without rehearsing, we began taping.

Opening Night Jitters

As I read the first few finals, a whole array of issues began to emerge about using case studies for evaluation purposes. Foremost among these was the very practical concern of how I was going to grade them. Though I had indicated the approximate length (400–700 words) that I expected, students' answers varied from under one handwritten page to five complete pages. They also ranged dramatically in sophistication. Some were extremely informal, moving from one topic to another apparently randomly. Others reflected a carefully conceived organizational scheme, raising issues within the context of a developed theoretical structure, as suggested in excerpts from three students' papers:

> *...Another thing, Steve, is your rules and expectations. There should be no question as to what students are expected to bring to class....*

> *...Steve, you need to spend some time going over your classroom rules and procedures. Students seem to come to class totally unprepared to work. And then you reward them by letting go to the lockers (or wherever!) to get their books. You've got to lay down the law and then enforce it.*

...Your handling of the students who did not have books was a major rein-
forcement error. You made the consequence for not bringing a book to class an
unescorted stroll around campus. Though I wasn't able to see whether you moni-
tored students' return, simply letting them out of class is likely to encourage
students to come to your classroom unprepared. In fact, I'm surprised anyone
brings their book!

In my rush to get the video made to use that semester, I had given scant
thought to the criteria I would use to assess students' papers.

As for any form of written evaluation, I also was concerned about whether
the final gave all students the opportunity to express what they had learned
during the course about classroom management. In developing the final, I had
tried to address this concern by having students write their responses as an
informal letter to a colleague. I hoped that this form would be more accessible
to all students, especially non–native speakers of English. I also included several specific guidelines for the exam to direct students' attention to what I wanted
them to do. It was apparent from reading the examinations, however, that students' responses varied widely. I wondered whether those exams that I responded more positively to showed greater depth of understanding of management issues or simply reflected a more refined ability to organize and express ideas in written form.

A broader concern was determining what the examination actually measured. My experiences with students in other classes had highlighted for me
differences between academic skills and the ability to apply knowledge within
actual classroom settings. In using case studies in other classes, I had often
seen individuals who could provide brilliant analysis of cases. They were quite
capable of identifying salient issues and applying appropriate theoretical perspectives in discussing the case. Many of these individuals, however, had a
great deal of difficulty in employing even the most rudimentary instructional
or managerial techniques to their own classrooms. Other beginning teachers
that I had supervised intuitively seemed to choose appropriate actions in the
classroom. Some of them, however, seemed unable to reflect upon their own or
others teaching, either within the university classroom or on their own cam-
puses. As I read over the students' papers, I wondered whether the final was
gauging the ability to apply knowledge to specific classroom settings or simply tapping into their skill in analyzing cases.

This issue of using cases for evaluation was complicated by the difficulty of
knowing what students learned from cases. As I pondered how to grade the
finals, I was reminded of the continuing discussion in academic circles around
the issue of what makes up teacher knowledge and how teachers acquire "expert knowledge" (Floden & Klinzing, 1990; Lampert & Clark, 1990; Leinhart,
1990; Doyle, 1990). I was pessimistic that I could resolve this question before
the semester's grades were due. But before moving on, I turned to another

source of information—student questionnaires—to shed additional light on my dilemma.

The Critics' Reviews

Immediately following the final, I asked students to fill out a questionnaire that solicited their reactions to the examination. The directions for the questionnaire explained that the video case was an experimental technique being used to evaluate what they had learned in the class. The questionnaire contained three open–ended questions that asked students to comment on the final.

In analyzing their responses to the first question (a general prompt to elicit their response to the final), several things were immediately apparent. Many of the comments suggested that, at least on a surface level, students liked the final. More than a dozen students mentioned that the exam produced far less anxiety than other types of final exams. "It was far less nerve–wracking" noted one student. Another student expressed similar sentiments. "I was more relaxed and confident, she said." Yet another student gave the experience high praise, saying, "It seems to lessen the anxiety that I usually feel….It was almost enjoyable." I was pleased, as most students seemed to view the exam positively. I moved on to the second question that probed their ideas on specific benefits that the video case final might possess, still hoping for clues on how to evaluate this stack of papers.

While I was to be disappointed in solving my grading riddle, students did provide an array of insightful comments. For many students, the video format seemed especially helpful. Several students commented on the visual aspect of the final. "Seeing something," said one, "makes things much more clear." Another student agreed, stating "You witness an actual situation. This helps in understanding *fully* what is going on." For a generation brought up on television, the video seemed a familiar, almost comforting addition. One student observed that the experience prodded her to produce even higher levels of work. "A sight and sound experience breaks up the writer's block which may be caused by staring at an exam sheet in a silent room." Said another in talking about the video, "I was 'freed up' to express what I learned in an interesting way."

Not all students were overly enthusiastic about the video format. A few students grumbled that it was very similar to other finals they had taken. One commented, "This *is* a traditional final — it's an essay. The prompt is just a video." Another expressed a similar sentiment saying, "I've had a number of finals which require writing an essay on some situation. Whether it be a video or a written situation doesn't make much difference to me. I'm not sure if making a video makes a situation any more 'real.'"

A great number of students noted the final examination asked them to use knowledge in a different way than traditional evaluations. Several cited the comprehensive nature of the exam. As one student said, "It...asked you to reflect on all of your learning experiences at once. Traditional finals seem to most always test you on part of the whole." The video final also seemed to avoid the fragmentation that often occurs in examinations. Many students remarked that the exam encouraged them to think of the diverse topics and activities addressed in the course as a unified whole. In this vein, one student explained, "We can see how all that we learned relates together to work or to create major problems." Added another, "It ties everything together into one whole piece."

Students also seemed to feel that the examination focused upon the central elements of the course and classroom management. "I like not dealing with nit–picky specifics and getting to the major concepts," said one student. Another echoed a similar sentiment in noting, "(It) tested what I know, not what I don't know. Not trivial, like a multiple–guess test."

In other comments, students observed that the examination asked for a sophisticated response from them. Many students sensed that they were being encouraged to "apply" what they had learned to a specific situation. As one student stated, "I was able to synthesize and apply my knowledge — I never feel that way on a 'traditional' final." These comments by students suggested that the exam asked them to perform in markedly different ways than most examinations. One student noted, "It was more interesting, certainly more challenging....It is very close to real world application of knowledge." Another added, "Reading techniques and hearing lectures are one thing; but actually applying these techniques is another." A third student, elaborating on these ideas, said, "The video requires you to observe, absorb, organize...to tailor your premeditated answer to a real–life situation with real variables instead of simply "locating" an answer to fit a contrived scenario."

The exam seemed to honor knowledge learned outside of the university classroom, as well. Students felt that they were granted permission to draw upon their own teaching experiences in responding to the final prompt. One student noted, "It allows us to build on our experiences as well as the classroom management techniques that we have been taught."

Another surprising aspect of the exam was the degree to which students identified with the scenario. Many of the problems that Steve was experiencing evoked their own struggles in the classroom. One student noted, "I saw many incidents with which I could identify." Another added, "As exaggerated as the video was, most of us probably saw something that we have on one occasion or another been guilty of...." Several people felt the video encouraged them to reflect upon their own practice. "Watching a classroom scenario," wrote one student, "allowed me to self–evaluate myself as well." For others who were now finishing their first semester of teaching, the video seemed to pose a marker against which they could gauge their own progress. "I was much more able to reflect," said one student, "by seeing an example of what I was probably like in the beginning...." One of the most striking comments came from a student who seemed to have been especially touched by the video. "I took this more personally..." she said. "What I think happened was that as I was writing to Steve, I actually started writing to myself. This gave me a chance to see where I had been in the beginning of my learning process and compare it to where I am now."

Having almost forgotten my grading dilemma, I eagerly moved on to the third question that asked students to cite problems or suggestions that they thought this video–case approach might have. To my relief, most students identified few difficulties with the final. A few suggested that the exam was so different from traditional approaches, that some students might object to it ("hard–core, right wing conservatives," as one student wrote).

Others, however, had less flattering things to say. Several students were clearly annoyed that the video was not authentic. "I resented the fact," said one, "that it was a setup. It would have been much more insightful if we had viewed a *real* situation. After a while I felt that the video was so over the top that I wasn't taking the assignment seriously." I pondered these comments, and tried to dismiss them. This student, however, was not alone in her criticism. "I think it should be a *real* classroom," another student stated. "The video was very unrealistic," noted another, "and was such a staged act that it was almost slapstick."

As I read on, my dreams of a career in the movies slowly vanished. "There was too much going on in the video to give a serious answer," retorted one student. "It doesn't show the whole class," complained another. Other California reviewers volunteered their critiques. "This specific video really tries the nerves after a day at work!" commented another student. "I wanted to scream after a while about his class," said a fourth. I brightened for a moment: maybe horror films! My ego slightly bruised from these critiques of my artistic skills, I was nevertheless buoyed by their comments, and I returned to my grading with confidence.

It seemed that the final's flaws as an evaluation tool were no more numerous than any other attempt to administer a summative evaluation of a complex collection of knowledge, skills, and attitudes. In fact, according to students' comments, the video case had taken several steps toward addressing many concerns that university students held about course finals. Nevertheless, for the Spring 1993 semester, I took the easy way out in solving my grading dilemma: if a student took the final exam, he or she received full credit. The final constituted only 10% of the grade, I reasoned, and it was highly experimental. I would wait until the next semester to grapple with how to evaluate students' responses to the case.

Taking It on the Road

After having used this video case for three semesters, many issues remain unresolved, and others have emerged that raise continuing questions about using cases for evaluation. The use of video cases brings some of these questions into even starker relief.

Students' responses to the video final over the last three semesters have driven home the importance of context for the case. Though students repeatedly noted the power of the video in providing a rich, textured picture of the classroom, their responses also highlighted the need for greater understanding of the contextual elements that influence the classroom. Aspects of the broader framework in which the class exists—the social and political structure of the school, the personal context of professional staff, the background of students, for example—are not immediately obvious in the video. As a variety of critics have noted, these considerations have a dramatic effect on the school experience. Those individuals who use video cases, as well as those using written cases, must be careful to avoid decontextualizing the situation and, by inference, the solutions to complex, multi–layered problems.

An additional issue in using cases for evaluation purposes is the choice of the cases. When professors or training leaders work with cases in instructional settings, they usually have the opportunity to orchestrate or mediate discussions. By questioning or probing, those elements of the case that are of particular relevance to an audience can be highlighted, while other aspects downplayed. Unlike these classroom discussions, when used for evaluation, a case must be capable of standing on its own. The link between what the case is about and the knowledge, concepts, or skills to be evaluated must be apparent and accessible to the reader or viewer. This clarity must be achieved without losing the power inherent in cases of expressing an intricate, textured reality subject to numerous interpretations. Casewriters face a special challenge in artistically combining these conflicting demands.

Despite the growing availability of a range of cases, finding or developing cases that address central elements of a course is not always easy. This is compounded greatly by the use of video. The logistical concerns of equipment and timing make it unlikely that an outsider, armed with a video camera, is likely to be in a classroom when a critical incident occurs. Scripted cases, like the one used for the examination, however, also raise concerns. During the first semester, several students objected to the "staged" feel of the video. In subsequent semesters I addressed this issue of reality versus role–playing in the case directly. Students were told that, while these were an actual classroom with a real teacher and students, this was not a tape of a unplanned class. Instead, the class was responding to a broad outline of several incidents that were then taped. After giving this information to students before the viewing of the tape, the number of comments about this issue were reduced dramatically. I suspect that this additional information allows students to more easily suspend belief and focus upon other aspects of the video. Nevertheless, the larger question of the source for cases, video or written, remains a tantalizing one, around which a vigorous debate is needed.

The use of video cases for evaluating students' learning is at the beginning stages. My experiences using video cases in my classes suggest that it has a power and immediacy that may push the boundaries of cases even further. While riddled with unanswered questions, it nevertheless poses interesting possibilities for helping us understand how teachers learn and reflect upon complex skills, tasks, and frameworks within the unpredictably and challenging world of classrooms.

References

Doyle, W. (1990). Classroom knowledge as a foundation for teaching. *Teachers College Record, 91*, 347–360.

Floden, R.E. & Klinzing, H.G. (1990). What can research on teacher thinking contribute to teacher preparation? A second opinion. *Educational Researcher, 19*(4), 15–20.

Lampert, M. & Ball, D. L. (1990). *Using hypermedia technology to support a new pedagogy of teacher education* (Issue Paper 90–5). East Lansing: National Center for Research on Teacher Education, Michigan State University.

Leinhart, G. (1990). Capturing craft knowledge in teaching. In J. Calderhead (Ed.), *Teachers' professional knowledge* (pp. 145–168). London: Falmer Press.

Shulman, L. S. (1992). Toward a pedagogy of cases. In J. H. Shulman (ed.), *Case methods in teacher education* (pp. 1–30). New York: Teachers College Press.

Sykes, G. & Bird, T. (1992). Teacher education and the case ideal. *Review of Research in Education* (Vol. 18). Washington, DC: American Educational Research Association.

Kim Trimble is an associate professor in the Department of Teacher Education at California State University, Dominguez Hills. Formerly a junior high and high school social studies teacher, he has also taught English as a Second Language at the high school and university level. Professor Trimble has co-authored an intermediate Spanish conversation book and writes regular reviews of social studies technological materials. He presently serves as the West Coast Coordinator for the National Coalition for Equality in Learning, a consortium of school districts from around the country working on school reform issues.

Using The Case Method in a Foundations of Education Course

Mary M. Williams

In my foundations classes in the Teacher Education Program, preservice teachers examine commercially–generated cases dealing with philosophical and ethical decision making, social issues, leadership and administration, and effective teaching and school situations. Analyzing cases prepares preservice teachers for the real world of schooling because it requires them to be active and reflective in the learning process, constructing their own professional knowledge base. Internalization of the methodology also prepares preservice teachers to assume responsibility for dealing with classroom problems as they arise.

After taking the foundations course, many preservice teachers report that they better understand the connections between research and practice — they see how the readings can be applied in real school situation. Case methodology has become invaluable in my foundations courses as students struggle for the first time with school related problems and issues from a teacher's perspective. There has been a qualitative shift in students' sense of efficacy that I attribute to the case method, because no other changes (e.g., text, content) have been made in my sections of the course.

Rationale for Using the Case Method in a Foundations Course

For years, many foundations professors have used a traditional approach, i.e., lecture, readings, recitation, with some seminars and group activities. Most foundations experts hold a perennialist position, seeing their responsibility as passing on the core knowledge to the next generation of teachers. Yet, this core foundational knowledge has been difficult for students to apply in current school situations. So, we lecture to be sure students are exposed to the content.

I am certain that most professors, including myself, like to believe that students learn a great deal from our lectures, especially when we get their applause. While an offhanded student comment would occasionally raise questions about the usefulness of the foundational education courses, for a long time I laughed these off and confidently continued with my lectures, convinced that their criticisms were directed at other instructors and not me. After all, I reasoned, my models and mentors throughout the years had used a lecture–based approach and I was a successful student in this type of learning environment. I believed that if I could be successful, so could my students, if they worked hard enough.

Four years ago, however, several events occurred that convinced me to examine my assumptions and begin to use case–based pedagogy in my classes. First, I was preparing to teach courses in educational psychology. As part of my background reading, I undertook an in–depth study of research on learning theories. I also observed two of my colleagues who were using cases to co–teach a graduate educational psychology class. With these two events as background, I decided to experiment with case methodology in one of my own graduate classes.

The impact of this instructional methodology on student learning was readily apparent. I was struck by how students engaged one another in lively debates, convincingly defending their assertions with references to theories and research. In comparison to previous classes where I lectured, these preservice teachers were gaining a much deeper understanding of educational concepts about which we were reading and applying them skillfully to practical situations. I marveled as I watched the theories of constructivism and meaningful learning that I had been studying come to life in my own classroom. By the end of the full class discussion of the case, I was considering how to incorporate the case method into other classes more formally and frequently.

The Case Method

In trying to understand the success of these teaching techniques, it is helpful to draw upon learning theories, especially constructivism. While contemporary case methods have their roots in the Harvard Business School Case Study approach, many of the theoretical underpinnings of case methodology can be found in the constructivist view of meaningful learning. In applying this approach to teacher preparation, genuine teaching and schooling situations are the topics of inquiry and dialogue to explore shared experiences in light of theory or research (Silverman, Welty and Lyon, 1992).

Constructivist Learning Theories

Constructivist learning theories indicate that students do not learn best by teachers telling them what they should know. Lectures may inspire, but according to Bruner, Vygotsky and Piaget (Biehler & Snowman, 1993), meaningful learning takes place when students actively create knowledge structures (e.g., rules, concepts, hypotheses, schema) from their interpretations of experience. These interpretations are influenced by such factors as the learner's age, gender, race, ethnic background, and knowledge base (Biehler & Snowman, 1993) and are facilitated by social interactions with peers and adult guidance within the learner's zone of proximal development (Vygotsky, 1978).

The case method in the college classroom directly reflects several aspects of constructivist learning theories:

- the use of realistic educational problems and conditions in context;
- an emphasis on perspective taking and understanding multiple perspectives;
- student's active cognitive engagement (analyzing data, finding problems, formulating and testing hypotheses, developing and evaluating solutions) on their own and with peers;
- the use of a method for solving problems that can be transferred to future educational experiences;
- a supportive mentoring system that encourages students to become independent learners, taking on more and more responsibility for their own learning; and
- a classroom environment that is collaborative and supportive, where students can risk sharing ideas.

Facilitating Learning with the Case Method

Learning at a high cognitive level involves deep levels of understanding, application, and transfer. Constructivist theories suggest that this kind of learning can most easily take place when students construct their own knowledge and take responsibility for their learning. Case pedagogy effectively engages preservice teachers by providing a common context and process for applying foundational theories and research to complex, realistic classroom and school–wide situations. As they analyze a case, preservice teachers participate at high levels, learning more that is longer lasting because they are engaged within their zone of proximal development.

Through perspective discussion, problem identification, and evaluation of solutions, students learn to use a problem–solving heuristic that helps them be more aware, reflective, and respectful of their own and each others' ideas. They learn how to listen and how to share their ideas in thoughtful ways and become tolerant of multiple perspectives. Preservice teachers appear to thrive in this form of collegial environment. They become team players, practicing collaborative forms of interaction, as they work together to solve real school and classroom problems. The skills learned during the case process can be transferred to educational settings.

Using the Case Method in a College Classroom

In my foundations classes in the Teacher Education Program, preservice teachers examine commercially–generated cases dealing with philosophical and ethical decision making, social issues, leadership and administration, effective teaching, effective schools, and first–year teacher issues. Each case is chosen for its ability to generate discussion around issues from the course readings. I use between six and eight cases throughout the semester, with a case analysis as a performance based final exam.

Procedures for Using the Case Method

Roles and responsibilities for learning in classrooms where cases are used differ markedly from traditional classroom settings. For effective learning to occur, students must assume greater responsibility for their own learning. Students must prepare for class meetings by reading cases and other assignments and developing a preliminary analysis before class. The professor's responsibilities also change. As for many other courses, the professor must provide relevant readings and preparatory questions for students. An additional and critical responsibility, however, is to establish a collaborative and supportive class environment where students may share their ideas and beliefs as they present their prepared analyses and evaluate each others' solutions.

To illustrate these changing roles, I will describe how I use the case of Brenda Forester (Silverman, et al., 1992) to illuminate and apply foundational principles in my classes. Students in the Foundations Class begin by reading a textbook chapter about the established philosophies of education. Prior to reading, they are asked to reflect on pre–reading questions. As they read, they must choose a philosophy that matches their beliefs and come to the next class prepared to defend their choice. In class, students complete a goal setting exercise. In this activity, students individually prioritize educational goals. In groups, they are then asked to draw on their chosen philosophy and reach consensus on these goals. Thus, prior to analyzing a case, students spend a significant amount of time reading, reflecting, and prioritizing philosophical principles and educational goals.

The Case

Now students are ready to apply their knowledge of educational philosophy to an authentic classroom situation. They do this by examining the case of a college undergraduate (Brenda Forester) who is going through the process of clarifying her philosophy as she prepares to become a teacher (Silverman, et al., 1992). Brenda is experiencing dissonance between the models of progressive teaching in some of her university education classes and her own former, traditional educational experiences. Like many of the students in my own classes, Brenda faces a philosophical dilemma in developing a personal approach to teaching.

Student Analysis of the Case

Students use the following procedure for each case that they analyze. After reading the text chapters assigned, they read the preparatory questions and then the case itself. Next, as preparation for writing their analysis, students reread the text to delve beyond the surface layers of the case to understand the underlying problems facing the teacher. Students then identify and write the short–term and long–term solutions for each problem, supporting them with references to theory and research from authoritative sources. Instead of falling back upon their experiences as their only guide, students make their assertions more powerful by grounding them in theory and research from the textbook.

Then, students are asked to reflect in writing on potential consequences of the solutions they have offered. This preparatory work is essential for students to gain from the subsequent discussion and in–class analysis and reflection.

As students come to class with this three–to–four–page written case analysis, the class discussion can focus upon high–level questions. Having previously thought carefully about the case, students generally enrich the discussion with reasoned insights and suggestions. As they are able to participate thoughtfully, they take greater ownership of both the process and solutions. Because student preparation and participation is important, it counts for thirty percent of their final course grade. If they remain open–minded, each student leaves the class with twenty to thirty more ideas than they came in with. After the discussion, students take ten minutes to reflect, writing a note to me about what they have just learned. They are given specific questions to respond to that ask them to make additional connections to theory or research. These reflective notes are submitted with the analyses they had prepared outside of class.

During class discussions my role is not traditional. I ask questions, listen, encourage, facilitate, guide, prompt and clarify. I do not offer answers, because there is no 'one right answer' for Brenda. When there is an oversight, error or explicit misconception, however, it is my job to step in and clarify or press students to support assertions they have made.

Successful Implementation: Case Method Evaluation

I use a variety of sources to evaluate the quality of my case method teaching and students' learning. I invite other professors to observe my classes and give me feedback and suggestions. I continue to observe and learn from veteran instructors who use the case method. I videotape my case discussions frequently and review the tapes. These provide me with an opportunity to reflect and generate ideas about how to improve my approach.

I have also gathered a great deal of evidence of the effects of the case methodology by carefully observing my students. In each foundations course that I have taught, cases seem to increase dramatically students' abilities to analyze, apply, and reflect on important educational issues. I am amazed to observe that students persuade each other with thoughtful arguments grounded in the research and literature. I have never before experienced such high levels of student engagement and interaction.

In addition to helping preservice teachers bridge the gap between theory and practice, the case method also encourages students to become more open–minded, thoughtful and reflective. Students, especially graduate students, come to schools of education with many preconceived notions about what should work in schools. One of our primary responsibilities as teacher educators is to help students break down these misconceptions. The power and the ambiguity of cases seems to encourage them to become less convinced that their earlier ideas may represent the only truth. In the process, students also become more open about receiving help and support.

My sense of the success of case methodology is further reinforced by comments from students. While I use cases in other classes that I teach, this method seems to have the greatest and most dramatic impact upon students in foundations classes. On informal surveys, these students regularly report discovering important insights and connections between course readings and classroom experiences. Before taking the foundations course, many preservice teachers state that they see little use for theory and research. After taking this entry level course, students recount that they better understand the connections between research and practice. They tell me that they see how the readings can be applied in real school and classroom situations, and they report that they are grateful for the shared experience. While students often maintain that it is the most difficult approach they have ever been exposed to, they also recognize that it is an invaluable tool for comprehending school related problems and issues from a teacher's perspective.

Cases also seem to help students organize the course content more coherently. Before I used the case method, many students became overwhelmed with the multitude of issues and conflicting forces impacting schools. More recently, after using cases, students report that they understand their job as teacher will be more complicated than they had ever realized. Nevertheless, they express a confident desire to take on the responsibilities of this important job.

Case Method Support Group

For my own professional development, I participate in a support group for professors using the case method in their education classes. Each semester, faculty who use the case methodology meet monthly to discuss issues, techniques, style, and approach. The meetings allow us an opportunity to share the issues we grapple with as we work to become effective case teachers. Faculty members, for example, distribute their syllabi to peers to illustrate how they integrate case studies into their courses. During meetings throughout the semester, we discuss diverse issues that have emerged in using cases in our classroom. Some of these are practical concerns, like grading student participation, posing opening questions, developing engaging assignments. Others focus on broader topics, such as students' rights and responsibilities in a discussion, preparing case teaching notes, and balancing teacher and student control of discussions.

Should you decide to use the case method in your foundations of education course, it is important to get support in order to use the method effectively with your students. This support might come in the form of workshops, observations, team teaching, or peer video reviews. I caution you to "ACCEPT NO SUBSTITUTES." The case method applied incorrectly can have a devastating effect. The use of cases that are pedantic, simplified, or moralizing can stifle the higher levels of thinking that are required for deep understanding to occur. Also, a professor who does not make appropriate assigned readings, who does not respect student contributions, or who has predetermined correct answers will prevent higher–level learning from happening.

With the help of the case method, students will learn the core knowledge which they can and will want to take with them as they begin to teach! Then, Foundations of Education might once again become the most important class preservice teachers take.

References

Biehler, R. & Snowman, J. (1993). *Psychology applied to teaching*. Boston: Houghton Mifflin.

Ryan, K. and Cooper, J. (1992). *Those who can, teach* (6th edition). Boston: Houghton Mifflin Company.

Silverman, R., Welty, W., and Lyon, S. (1992) *Case studies for teacher problem solving*. New York: McGraw–Hill.

Vygotsky, L. (1978). *Mind in society: The development of higher mental process*. Cambridge, MA: Harvard University Press.

Woolfolk, A. (1995). *Educational psychology* (6th edition). Boston: Allyn & Bacon.

Mary M. Williams is an associate professor of Education at Pace University. She is an associate with the Center for Applied Ethics at Pace and the Moral Education Seminar at Columbia University. Dr. Williams teaches philosophy and history of education, teacher effectiveness, curriculum and assessment, educational psychology, global perspectives, and reading and children's literature. She has created courses in middle level development, multicultural education and diversity, and she supervises student teachers.

Dr. Williams has conducted extensive research in order to evaluate the effectiveness of the formal and hidden curriculum in classrooms. She works on research teams to conduct pilot studies, develop curriculum, and evaluate teacher effectiveness and student learning. Dr, Williams is currently working on the National Commission on the Moral and Ethical Dimensions of Teaching, the Character Education Partnership, and the ASCD Character Education Network to develop, implement, and evaluate character education programs.

Dr. Williams has given numerous national and local workshops and presentations about her research and is the Deputy Executive Director of the newly formed International Society of Educational Administrators. She has a book in press, *Character Education and Teacher Education* and two works in progress: *Respect: How to Get It!* and *Character Education & Multicultural Education: The Best of All Worlds.*

Just in Case: Reflections on Learning from Experience

Lee S. Shulman[1]

This chapter introduces the functions of case–based learning in teacher education as a response to the dual problems of learning from experience and bridging the gap between theory and practice. After describing the ways in which the author uses cases in his own teacher education practices (as a case–in–point), three conceptual issues are addressed: the structure of a case; the connections between cases and theory; and the psychological principles that govern case–based learning. The chapter concludes with a discussion of the role of teacher communities in case writing and learning, and with a re–examination of cases as accounts of the interplay between design and chance.

This book is filled with contributions from leading educators who both use cases and think about them. I also fall into that category. I use cases regularly in my teaching of both new and veteran teachers. I also think about them obsessively, wondering why they work so well at some times, and so marginally at others. This chapter represents my attempt to subject my own case methods to a reflective analysis, and to connect the use of cases to a broader arena of educational and psychological theory.

I begin with a reconsideration of the functions of cases in the education of teachers and the pedagogical and professional challenges that cases are intended to address. I will describe in some considerable detail the ways in which I have been using cases — both reading cases and writing them — in my own pedagogy of teacher education. This account will itself serve as a kind of case–in–point, an instantiation of a particular strategy of case method in teacher education which can then serve as a touchstone for the analyses that follow. I will then examine the example from two perspectives: the structure of case (or what makes a story function as a case); and the theoretical principles of learning and teaching needed to explain why cases can function in powerful ways pedagogically. I will conclude with reflections on the role of cases in the creation of teacher communities.

Working with Cases

I work with case methods in teacher education for a number of reasons. First, I believe that the admonition that practitioners should reflect on their own practice is both absolutely correct and painfully demanding. Discerning the object of reflection — which kind of experience is "case–worthy" — is a nontrivial challenge. Should I reflect on the problems of a particular child, on the complexities of a lesson, on the subtleties of an interaction, or the unfolding of a teaching episode? How can I keep an event in focus long enough to engage in reflection with respect to it? Using cases as the unit of reflective analysis may aid in organizing the process of reflection as a firm component of teacher education programs.

Second, too much of teacher education is unbearably generic, offering vague general principles and maxims that purport to apply broadly to a vast range of situations. A case of instruction is — by definition — *situated* in place, time *and* subject matter. If the case is faithful in its particularities, it cannot ignore the subject– and situation–specificity of teaching, because we are always teaching some *subject matter* to some *student(s)* in some *context*.

Third, the essential feature of teaching is its uncertainty and unpredictability. Teaching cannot be directed by formal theory and lockstep national syllabi, yet remain responsive to both student insights and misconceptions. Moreover, as our educational goals increasingly emphasize higher–order thinking and reasoning and student collaborations around real problems, the education of teachers must emphasize their development of flexibly powerful pedagogical understanding and judgment. Therefore, discourse on teaching must go beyond broad principles and propositions as its objects. Knowledge of teaching is comprised of combinations of cases and principles. We intend for our students to develop a repertoire of cases which can help to guide their thinking and reflections on their own teaching. They can then use their experience with cases, their own and those of others, as lenses for thinking about their work in the future.

Most other professions already structure much of their clinical knowledge in terms of some sort of case format for both the documentation of practice and the organization of instruction. Professions that divide their work into case–like segments include law, medicine, nursing, social work, architecture, even business. These cases then serve as the building blocks for professional reasoning, professional discourse, and professional memory. Cases may have many advantages over arrangements of expository rules, standards or maxims. For example, they take advantage of the natural power of narrative ways of knowing, a topic that has been addressed with considerable vigor by psychologists such as Jerome Bruner (1986). They also appear to fit well with the intuitions of practitioners.

The great challenge for professionals who wish to learn from experience is the difficulty of holding experiences in memory in forms that can become the objects of disciplined analysis and reflection. Consider the possibility that cases are ways of parsing experience so that practitioners can examine and learn from it. But teachers are typically confronted with a seamless continuum of experience from which they can think about individual kids as cases, or lessons as cases, but rarely coordinate the different dimensions into meaningful experiential chunks. Case methods thus become strategies for helping teachers to "chunk" their experience into units that can become the focus for reflective practice. They therefore can become the basis for individual teacher learning as well as a form within which communities of teachers, both local and extended, as members of visible and invisible colleges, can store, exchange and organize their experiences.

In this chapter, I offer one model of case method in teacher education. It does not depict *the* case method, for no such enterprise exists, in spite of the claims of some educators. Instead, I shall present a particular example of how cases are used in teacher education, an example that combines: 1) the study of cases written by others, 2) the crafting of one's own written cases, 3) the process of commenting upon and discussing the cases written by other members of one's teaching community, and 4) the beginnings of a case literature for teacher education.

I will follow this account with three exercises in theory development. First, I will ask what counts as a case. What are the elements of those narrative accounts that are more than stories and can function educatively as teaching cases? Second, I examine the much–misunderstood connections between cases and theory, attempting once again to explain how cases can draw their pedagogical power *from* theory without cases being *about* theory. Third, I will address the question of learning from cases. If cases — as forms of narrative — have a certain structure and form, what are the principles that describe how and why they can serve as an educative medium for professional learning? I conclude with a discussion of the connections between conceptions of case method and an emerging image of teachers as members of learning communities. I begin with a description of one type of case method for teacher education: The Analysis–Construction–Commentary–Community Cycle.

An Example of Case Methods

Case Reading and Discussion

I begin my course on "Foundations of Learning for Teaching" each year by having my students read a case written by Vickie White (1988), describing her experiences as a first–year intern teacher in Los Angeles. The case, taken from Judy Shulman and Joel Colbert's (1988) *Intern Teacher Casebook,* is titled "One Struggle After Another," and describes Ms. White's experience in attempting to teach Shakespeare's *Romeo and Juliet* to a class of inner–city African–American adolescents, in a secondary school located in the same general area of south east Los Angeles in which Vickie herself grew up.

Vickie describes in poignant detail her increasingly frustrating attempts to engage her students in the complexities of language and plot of Shakespeare's masterpiece. Her students challenge Vickie at every step. "Why do we have to read this?" "This is too hard to read." She assigns scenes for homework, and very few students complete the assignment. She works with a group of university friends to make a tape recording of the play for the students to hear the power of the Shakespearean language. Her students complain that one character's voice is too nasal and that her friends sound like they are white (they are; Vickie is not.). The narrative is a tale of trial and error, of difficulty and repair. In the end, Vickie seeks assistance from more experienced teachers, who suggest alternative ways for her to teach *Romeo and Juliet* to her class.

When my own students, themselves first–year intern teachers of English (including literature and drama), mathematics, science, foreign language or social studies at the secondary level, have finished reading the case, I ask them how they would characterize Vickie's situation. They begin to analyze her circumstances ("She's never really thought about why she is teaching Shakespeare. Telling the students they must learn it because it is in the California state curriculum won't satisfy them." "Her situation is typical. I teach social studies and I have problems like that regularly."). Soon they begin to connect Vickie's experiences to their own. As dialogue among the students develops, two kinds of response are typically offered: the analysis of Vickie's case leads students to invoke more theoretical principles ("She has forgotten that you must begin where the kids are." "She has not diagnosed the students' prior knowledge, abilities or interests adequately." "She should have thought through her goals and rationale more thoroughly, and she should have asked for help from her mentors in a more timely manner."); and students use the occasion of Vickie's story to begin telling stories of their own about their own experiences in teaching.

At this point in the analysis, we begin to introduce a theme that becomes a recurrent refrain in all our work with cases. "What is this a case of?", we ask incessantly. How would you characterize this account in relation to other accounts, to your own experiences, and to conceptual or theoretical categories with which you are familiar? "What is this a case of" is a locution whose purpose is to stimulate students to initiate the intellectual work that makes cases powerful tools for professional learning. They must learn to move up and down, back and forth, between the memorable particularities of cases and the powerful generalizations and simplifications of principles and theories. Principles are powerful but cases are memorable. Only in the continued interaction between principles and cases can practitioners and their mentors avoid the inherent limitations of theory–without–practice or the equally serious restrictions of vivid practice without the mirror of principle.

The answer to "what is this a case of?" is rarely singular. That is, rarely if ever is a particular account related to only one theoretical, conceptual or descriptive category. Indeed, part of the power of cases rests in a given case's capacity to be related to multiple categories and to numerous other instances. Because of their complexity, contextuality and richness, cases provide excellent opportunities for learners to "criss–cross the landscape" of theory and practice (Spiro, Coulson, Feltovich and Anderson, 1988) linking experiences to ideas in a network of associations. Were it grammatically correct, I would prefer asking the question "what are this a case of?" Later in this chapter, I shall return to "what is this a case of" in a discussion of the connections between cases and theory.

Vickie's case is but the first of a series of cases that we read and discuss during the first few weeks of the course. Some cases are written by intern teachers like themselves. These cases may be taken from casebooks, but increasingly I draw from cases that have been written by their predecessors in this same program. Other cases have been written by veteran teachers. Still others have been written by researchers like Deborah Ball (1993), Magdalene Lampert (1990) or Suzanne Wilson (1992) who conduct research on their own school teaching. Although the students are not aware of it at the time, I select those first few cases carefully, with special attention to their organization, their focus and their tone.

Case Organization

For my purposes, I try to ensure that each case has roughly the same focus and plot. Each case must be a narrative about *the teaching of subject–matter.* It must dwell on a teacher's attempts to teach some particular body of knowledge, skill, understanding or appreciation to a group of students, whether directly, by discovery or through some project or simulation. It is not a case of a troubled child, nor primarily a case of classroom management problems, nor of a confrontation with parents, principals or fellow teachers. Though each of these is a worthwhile topic, in principle, I am interested in engaging my own students in the careful contemplation of the complexities of substantive pedagogy, in which a teacher is attempting to teach something he or she understands reasonably well to a group of students. This is a nontrivial specification, since if you ask a teacher to tell a story about teaching, it is not typical that you are told about the teaching of subject matter. I believe that cases can be classified into genres, much like types of writing or literature. This particular genre can be called "instructional cases of subject matter."

The plot of each case[2] must revolve around a plan that goes awry, an intention unfulfilled or some surprise that disrupts the expected scenarios and requires that the teacher re–examine, re–plan, revise or otherwise reflect on her original plans and modify them in some way. Thinking in dramaturgical terms, *Act I* of each case sets the scene by laying out the context of the classroom and students, describing the intentions, the dreams, the hopes and plans for the unit or course of instruction, and exploring the content to be learned fully and critically. *Act I* ends on a note of hope and high expectations as the goals of instruction and the expected scenario of teaching and learning are portrayed.

Act II of the case provides an account of what actually happened, complete with unanticipated problems and difficulties. It should be rich in the detail of classroom dialogue and interaction. This act ends in a state of tension, uncertainty and unresolved conflict.

Act III resolves the tension in some fashion, either by describing the actions that were taken to relieve the difficulties, or by sifting through emerging insights about why the problems occurred as they did. *Act III* is the resolution, the recapitulation and the reflection, through which we begin to discern the teacher's current grasp of the issues and how the resolution (or the resignation to the absence of any resolution) has left the teacher with a different level of understanding than she had before. Each of the cases they read, whether written by a teaching novice or by a veteran expert, more or less follows that set of guidelines: a focus on the teaching of substance and a similar narrative plot of plans, disruption of the intended, and resolution or reflection on the outcomes and consequences for the students and for the self.

As I observed earlier, a case of subject matter pedagogy is a particular genre of case, not the only legitimate type of case. I am convinced, however, that if teachers are to learn from experience — whether their own or vicariously through the case–based experiences of others — they must learn to parse the flow of experience into the structure of cases. They must learn a syntax, a grammar of cases, which provides a set of terms within which they can organize and analyze their understanding of experience. If they can see the structure in cases they read, they can begin to see the structure of cases in their own lived experiences. For this reason I begin with the analysis of instructional cases, all of which share the same overall plot or structure.

There is another feature to the cases our students read. They are largely "self–disclosing. That is, the case is a first–person account of an episode of teaching, an episode that may well have extended over several days or weeks, in which the narrator has experienced some form of surprise, difficulty or clear failure. The essence of the case is in the problem, the surprise or the failure. The case writer presents his account of the difficulties without embarrassment, much as physicians learn to present difficult cases for clinical–pathological conferences. The case is educative precisely because it is built around some form of failure or surprise, requiring a comparison of intentions and outcomes, and demanding either improvisational or deliberative responses to the problems.

As we have come to see, by reading and discussing such cases, we begin to "detoxify" the recounting of failures and make the possibilities for learning from such experiences more real. We try to help our students celebrate their failures if they can learn from them, rather than denying them to avoid embarrassment. There is a research monograph written about learning in the surgical residency, that carries the wonderful title, *Forgive and Remember* (Bosk, 1979). The title communicates the message that internships are occasions in which errors must be made. They will be forgiven only if they can be remembered, reflected upon and become a source of learning. "Forgive and forget" is a motto for good relationships without growth. "Forgive and remember" is a slogan for all practical internships and an inspiration for those who would learn from cases.[3]

Case Writing

Following the model of Judy Shulman (1991) and her extensive research on teachers as *case writers*, I next ask my students to examine their own teaching experiences to find personal instructional cases they can write. If the discussions stimulated by the case reading have been successful, the students should now be able to locate cases within the remembered flow of their own teaching experiences. They are asked to write subject matter instructional cases that follow the plot structure of the cases they have been reading. All of them write such cases over the period of about a month, usually in early February. They have been teaching two classes each day since September and continue teaching for two hours each morning. They almost always have enough experiences from which to write their own case.[4]

One example of such a case is Mark Ellis's case of teaching the mathematical concept of "pi", which he wrote during the Winter of 1992, while serving as a teaching intern. Mark was teaching 10th grade geometry and understood that all his students had already encountered "pi" in their earlier mathematical learning. But he was convinced that they viewed pi as an arbitrary constant, which held the value 3.14159.... for no particular reason other than that some Greek mathematician had defined it that way. Mark wanted his students to understand that pi was a ratio, that it was a rational number and that its identity rested on the universal relationships that held among the circumference, the diameter and the area of a circle.

As Mark wrote his case, he lays out his analysis of the instructional challenge, and of his recognition that an understanding of ratio necessarily rested on understanding the concept of proportion, and proportion rested on notions of scale. As he began to draw examples of representing scale in a proportional way, he designed demonstrations and discussions of scale models, architectural drawings, maps and other artifacts in which the idea of scale is central. Mark's analysis of the complexity of both the concepts of the subject matter and the strategies of instruction are compelling. So ends *Act I*.

Mark then describes how the actual instruction unfolded and proceeded. At some points students failed to know things that he had thought elementary. At other points, his examples and exercises seemed to work almost too well. Did the students really understand, or were they operating with a delusion of comprehension? As *Act II* ends, Mark has concluded his teaching of the unit on pi and has given the students an essay final examination, which includes an open–ended question on the meaning of pi. As he reads the answers, his heart sinks. Only two of the students' responses reflect anything but the most superficial understanding of pi. His heart sinks as the "curtain" falls.

The final section of the case does not resolve the problem in a simple way. Mark does not re–teach pi and achieve his goals in some miraculous manner. But he analyzes the student responses carefully, reflects on his assumptions and anticipations, and develops a theory that accounts for his experience and suggests a strategy to employ the next time, an approach based on his inferences regarding the persistence of the students' prior knowledge of pi in the face of his attempts to modify or even eradicate their earlier ideas. His reflective analysis brings together his technical and theoretical understanding of the power of prior knowledge and preconceptions on student understanding, and his personal reflections on his own and his students' intentions and actions.

Case Commentary

The students write cases of this sort based on their own teaching experiences. They have now applied the syntax of the cases they have read to telling the stories of cases they have themselves lived. They have moved from reading and discussing the cases of others' experiences to the writing of their own cases. They are now ready to move to the next level of exchange, case discussion and commentary. Once a narrative has been completed, the initial stage of reflection has been initiated.[5] The reflective processes undertaken to capture the features of one's own practice for case writing are essentially intrapersonal (even though they have probably been stimulated by some pre–case conversations with peers or supervisors). We now have the students exchange the first draft of their cases and prepare written commentaries on each other's case. We thus move from individual reflection to socially mediated reflection, from introspection to conversation.

Case Conversations

Cases with commentaries can now be circulated for broader conversations within the community of those learning to teach. At this point, the direct experiences of some members of the group can be shared with others who experience them vicariously as cases. We now create contexts for small–group conversations among students regarding cases they have written and read. There is no question that such conversations are experienced as stimulating and enlightening by the participating students. Based on these conversations and commentaries, each case–writer now re–drafts the case into a new and improved version. We have barely begun to explore why certain types of conversation are particularly fruitful and stimulating while others stimulate yawns and worse.

Case Conferences and Case Literatures

Once teacher–written cases have emerged from the private property of their authors, have been enriched by commentaries and become the foci of conversations, they become candidates for inclusion in the discourse of the larger pedagogical community. In our course, we employ two related approaches to creating a community around teacher–written cases. We have experimented

with small teacher conferences or congresses where we bring together participants in teacher education programs from different institutions who make presentations on their own cases and then discuss them jointly. This is a provocative experience for young teachers, who begin to see their work as a form of
scholarship that can be shared with other members of the profession.

We also collect the cases that have been written and publish an annual
casebook from the teacher education program, organized by subject–specific
categories. These casebooks cam be read by all members of the graduating class
of teachers, and a copy is placed on permanent deposit in the library of the
program. A number of the cases are selected for inclusion in the reading materials for future generations of teacher education candidates. In this way, each
group of teacher education students leaves a legacy of cases for those who
follow.

As we continue to collect instructional cases written by teachers as well as
by others, we can begin to discern the outlines of a case literature for subject–
specific teaching. We have several cases on the teaching of "democracy" or
"feudalism" in history and social studies; several cases on the teaching of logi-
cal argument or proof in geometry, or of zero in arithmetic. I envision the even-
tual development of large bodies of subject–specific cases with commentaries,
organized perhaps the way chessbooks present the variety of ways in which
particular openings can be pursued, or particular endgames can be contem-
plated. By collecting and organizing a multiplicity of subject matter cases, with
analyses and commentaries, we will provide rich food for thought to both inexperienced and experienced teachers. Moreover, as new teachers become more
experienced at seeing their own teaching and that of others in terms of cases, I
suspect that they will also become more adept at making analytic sense of different genres of case, written in different ways and from different perspectives.
The purpose of scaffolding is to provide support for structures that are incom-
plete or immature. As they continue to develop as teachers, they will depend
less and less on the particular structures they employ earlier in their educa-
tions.

Having described in some detail the manner in which I work with cases, I
can now turn to three related questions. First, what are the attributes of a narrative that make it worthy of the designation "case?" That is, what story do
cases tell that distinguish them from mere anecdotes? Second, what are the
connections between cases and theory? Third, what are the theoretical reasons
why cases "work?" Can we relate our emerging theory of case methods to
more general principles of teaching and learning?

❂

Conceptions of Cases:
Attributes, Theory and Principles

Attributes of a Case

The essence of any case is *chance*. In remarks to one of the annual case conferences organized by Judy Shulman and the Far West Laboratory, Judith Kleinfeld of the University of Alaska recalled Jerome Bruner's (1986) observation that a narrative is an account of the "vicissitudes of human intention" (p. 16). To call something a narrative is to assert that it tells of the encounter between a plan and an accident, between a goal that was pursued and an impediment that delayed or interrupted the quest. In a fundamental way, narratives are the children born of a liaison between design and chance.

Imagine the following account: "Little Red Riding Hood went into the woods to bring lunch to her grandmother...and she did." That is hardly a compelling narrative. It's hardly a story at all. But change the account to "Little Red Riding Hood went into the woods to bring lunch to her grandmother...and she *happened* to meet the Big Bad Wolf." Enter vicissitudes and you have a narrative. Enter chance and you have the makings of a case. The connection of case and chance is no accident. The Oxford English Dictionary tells us that one of the etymological roots of "case" is the idea of "chance." Thus, we employ locutions like "just in case" to describe situations when we must prepare for the unpredictable. We bring along an umbrella "in case" it rains, that is, on the *chance* that rain might fall.

I would argue, however, that an educative case is more than a good narrative, more than a clever juxtaposition of intention and vicissitude. An educative case is a form of communication that places intention and chance into the context of a lived and reflected experience. A case doesn't just happen; it creates conditions that demand of its narrator (or protagonist) that she both render judgments among alternative tacks and act on those judgments. A case has consequences. One learns from deliberating reflectively on the connections among the elements of a case. Thus, an educative case combines at least four attributes or functions: intention, chance, judgment and reflection. They are the functions that explain or delineate the educative power of cases for learning to engage in any practice:

- **intention**: The existence of a formal or tacit plan, itinerary, or purpose.
- **chance**: The plan is interrupted by a surprise, by a "glitch", by the unexpected.

- **judgment**: In the face of uncertainty and surprise, the actor must exercise judgment, because no simple answer is available.
- **reflection**: Examining the consequences of action taken in light of judgment and learning in a way that produces the basis for a new plan or intention.

First, there has to be an intention, a plan of action. There is no case if there has been no plan, no itinerary, no sense of a path to be taken. A case is a "chance" event, a disruption of the itinerary. So we have a path that has been set out upon, and a chance event or events that disrupts the plan, that occludes the anticipated flow of experience. The blocking of intention provides the foundation for reflection, thought, and deliberation.

This sense of a case is quite consistent with Dewey's (1938) concept of inquiry. Dewey argues that thought is a response to the blocking of habit. Only when our habitual or reflexive modes of behavior fail to attain the desired goals, do we then begin to think about what to do. We have educative experiences when we are obligated to reflect on our actions and strategically select new paths because our habitual paths have been blocked. A case, therefore, is an account of an experience in which our intentions have been unexpectedly obstructed, and the surprising event has triggered the need to examine alternative courses of action. Surprise becomes the impetus for thought, and reflection on our responses to the surprise and the consequences that flow from our actions, become the basis for new learning.

We do not learn from experience; we learn by thinking about our experience. A case takes the raw material of first–order experience and renders it narratively into a second–order experience. A case is the re–collected, re–told, re–experienced and re–flected version of a direct experience. The process of remembering, retelling, reliving and reflecting is the process of learning from experience.

Cases and theory

To assert that a narrative is a *case* is to engage in an act of theory. When I first made that claim (Shulman, 1986), I created more misunderstanding than was stimulated by nearly any statement I have ever written. I do *not* mean that cases are, in themselves, inherently theoretical. Nor do I mean that the purpose of cases is to teach theory. Instead, I am claiming that any story that can be called a case must be arguably a case *of* something. It must be seen as an exemplar of a class, an instance of a larger category.

For this reason, the key move made in teaching with cases occurs when instructor and students explore the question, "what is this a case of?" As they wrestle with this question, they move the case in two directions simultaneously. They connect this narrative to their remembered (personal) experiences or to vicariously experienced cases written or recounted by others, thus relating this particular case to other specific cases. They also connect this narrative to categories of experience, to theoretical classifications through which they organize and make sense of their world.

First, an encounter with a case invites both the reader and the author to forge connections between this narrative and other narratives. Note that I say we are connecting narratives, not the experiences themselves. The transformation of an experience into a narrative is itself an act of selection and conceptualization. In converting a first–order experience into a second–order experience through narrative, an author has chosen to frame an experience in a particular way, has placed that experience in more general terms. When the reader of a case connects that narrative to his or her own experiences, a second kind of selection has taken place. Like story–swappers who respond to a tale by stating, "That reminds me of when...", one person's narrative connects with other narratives. A story about a classroom simulation that went awry elicits yet another account of a similar problem. An account of a social studies groupwork project in which a hitherto silent ESL student suddenly blossomed and stepped forward in a leadership role generates a second story of group processes, or of blossoming students or of surprises from language–minority students. It appears to be a characteristic of our species that stories explicitly breed yet other stories and, implicitly, the categories of analysis that connect stories to one another conceptually. Even in the concrete act of narrative, underlying theoretical categories emerge and often become explicit.

There are four processes at work in learning from the writing and contemplation of cases. These are *enactment, narration, connection* (or recounting) and *abstraction*. Stories begin in the raw experience itself, are transformed into cases through narration, become part of a network of narratives through connections with other cases, and both enrich and are enriched by theory when they are analyzed, interpreted and/or classified in the teachers' conversations.

Principles of Learning from Cases

Most educators who work with cases and case methods do not spend much time worrying about the structure of cases or their development, as I have in the previous two sections. Educators tend to emphasize case *methods* rather than on the cases themselves. As we review the variety of approaches to the study, discussion, writing and interpretation of cases described in this volume, we may begin to discern a set of principles that underlie the extended family of case methods, even acknowledging their great diversity. Are there a small set of principles that might explain the efficacy of case methods for stimulating and effecting significant learning among those who work with them? At the risk of sounding as if all my first principles fall into groups of four (in other papers they come out in threes), I shall now offer four constructs that may account for the efficacy of case methods.

I draw these principles from the current research that Judith Shulman and I are conducting on communities of learners and teachers in schools. After observing the workings of several classrooms in which Brown and Campione's "community of learners" (Brown, 1994) concepts have been implemented, and the apparently remarkable levels of student learning that resulted, the remarkable Jerome Bruner (once again!) offered four ideas on which he claimed these approaches appear to rest (Bruner, 1994). I have modified and adapted these principles to serve our current purposes, but they remain quite close to Bruner's original formulation. They are fitting in this context because, I believe, the varieties of effective case methods create conditions of learning that are quite consistent with those achieved in communities of learners.

The four principles that seem to characterize the conditions for effective, substantive and enduring learning are: *activity or agency*; *reflection or meta–cognition*; *collaboration*; and the formation of a supportive *community* or a sustaining culture. To elaborate, authentic and enduring learning occurs when:

- learners are *active* agents in the process, not passive, an audience, clients or collectors. This is a modestly constructivist claim, implying both a view of cognition as the active construction of meaning by learners who take responsibility for making sense of their world, as well as a physical construction of understanding through writing, project work, the manipulation of their environment and research–like activities.
- learners not only behave and think, but can "go meta–," that is, can *reflectively* turn around on their own thought and action and analyze how and why their thinking achieved certain ends or failed to achieve others. Metacognition — consciousness of how and why one is learning particular things in particular ways — is the key to deep learning.
- learners engage in *collaboration*, working together in ways that scaffold and support each others' learning, and in ways that supplement each others' knowledge. Collaboration is a marriage of insufficiencies, not exclusively "cooperation" in a particular form of social interaction. Moreover, there are difficult intellectual challenges that are nearly impossible to accomplish alone, but are more readily addressed with others.
- learners are scaffolded — that is, supported, legitimated and nurtured — in the processes of activity, reflection and collaboration within a *community* or *culture* that values such experiences and creates many opportunities for them to occur and to be accomplished with success and pleasure. Such communities create "participant structures" that reduce the labor–intensity of the activities needed to engage in the most daunting practices that lead to teaching and learning.

These principles were originally applied to explaining why students who participated in communities of learners were successful in their work. However, I would claim that these same principles apply to both new and veteran teachers who are learning from cases. First, whether as case analyst or as case writer, the case learner becomes an active agent in his or her own understanding. When a student is wrestling with a case, whether as an occasion for analysis or a stimulus to reflect on his own experience as a prelude to writing, active agency is engaged. Second, cases are inherently reflective. They begin with an act of re–cognition, of turning around on one's own lived experiences and examining them to find events and episode worthy of transformation into telling cases. Even when the goal of case learning is not case writing, the discussion of cases eventually stimulates reflection on one's own experiences and reactions.

Third, case methods nearly always emphasize the primacy of group discussion, deliberation and debate in the examination of a case. The thought process of cases is dialogic, as members of a group explore different perspectives on the nature of the problem, the available elective actions or the import of the consequences. In the example of case–based teaching I offered above, the interaction of activity, reflection and collaboration is apparent. But what of community or culture?

Teaching and learning with cases is not an easy pedagogy. Active learners are much more outspoken and assertive than are passive learners. They are less predictable than their more passive counterparts, as they investigate their options, explore alternative interpretations and challenge prevailing views. Since cases encourage the connections between personal experiences and those vicariously experienced through the narratives, the directions in which discussions might develop are rather difficult to anticipate, further complicating the pedagogy. Finally, the collaborative mode of instruction once again reduces the authority of the teacher and vests a growing proportion in the initiatives of students. Taken together, the enhancement of agency, reflection and collaboration make teaching more complex and unpredictable, albeit by reducing the authority of the teacher and his ability to plan for contingencies. When uncertainty increases and power is distributed, the need for a supportive culture or community becomes paramount for teachers and students alike. A supportive culture helps manage the risk of contemplating one's failures and reduces the vulnerability created when one candidly discusses a path not taken. A supportive culture engages each member of the community in parallel risks. It celebrates the interdependence of learners who will rely on one another for both insights and reassurance. A learning environment built on activity, reflection and collaboration — which is an apt characterization of a well–functioning case–learning and case–writing community — proceeds smoothly only in the presence of a sustaining culture and community.

Learning from Experience: A Recapitulation on Cases and Communities

I began this chapter with the assertion that case methods were a particularly potent instructional vehicle for accomplishing that most difficult of learnings, that which derives from the inspection of one's own experience (see Figure 1). After a brief discussion of the ways in which cases address the challenge of experiential learning, I offered an extended account of my own method of teaching with cases within a teacher education program. In this approach, which I have called the Analysis–Construction–Commentary–Community Cycle, students progress from reading the cases of others analytically, to drafting their own cases, to commenting on one another's cases in small case discussion groups that lead to new drafts of the same cases, to the presentation and discussion of cases in writing and orally within larger communities.

I then offered three sets of principles for examining the nature of cases and case methods. I first argued that a case was a narrative with a particular formal organization, composed of intentions, chance, judgment and reflective analysis. A case narrative depicts the protagonist's intentions and intended path, portrays the surprises and accidents that impeded direct movement toward the goal, explores the judgments and reasoning that contributed to the choices subsequently made, and then, in the light of the consequences of the elective actions, reflects on the wisdom of the choices and their grounds. All the components are needed for a case. Without intention, there can be no surprise. Without chance, there is no narrative. Without judgment, there is no thinking. And without reflection, there is no analysis of the ebb and flow of the engagement and hence, no learning from experience.

I then explored the mischievous contention that declaring something a "case" was an inherently theoretical claim. In this section I elaborated on the argument that both crafting and learning from cases involved a dialectic between first–order and second–order experience, between the direct undergoing of an event and its reconstruction in narrative. This transformation of experience to case is mediated by the question "what is this a case of?" The answers emerge from connecting one's own case to other cases — relating stories to one another — and from relating cases to larger theoretical categories of which they are instances. Thus every case, in its particularity, derives its "case–ness" from its connections to other cases and to organizing principles or theories.

But the structure of a case is only part of the story. A few pages of prose cannot alone educate. Cases are taught and learned using a small range of methods. I go on to assert that these methods share in common a set of learning principles that account for the effectiveness of all learning within learning com-

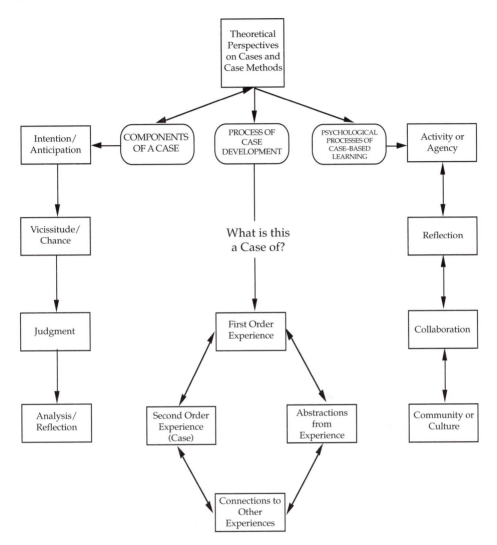

Figure 1: Theoretical Perspectives on Cases and Case Methods

munities: activity, reflection, collaboration and culture. The methods of case teaching share an affinity for those principles of learning, as well they should.

Communities of Teachers

Which brings us to the centrality of *community* to the efficacy of the "case idea." Cases become educative for teachers within teaching communities. Learning from experience is nearly impossible without the scaffolding of others, their alternative views, their complementary perspectives, their roles as active listeners and critical friends. If "collaboration" is one of the key inner principles of effective and enduring learning, then "community" is its external scaffolding, which keeps the structure erect in spite of the tensions of the processes that occur within it (Shulman, 1989). When McLaughlin and Talbert (1993) identified the conditions that permitted teachers at the secondary school level to teach with understanding, they identified the critical importance of communities and networks, within and across institutions, for sustaining the difficulties of adventurous teaching. Cases can be a critical element of the glue that holds such communities together and gives their deliberations substance and form.

Just in Case...

So much of teacher education emphasizes the importance of playful intention and disciplined improvisation. Lesson planning, unit planning, test design, classroom organization and management all attest to the essential character of planfulness and preparation in the success of teachers. But design is less than half the story. Teachers learn quickly that the heart of teaching is developing the capacity to respond to the unpredictable. Teaching begins in design, but unfolds through chance. And cases — as the narrative manifestations of chance — offer teachers the opportunities to contemplate the variety of ways in which the unpredictable happens. Case–based teacher education offers safe contexts within which teachers can explore their alternatives and judge their consequences.

John Dewey argued, in his classic essay, "The Influence of Darwinism on Philosophy,"(Dewey, 1910) that Darwin signaled the emergence of a new era of modern science with his theory of natural selection and evolution, when he demonstrated that it was chance, not design, and variation, not fixedness, that explained why the biological world had evolved as it had. The secret of adaptation is the species' response to and management of chance through the nurturing of variability, flux and change. Similarly, case methods bring the vicissitudes of intended practice front and center, so that teachers might learn to respond and manage pedagogical chance adaptively and successfully. Cases and case methods are surely no panacea for the challenges of teacher education. But in the needed redesign of teacher education programs at all levels, they will occupy a central role.

References

Ball, D. (1993). With an eye on the mathematical horizon: Dilemmas of teaching elementary school mathematics. *Elementary School Journal, 93*(4), 373–97.

Bosk, C. L. (1979). *Forgive and remember*. Chicago: University of Chicago Press.

Brown, A. L. (1994). The advancement of learning. *Educational Researcher, 23*(8), 4–12.

Bruner, J. S. (1986). *Actual minds, possible worlds*. Cambridge, MA: Harvard University Press.

Bruner, J. S. (1994). *The humanly and interpretively possible*. Paper presented at the American Educational Research Association, New Orleans.
Dewey, J. (1910). *The influence of Darwinism on philosophy and other essays*. New York: Henry Holt & Co.

Dewey, J. (1938). *Logic: The theory of inquiry*. New York: Henry Holt & Co.

Lampert, M. (1990). When the problem is not the question and the solution is not the answer. *American Educational Research Journal, 27*(1), 29–63.

McLaughlin, M. W., & Talbert, J. E. (1993). *Contexts that matter for teaching and learning*. Stanford, CA: Center for Research on the Context of Secondary School Teaching, Stanford University.

Shulman, J. H. (1991). Revealing the mysteries of teacher–written cases: Opening the black box. *Journal of Teacher Education, 42*(4), 250–262.

Shulman, J. H., & Colbert, J. A. (1988). *The Intern Teacher Casebook*. San Francisco: Far West Laboratory.

Shulman, L. S. (1989). Teaching alone, learning together: Needed agendas for the new reforms. In T. M. Sergiovanni & John H. Moore (Eds), *Schooling for tomorrow* (pp. 166–187). Boston: Allyn and Bacon.

Spiro, R.J., Coulson, R.L., Feltovich, P.J. & Anderson, D.K. (1988). Cognitive flexibility theory: Advanced knowledge acquisition in ill–structured domains. In *Tenth annual conference of the cognitive science society* (pp. 375–383). Hillsdale, N.J.: Erlbaum.

White, V. (1988). One struggle after another. In J. H. Shulman & Joel A. Colbert (Eds.), *The intern teacher casebook* (pp. 12–13). San Francisco: Far West Laboratory.

Wilson, S. M. (1992). A case concerning content: Using cases to teach about subject matter. In J. H. Shulman (Ed.), *Case methods in teacher education (pp. 64–89)*. New York: Teachers College Press.

Notes

[1] Preparation of this chapter was supported by grants from the Mellon Foundation (for the project "Fostering a Community of Teachers and Learners") and the Spencer Foundation (for the project "Toward a Pedagogy of Substance"). I am grateful to both foundations for their support; they bear no responsibility for the chapter's contents or its claims.

[2] Readers will discern that this form of case is quite different from the business school model. It presents students with a full narrative accompanied by an analysis and often commentaries, rather than the open–ended problem–solving case preferred by those teacher educators who prefer the business school model.

[3] Some colleagues argue that I place too much stress on exclusively asking for cases of surprise or failure. They claim that teachers need to contemplate success and accomplishment in addition to disappointment and the unexpected. They are probably correct. I have not yet had the opportunity to experiment with different kinds of case and their relative efficacy.

[4] Some may argue that imposing a structured genre on teacher case–writing stifles their creativity and is unnecessary. I disagree. Writing to a genre specification is done widely in the field of creative writing, and does not appear to limit the inventiveness of writers.

[5] In this analysis, I build upon Judy Shulman's (1991) four–stage model of case–based reflection. She posits the first stage as the direct experience of the event, the second stage as the joint reflection on the event by the actor and a

case editor or mentor out of which emerges the written case itself; the third stage as the case with written commentary, which is now a part of a broader education community; and in the fourth stage the case is part of the broader case literature, now an element in the community of educators.

Lee Shulman is the Charles E. Ducommun Professor of Education and Psychology at Stanford University. A native of Chicago, he received his Ph.D. from the University of Chicago. He was previously (1963–82) on the faculty of the Michigan State University where he was Professor of Educational Psychology and Medical Education and founding co–director of the Institute for Research on Teaching. Shulman is a former President of the American Educational Research Association as well as immediate past–president of the National Academy of Education. He has received AERA's career award for Distinguished Contributions to Educational Research and the American Psychological Association's E.L. Thorndike Award for Distinguished Psychological Contributions to Education. His current research is on the improvement of teaching in both K–12 and university settings, new approaches to the assessment of teaching, and in the methods and quality of educational research.